Pests and Diseases

Other Publications:

Pests and Diseases

by
RICHARD H. CRAVENS
and
the Editors of TIME-LIFE BOOKS

Watercolor Illustrations by
Robert E. Hynes

TIME-LIFE BOOKS, ALEXANDRIA, VIRGINIA

Time-Life Books Inc.
is a wholly owned subsidiary of
TIME INCORPORATED

FOUNDER: Henry R. Luce 1898-1967

Editor-in-Chief: Hedley Donovan
Chairman of the Board: Andrew Heiskell
President: James R. Shepley
Vice Chairman: Roy E. Larsen
Corporate Editor: Ralph Graves

TIME-LIFE BOOKS INC.

MANAGING EDITOR: Jerry Korn
Executive Editor: David Maness
Assistant Managing Editors: Dale M. Brown, Martin Mann,
John Paul Porter (acting)
Art Director: Tom Suzuki
Chief of Research: David L. Harrison
Director of Photography: Melvin L. Scott
Planning Director: Philip W. Payne (acting)
Senior Text Editor: Diana Hirsh
Assistant Art Director: Arnold C. Holeywell
Assistant Chief of Research: Carolyn L. Sackett

CHAIRMAN: Joan D. Manley
President: John D. McSweeney
Executive Vice Presidents: Carl G. Jaeger (U.S. and
Canada), David J. Walsh (International)
Vice President and Secretary: Paul R. Stewart
Treasurer and General Manager: John Steven Maxwell
Business Manager: Peter G. Barnes
Sales Director: John L. Canova
Public Relations Director: Nicholas Benton
Personnel Director: Beatrice T. Dobie
Production Director: Herbert Sorkin
Consumer Affairs Director: Carol Flaumenhaft

THE TIME-LIFE ENCYCLOPEDIA OF GARDENING

EDITORIAL STAFF FOR PESTS AND DISEASES:
EDITOR: Robert M. Jones
Assistant Editor: Sarah Bennett Brash
Text Editors: Bonnie Bohling Kreitler, Bob Menaker
Picture Editor: Jane Jordan
Designer: Albert Sherman
Staff Writer: Susan Feller
Researchers: Marilyn Murphy, Judith W. Shanks,
Reiko Uyeshima
Art Assistant: Edwina C. Smith
Editorial Assistant: Kristin Baker

EDITORIAL PRODUCTION
Production Editor: Douglas B. Graham
Operations Manager: Gennaro C. Esposito
Assistant Production Editor: Feliciano Madrid
Quality Control: Robert L. Young (director),
James J. Cox (assistant), Michael G. Wight (associate)
Art Coordinator: Anne B. Landry
Copy Staff: Susan B. Galloway (chief), Tonna Gibert,
Elizabeth Graham, Florence Keith, Celia Beattie
Picture Department: Dolores A. Littles, Barbara S. Simon

CORRESPONDENTS: Elisabeth Kraemer (Bonn); Margot
Hapgood, Dorothy Bacon (London); Susan Jonas, Lucy T.
Voulgaris (New York); Maria Vincenza Aloisi, Josephine du
Brusle (Paris); Ann Natanson (Rome). Valuable assistance
was also provided by Jane Rieker (Boynton Beach, Fla.) and
Carolyn T. Chubet (New York).

THE AUTHOR: Richard H. Cravens has combined a career in journalism with a longtime interest in gardening and agriculture. He first became aware of plant pests and diseases as a teenager harvesting grain in his home state of Kansas. He later did graduate work in cultural ecology at the University of New Mexico, then was a staff writer for the Associated Press and for TIME-LIFE BOOKS.

THE ILLUSTRATOR: The work of Robert E. Hynes, who created the paintings of insects and plants beginning on page 84, has appeared in many publications, including the *National Geographic U.S. Atlas* and *World* magazine. Mr. Hynes has taught drawing at the University of Maryland, where he earned a Master of Fine Arts degree. He designed and painted the prehistoric insect diorama for the Smithsonian Institution's Museum of Natural History in Washington, D.C.

GENERAL CONSULTANTS: James Underwood Crockett, author of 13 of the volumes in this Encyclopedia, co-author of two additional volumes and consultant on other books in the series, has been a lover of the earth and its good things since his boyhood on a Massachusetts fruit farm. He was graduated from the Stockbridge School of Agriculture at the University of Massachusetts and has worked ever since in horticulture. A perennial contributor to leading gardening magazines, he also writes a monthly bulletin, "Flowery Talks," that is widely distributed through retail florists. His television program, *Crockett's Victory Garden,* shown all over the United States, is constantly winning new converts to the Crockett approach to growing things. Dr. Emil M. Mrak, mycologist, is Chancellor Emeritus at the University of California at Davis and Chairman of the Science Advisory Board of the Environmental Protection Agency. Dr. Robert Pristou, plant pathologist, is Associate Professor of plant pathology at Virginia Polytechnic Institute and State University in Blacksburg. Dr. Allen L. Steinhauer, entomologist, is Professor and Chairman of the Department of Entomology at the University of Maryland, College Park. Dr. Leslie O. Weaver, plant pathologist, is Professor in the Department of Botany, University of Maryland, College Park.

THE COVER: A spotted cucumber beetle, *Diabrotica soror,* shown 20 times actual size, feeds on a petal of a sunflower. The insect devours many kinds of plants and also is feared by gardeners as a carrier of plant diseases. The photographer, Edward S. Ross, former Chairman of the Department of Entomology at the California Academy of Sciences in San Francisco, now devotes much of his time to writing and photography.

Other contributors to this book were Linda Tokarz Anzelmo, Dixie Taylor Barlow, Richard C. Davids, Jane Opper, Barbara Ann Peters, Kelly Tasker, Glenn White and Sue Hillaby Young.

CONTENTS

To His Grace *Cha.ˢ Lenox* *Duke of Richmond.*
This Plate is humbly Dedicated. by his Grace's most Obliged & Obed.ᵗ Hum.ᵇˡᵉ Serv.ᵗ
Moses Harris.

EN LA ROSE JE FLEURIS

The common sense of garden defense 1

During all the millennia that man has planted and harvested he has needed every wit and resource he could muster to save his crops from insects and diseases. Most of his ancient efforts were futile. Farmers tried magic incantations, prayer and desperate measures such as banging drums loudly to drive off devastating swarms of locusts. In one poignant Old Testament verse, Joel laments: "What the cutting locust left, the swarming locust has eaten. What the swarming locust left, the hopping locust has eaten, and what the hopping locust left, the destroying locust has eaten."

Plant diseases are not as dramatic—or as evident—as a swarm of locusts, but they also have marred and shaped the course of history. King Solomon prayed for deliverance from "pestilence, blight and mildew." And when a potato blight struck Ireland in the 1840s half a million people starved to death and another million emigrated to North America.

The ancients of Biblical times and the stricken Irish potato farmers had no truly effective chemical remedies. Homer mentioned "pest-averting sulfur," and some 600 years after Homer, in 200 B.C., Cato recommended fumigating diseased grape vines with a mixture of olive oil, sulfur and bitumen (pitch). Sulfur, in some forms, is still in use today and powdered tobacco, the predecessor of today's nicotine sulfate, was used to destroy plant lice as early as 1763. But it was not until about 100 years ago that the first really effective chemical weapons appeared. One was Paris green, an arsenic compound that checked the ravages of the potato beetle. The other was Bordeaux mixture, a blend of copper sulfate and hydrated lime, which was found to be effective against many fungus diseases. These two hazardous poisons dominated a meager arsenal of pesticides until DDT was introduced some 70 years later.

Today, man has to contend with the same 100,000 plant diseases and 1,000,000 kinds of insects that his ancestors did.

The Aurelian, a 1766 English handbook for fanciers of butterflies and moths, extolled their beauty in delicate drawings such as this but also recognized the havoc they can wreak in their voracious larval stage.

Fortunately, only a small number of pests and diseases are likely to strike in any one area, and there are approximately 1,000 fungicides, bactericides and insecticides with which to combat them.

When DDT was introduced in the United States for civilian use in 1947, many gardeners saw it as their ultimate weapon. It was first brought into full-scale use against larvae of the *Anopheles* mosquito, and proved dramatically effective in eliminating or greatly reducing malaria in much of the world. DDT also was found to be lethal to roaches, lice and a large number of garden pests. As a pesticide, it could be sprayed on plants or it could be dusted on soil. In various forms it also was incorporated into clothing for mothproofing and added to household paints to protect against cockroaches, silverfish and fleas. Within a few years of the introduction of DDT, various other broad-spectrum pesticides were developed, including parathion, TEPP and diazinon.

TOO MUCH OR TOO LITTLE?

The development of these pesticides brought with it the phenomenon of the shotgun gardener, who bombards his plants with a variety of dusts, sprays and oils at the first sign of infestation. At the other extreme, this overuse of pesticides brought forth the dedicated purist, who goes to a great deal of trouble to establish his garden and then declines to use any chemical means to protect it.

The latter course, despite its purity of purpose, can lead to great disappointment, as it did for a New York attorney who moved to New Mexico in search of a simpler life, which to him was epitomized by a garden. His first enthusiastic letters to former colleagues described a large home in a suburb of Albuquerque. And they told of the substantial amount of equipment and toil he was investing in a garden that spring. Soon, the letters described rows of tomato plants, beans, squash, lettuce and other comestibles, all thriving in the rich, red soil of the Rio Grande Valley.

Then all mention of the garden abruptly ceased. It was not until a friend stopped for a visit late that summer that his New York cronies found out what had happened. "It was a fine garden," the visitor related, "but the bugs got it all. Ted recognized grasshoppers and caterpillars but there were a lot more he couldn't identify. They chewed it to shreds, the whole garden. It was a disaster."

"Why didn't Ted kill the bugs?"

"He said he wanted a natural garden, farming the same way as the Pueblo Indians nearby," his friend responded. "He didn't want to upset the balance of nature. Or pollute. Now, he's convinced that civilization has so wrecked the environment that the insects are taking over. So," the urbanite added smugly, "he's switched from gardening to golf."

The transplanted lawyer failed as a gardener because he had never really gardened at all; he had merely provided a convenient picnic ground for all sorts of pests. His motives were pure, but his approach was naïve. If he had studied some of the Indians' methods more closely, he might still be swinging a hoe instead of a golf club. Like most growers of food, the Indians had lean years as well as years of plenty. When they were successful, it was partly due to luck—they were helpless in the face of pestilence or plague—but mostly due to good land management. The Pueblos planted their crops over the savanna-like terrain with intervening wild vegetation, which curbed the spread of afflictions from field to field. The lawyer's garden, on the other hand, adjoined others with similar vegetation, which encouraged the spread of pests and diseases that attack such plants. And while the Indians let their land lie fallow at regular intervals, thus cutting nourishment for lingering disease microorganisms and insect larvae, the lawyer planted immediately, heedless of any perils his untreated soil might harbor.

The basic principles of crop management the Indians employed are followed today by most successful gardeners. They keep their gardens clean and make sure their plants get adequate water, light, food and ventilation to increase resistance. Like the Pueblos— though more from scientific knowledge than mere experience—they realize that where they plant can be as important as what they plant. For example, root maggots, nematodes and fungi tend to build up in the soil season after season, specific ones feeding upon specific plants. If you keep shifting susceptible varieties to new locations periodically (a few feet away may do the trick), or if you replace

CROP ROTATION

By the 1850s, spraying had become one of the most effective methods of fighting garden pests and diseases, as is evident in this illustration from a contemporary handbook, *La Belgique Horticole*. Before spraying devices such as these were developed, gardeners painstakingly brushed or sprinkled their concoctions directly onto each individual plant.

them with more resistant varieties, destructive insects and disease pathogens in the soil will die out.

An occasional change of location, generally every three years, is important, particularly for eggplants, tomatoes and all of the crucifers, including cabbages, cauliflower, broccoli, Brussels sprouts and turnips. The cabbage maggot waxes in the soil adjacent to these plants, as do vegetable weevils and seed-corn maggots. Black rot, club root and nematodes also flourish with successive plantings of crucifers. Because these vegetables are so vulnerable to this combination of pests and diseases, end-of-season refuse should be cleaned up and disposed of, instead of being tilled under.

Many other good gardening practices and natural controls will be discussed in Chapter 3, such as attracting pest-eating birds and encouraging predatory insects like ladybug beetles and praying mantises, which help put down small invasions. But when a minor skirmish threatens to become a major attack, or when a disease takes hold and threatens to spread beyond a few plants, the wise gardener does not hesitate to zero in with precisely targeted chemical weapons. And he also realizes that some chemicals are as important in prevention as in suppression.

SCHEDULING CHEMICALS   Timing is an important factor in keeping a garden healthy with minimum use of chemical aids. If you dust or spray or otherwise destroy insects when they first appear, you can control them with a small amount of poison. Delay even a few days and you may vastly magnify the job. With some diseases, you can wait until the first symptoms appear before applying treatment. This is true of powdery mildew, which attacks a host of plants from African violets to lilacs, and botrytis blight, which used to be a terror in the days when only Bordeaux mixture was at hand. For many diseases, however, including black spot of roses, early and continued *preventive* measures—before any symptoms appear—are essential: spray the first leaves as they unfold and at weekly intervals thereafter. Azaleas, camellias and rhododendrons similarly need early protection before any sign of disease is evident.

The manner in which specific pesticides work will be discussed in Chapter 4 *(page 65),* and recommendations for dispatching specific pests and diseases are given in the encyclopedia *(page 85).* In general, insecticides kill on contact with the skin of the insect, through the stomach when ingested or through the breathing apertures when inhaled. Chlorinated hydrocarbons, such as DDT, and organic phosphates, such as malathion, kill by attacking the nervous system. Certain water-soluble insecticides called systemics, when applied to either the leaves or the soil, are absorbed and circulated within the plant, killing harmful sucking pests (aphids) and some chewing pests (beetles). Soil fumigants, used against nematodes, kill through the action of a lethal gas.

The efficiency of many of these pesticides has led some gardeners to use them as cure-alls instead of as weapons of last resort. One such compulsive sprayer in Massachusetts arrived at his weekly Rotary Club luncheon with a basket of resplendent peaches as his contribution to dessert. Each fruit was fat and round, its golden skin unblemished. How did he produce such marvels? He sprayed a bit more than usual, he admitted. In fact, he had sprayed 14 times during the season—about eight times more than necessary. Given the cost of the various chemicals, it was easy to calculate that the peaches were more expensive than any at the local supermarket.

The perfect peaches he served at that 1970 luncheon had been sprayed with DDT, among other chemicals. Today he could not use DDT, which was restricted by the Environmental Protection Agency (EPA) in 1972 because it was believed to be hazardous to the environment. In 1977, though, the federal government did allow DDT to be used at certain airports on both coasts: landing fields in California and airplanes bound for California were sprayed with it to keep Japanese beetles from spreading to the lush fields of the West.

Chlordane, once used almost as widely as DDT, is also restricted in many states, where its use is confined to subsurface termite control and certain quarantine programs such as those for the Japanese beetle and the imported fire ant.

Because the EPA restricted the use of many compounds, pesticide manufacturers began to develop new chemicals believed to be less harmful to the environment. These various pesticide chemicals are categorized under federal law as approved for general use (like over-the-counter medicinals) or as restricted (like prescription drugs); the latter are available only to farmers and commercial appliers who have demonstrated that they can use them safely and have a certificate to prove it. Such a certificate is issued by an EPA-approved, state-administered board only after the applicant has taken a course in the use of chemicals and has passed a written examination. Restrictions may be raised or lowered when new evidence of hazard or safety is presented; current information is made available through local agricultural agents.

Pesticides are restricted for several reasons, including direct danger to humans or to wildlife. The organic phosphate parathion, for example, is so toxic to man when inhaled that the applier is required by law to wear a respirator mask. A pesticide may also be restricted because of its persistence as a residue in soil or water.

LIMITING THE HAZARDS

FEDERAL CLASSIFICATIONS

The Great Plains grasshopper wars

Pioneers who settled the Great Plains were hardy folk, inured to summer drought and winter blizzard. But nothing in their experience could have prepared them for the trial they faced in the 1870s: a devastating plague of grasshoppers.

"They looked like a dense cloud of smoke," said one account. "As the cloud came nearer and nearer it obscured the sun and darkened the air like an eclipse. There was a continuous crackling and snapping sound which increased to a perfect roar . . . it was a cloud of grasshoppers."

The settlers viewed these "Rocky Mountain locusts" as a menace comparable to hostile Indians. The insects ate everything green except native grass, castor beans and cane. Even the paint on a house or a harness left carelessly outside were vulnerable to their voracious appetites.

There was no defense against the hordes. Farm families tried beating them with branches and brooms, to no avail. Smoke did not faze them. Crops were covered with protective straw or old blankets, but the grasshoppers burrowed through. Heavy rains, which drowned the pests by the millions, offered only occasional relief.

When the hoppers finally departed—as mysteriously as they had come—they had cut a swath of destruction from the Dakotas to northern Texas. The worst of the plague years, 1874, was afterward known as The Grasshopper Year.

Indians and grasshoppers were viewed as dual hazards in an 1874 cartoon that wryly dubbed them "Extra inducements to those who would go West at the present time."

A sketch of a grasshopper swarm stopping a Union Pacific train in Nebraska in the 1870s was based on fact. Railroad workers often had to shovel the pests from the warm rails, made so slippery by dead insects that the locomotive wheels could not gain enough traction to pull the train.

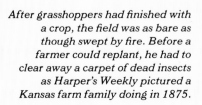

Swain Finch, a grasshopper-war veteran, shows how he battled the insects with a branch. The grasshoppers in this photograph were added to a glass-plate negative for a 1901 history of Nebraska. From all accounts the real swarms were much thicker.

After grasshoppers had finished with a crop, the field was as bare as though swept by fire. Before a farmer could replant, he had to clear away a carpet of dead insects as Harper's Weekly pictured a Kansas farm family doing in 1875.

Arsenic compounds such as Paris green, used for decades in orchards, have been restricted because they build up a lethal residue in the soil that will last for years unless it is dissipated by leaching or by natural erosion.

Unrestricted pesticides approved for over-the-counter sale are less dangerous than many household cleaning compounds. But like them, they can be hazardous if they are not handled with care. For instance, concentrated nicotine sulfate, which is made from the tobacco plant and used as a contact spray against aphids and other sucking insects, is very dangerous to humans if it is inhaled, ingested or absorbed through the skin.

TESTING A NEW POISON

Exhaustive tests must be conducted before the EPA will approve a pesticide. To qualify for general use, a chemical must be tested by the manufacturer for toxicity on at least two species of mammals, two species of birds, two species of fish and two species of shellfish. Its effect on plankton and soil microorganisms must also be studied. If it then appears that humans can be safely exposed to the compound, an independent laboratory—one not connected with the manufacturer—must conduct a further test before the product wins government approval. Altogether, testing a new pesticide takes about eight years, involves between two and three thousand laboratory animals (usually rats) and costs more than $5 million.

The manufacturer also is required to build another safeguard into all pesticide compounds: the pesticide you buy at your hardware store or garden center must be 100 times weaker than the level of concentration at which test animals showed adverse effects. This safety margin protects the user foolish enough to think that if a little chemical is good, double the amount is better. As an additional safeguard of your own, buy the smallest amount possible, certainly no more than you will use in one growing season. The small package will be easier to store, and it will be fresher—an important factor in the efficacy of nonresidual pesticides.

THE INFORMATIVE LABEL

Every pesticide carries an EPA registration number and explicit instuctions for use. Federal law holds the user responsible for following directions on the label; failure to do so can make the user subject to a fine or imprisonment. In the case of vegetable dusts and sprays, for example, only crops specifically identified on the label can be legally treated. The directions also indicate the method of application and the amount of time that must elapse between the application of the chemical and the harvesting of the crop. Though the fine print on the label may not make lively reading, the wise gardener will study it carefully and follow its advice to the letter, for his own protection and for the well-being of the plants in his garden.

Because EPA restrictions are constantly being updated, many manufacturers are packaging natural controls that are much less likely to be restricted or banned. One such product, milky disease, has proved highly successful against the Japanese beetle *(page 46)*. Another similar product is *Bacillus thuringiensis,* which causes a disease lethal to many caterpillars, particularly the cabbage looper, which preys on its namesake and many other vegetables.

Some gardeners prefer organic pesticides. One of the most widely distributed is rotenone, derived from the powdered roots of derris and cubé, plants long used by South American Indians to kill fish for food—the poison does not harm the Indians. Another organic compound is pyrethrum, derived from the flower heads of several species of chrysanthemums. Both pesticides are relatively nontoxic to warm-blooded animals and often are used indoors to kill mosquitoes and flies. They are useful on food crops nearly ready for harvest because they have little residual effect.

Yet another development in nonchemical pest control is the sterile-male technique. Males of the target species are sterilized in laboratories with gamma radiation, then released into the wild. Females that mate with these males produce no offspring. The overall reduction in pest populations in a short period can be dramatic. Unfortunately, this technique is not the panacea it once seemed to be, since it is most effective only against pests with a geographically limited range and those that are present in relatively small numbers. Among its successes, though, are the eradication of the screwworm, a livestock pest in Florida, and the Mexican fruit fly in California. Another procedure that is proving increasingly effective is the development of disease- and pest-resistant varieties of plants *(Chapter 3).*

TOLERABLE BLEMISHES

No gardener is going to win all of the battles that he must fight, no matter how scrupulous he is about sanitation, horticultural practices, spraying and the like. However, he does have one advantage over commercial growers. The latter must produce blemish-free crops to compete successfully in the marketplace, but the home gardener need not be so concerned about mere esthetics. For example, there is no reason to reach for the spray gun if your peaches are infected by scab: it does not alter either their flavor or their nutritional value.

The same rationale holds true for pest control. As a well-known horticulturist once told a skeptical garden club, "We have a phobia against anything that crawls or jumps, but some insects are helpful and others we can control. As for the rest, we've just got to live with them. After all, they outnumber us by the hundreds of billions."

Identifying marauders and maladies 2

A gardener whose yard is the pride of his neighborhood once tried to explain his success to a group of fellow enthusiasts. "I coexist with the bugs," he told them, and he recalled the advice his grandmother gave him years ago when she sent him into her garden in England: "If it moves slow, step on it; if it moves fast, leave it be—it will probably kill something worse."

He still follows that advice, allowing the fast-moving predators to feast on the pests in his garden. Ladybugs, praying mantises, wasps and other beneficial insects are welcomed as a vital part of natural control *(Chapter 3)*. But he also knows which insects are his enemies and how to spot them.

Large round notches in a leaf indicate to him that caterpillars have moved into the neighborhood. If a leaf has been chewed down to a skeletal state, he looks for beetles. Sucking pests also leave telltale signs: leaves that are wilted or curled up are the aphid's calling card, while yellowed leaves with tiny webs on their undersides can often be blamed on mites.

The shape of an insect's mouth is another way to distinguish friend from foe—if you can get a close enough look. Predators such as the ground beetle usually have long, pointed jaws that are well suited for grasping other insects, while plant eaters such as the grasshopper tend to have short, chunky mandibles (the first pair of jaws). This configuration can vary, though, with troublesome plant eaters such as weevils and curculios, which are beetles whose heads are prolonged downward and forward into cylindrical snouts. Complicating the matter is the fact that some insects are helpful to plants at one stage of their lives and injurious at another. For example, the larvae of the blister beetle do a good turn by consuming large quantities of grasshopper eggs, but the beetles themselves destroy a myriad of flowers and foliage.

The biggest problem for even the most experienced gardener,

Three insects familiar to every gardener crowd inside a squash flower. The pollen-covered bee helps to ensure a fruitful garden, but the cucumber beetle and the tiny aphid are pests that damage plants.

though, is differentiating among pest depredation, an unfavorable environmental condition and disease. A plant that turns reddish brown could simply need some water, it might be under attack from grubs at its roots, or it might be the victim of any one of hundreds of diseases. The following rules of thumb will help you to zero in on your plant's problem:

● When you see an unusual symptom occur simultaneously on several adjacent plants—yellowing, for example—you can assume that the condition is probably due to some environmental factor rather than an infection or infestation. But if the abnormalities, such as spots, blotches or severe wilting, are limited to a few plants, a disease is the likely culprit. (Diseases usually start small and then spread to adjoining areas.)

● Note the particular diseases and pests that attack each specific variety—and the geographic areas where they are likely to occur (*Chapter 5*). For example, if you are a California gardener and your foliage plants have been chewed into lacy patterns there are several pests that might be responsible, but Japanese beetles can be ruled out because there are so few Japanese beetles in California.

● Plants themselves are cooperative in sending out distress signals. Unlike many of the humans who tend them, plants neither exaggerate nor find cause to disguise their symptoms. When a plant is in trouble, it indicates clearly that something is wrong: growth may be slower than normal; buds and flowers may fail to appear or to develop properly; leaves, branches and stems may be discolored or wilted. But a plant obviously can convey only these and a few other simplistic symptoms—and the symptoms can indicate thousands of different pest and disease problems.

SEARCHING FOR SYMPTOMS

Fortunately, the home gardener will seldom need to contend with esoteric epidemics or rare pests. It is the relatively few widely distributed pests and diseases that concern him. Sometimes solving a garden problem is easy; when you spot a sunning grasshopper beside a chewed-up blade of sweet corn, you have a straightforward jaws-and-effect relationship. But if you have no real clues to your plant's malaise, it is best to apply first aid as if the problem were caused by an environmental deficiency—not enough water, too much sunlight or insufficient nutrition, to name three possibilities. If the plant does not respond rapidly to corrective modification of its environment, disease may be present, and the plant should be destroyed before it endangers its neighbors.

No one likes to lose a plant, though, and frequent inspections may nip potential trouble in the bud, so to speak. Don't be alarmed by minor deviations from the norm. A serrated leaf or a few brown edges or spots here or there may suggest only a single nocturnal visitor or a slight watering problem. Confined to one or only a few plants, such blemishes are generally unimportant.

Begin your inspection by checking your plants' overall appearance. Look for any gross irregularities, such as a section of a row that is not keeping up with the rest of the row or a grouping of leaves of a different color. Turn over leaves to examine the undersides, and take a close look at the junctions of branches and stems: these are the favorite gathering spots for aphids, Mexican bean beetles, whiteflies and many other pests. Close up, you will also have a chance to check for injuries, various types of fungi in the early stages of their development, and other anomalies.

Look near the base of the stem for swellings that may suggest the presence of gall producers such as nematodes, which are too small to be seen without a microscope. (An ounce of young strawberry roots, for example, may harbor as many as 100,000 nematodes during the growing season.) A pattern of darkened colors on the plant may be a sign that grubs and maggots are at work; you can check for them by scraping back a bit of soil at the plant's base, where they are usually found. In your search, be careful that you do not mistake a ladybug beetle, one of your garden's great benefactors, for its nastier look-alikes.

LOOK-ALIKES: TELLING FRIEND FROM FOE

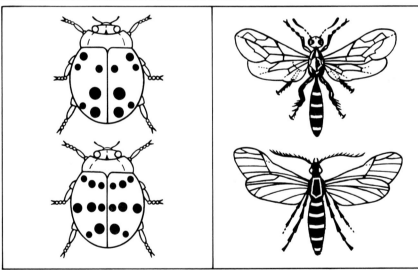

The Mexican bean beetle (bottom) is a destructive plant-eating pest often mistaken for a ladybug beetle. To tell them apart, count their spots; ladybug beetles have varying numbers, bean beetles exactly 16.

The moth of the peach tree borer (bottom) is a look-alike for the digger wasp, which preys on caterpillars and other pests. The destructive moth can be distinguished by its thicker middle, not at all a wasp waist.

On your inspection tour, take along a large tin can or wide-mouthed jar with several inches of water at the bottom. Beetles, caterpillars and other slow-moving feeders can be dispatched by swiping them into the can, where they will drown—or suffocate, if the jar has a lid. Make sure your swiping hand is gloved, because some insects, such as the aptly named blister beetle, emit poisons that can raise uncomfortable welts on bare skin. Some caterpillars are covered with bristles that can cause skin irritations.

One California gardener practices a kind of horticultural karate on cabbage aphids. "When they start on the tough, outer leaves," he says, "I cut the leaves off and stomp on them. Nobody likes the outer leaves, anyway, and I can dispatch a lot of aphids."

Aphids give themselves away by the sticky, silvery streaks of honeydew they secrete, but other pests are not as easy to spot. Understanding the pests' life cycles will help you identify many of them because often it is not the readily recognizable adult that does the harm, but its newly hatched offspring.

PATTERNS OF GROWTH

Insects develop in two different kinds of life cycles: either gradual metamorphosis or complete metamorphosis. The young of insects that develop gradually are almost identical to the adults except in size. During growth, only slight structural changes occur, such as the development of wings. The young of these insects are called nymphs. In complete metamorphosis, the insect goes through an intermediate stage of development: after hatching from an egg, the creature spends a period in a wormlike larval stage before becoming an adult. (The larvae of beetles are known as grubs, the larvae of flies are called maggots, and the larvae of moths and butterflies are known as caterpillars.)

Sorting out a pest's maturation process will also help you choose the right counterattack. Insects that develop by gradual metamorphosis tend to feed the same way throughout their lives, and what kills the adult will kill the offspring, too. But insects that undergo complete metamorphosis often inhabit entirely separate feeding sites as youngsters and as adults, and both stages may not be susceptible to the same controls.

Many insects pose little or no threat after they have reached the adult stage. "I like having a few colorful insects to watch," says one veteran gardener. "Several swallowtail butterflies may eat a few leaves but they are worth the damage. You just have to keep a close eye on their larvae." The offspring of these relatively harmless adults can damage a lot more than a few leaves, for in the early stages of life insects devote all their time to the business of eating. Nature has provided many of them with special protection, such as tough casings or safe dwelling sites within the soil, and in many cases the only clue that the noxious offspring are around is the presence of their very visible elders.

Some insects are easily recognized, like the tomato hornworm, which is comparatively large and feeds during daylight hours. In other cases, either the microscopic size or the feeding habits of the intruders make them difficult to see directly. These pests are usually recognized by the damage they cause.

Among the most visible garden pests are ants and grasshoppers. A trail of ants is too common a sight to trigger much alarm, but it should, because where there are ants you may find aphids. Some ants have the decidedly unhelpful habit of protecting these nuisances in order to eat the honeydew they secrete. And by themselves other species of ants such as the leafcutter ant of the Southwest can cause widespread damage.

The gardener who blames aphids for his plant's predicaments without actually seeing the pests—they are less than ⅛ inch long and often green—has a pretty good chance of being correct. Worldwide, there are thousands of varieties of these plant lice; they are attracted to all vegetables and to most other garden plants. Besides reducing plant vigor by sucking out the sap, aphids are agents in the spread of destructive diseases. Their honeydew secretions are an ideal medium for the growth of sooty mold, for example, a black fungus that spreads over leaves and interferes with the process of photosynthesis.

There is hardly a garden anywhere on earth that does not harbor at least a few aphids. Whenever you start seeing a number of them on a single plant, though, you should consider starting a spraying program, because aphids are among the most prolific breeders in the animal kingdom. Within a week or two, that same plant might be crawling with aphids numbering in the thousands.

Most nonscientists would probably call an aphid a "bug." But technically speaking, true bugs occupy a special niche in the vast world of insects. They are distinguished from other insects by front wings that are stiff at the base and membranous at the ends; they assault plants by piercing them and sucking out the sap. Several of these pests give off a foul smell when they are crushed; consequently the name "stink bug" is widely applied to many of them. One of the worst of these pests is the harlequin bug, a flat, ⅜-inch insect with bright red markings on a black shell, found mostly in the southern part of the United States. Nymphs of this species feed mainly upon vegetables such as cabbages, cress and turnips, but they will vary their diet with many other fruits and vegetables. Both adults and

HOMAGE TO A PEST

Cotton growers in the South spend millions of dollars annually to fight the boll weevil, yet there is a monument honoring this pest in Alabama. Its depredations shortly after the turn of the century were so severe that farmers turned in desperation to other crops. In Coffee County planters tried peanuts; skepticism turned to delight as they netted $5 million in profits the first year. To celebrate their good fortune, they built a fountain in Enterprise, Alabama, and had it inscribed: "In profound appreciation of the boll weevil and what it has done as the herald of prosperity."

BUGS THAT ARE TRUE BUGS

offspring are so voracious that they can kill off entire crops. Slightly larger, with a dull brown or light gray color, is the squash bug, which feeds upon all vine crops, injecting a toxic substance that turns plants black and kills the smaller vines. These insects reproduce prolifically, and the best way to stop them is to destroy their eggs, which are laid in distinctive brick-red clusters between the veins on the undersides of vine leaves.

Though not a bug, the grasshopper is another obnoxious intruder, ravenously devouring leaves and vegetables. In recent years, the careful administration of sprays and poison baits has reduced the chances of a recurrence of the swarms that ravaged the Great Plains states in the 1870s *(pages 12-13)*.

All of the aforementioned intruders have two things in common: they can be seen feeding upon the plant, and they all undergo gradual metamorphosis. The average gardener will have far more trouble, however, from some of the beetles, flies and moths, which undergo complete metamorphosis and include among their voracious offspring such destructive villains as cutworms, caterpillars, grubs and fruit maggots.

A MULTITUDE OF BEETLES

Beetles are the most varied and numerous members of the insect world—and of the animal kingdom. There are over a quarter of a million species of beetles, with some 26,000 different varieties in North America alone. And they pose a special problem for the gardener, who must differentiate between enemies and allies, for some beetles are useful, devouring insect pests and scavenging dead animal and vegetable matter. The firefly grub, for example, is omnivorous, numbering slugs, snails and worms among its victims. And the ground beetle should be a welcome guest in any garden because both adults and grubs feed upon several species of pests. Ground beetles usually are large and black, and are sometimes found resting under stones or moving swiftly across the soil. They have a particularly ferocious appearance but are among the best natural controls in your garden.

The worst beetle menaces assault plants both as adults above the ground and as grubs feeding within the soil. One way to identify a beetle problem is to note the occurrence of garden and yard problems simultaneously. Brightly colored Japanese beetle adults, for example, chew on the leaves and shoots of young vegetables and ornamentals. And their grubs feed on the roots of grasses, leaving bare or brown areas on your lawn. Apple and plum curculios, which, despite their names, are general feeders that ravage many kinds of fruit trees, are also highly destructive in both adult and larval stages. The plum curculio makes a typical crescent-shaped scar on fruit, while apple curculios signal their presence with closely spaced punctures. And the grubs of both varieties feed in the interior of the fruit. An important nonchemical means of controlling these beetle pests, and a number of fly maggots as well, is the prompt disposal of any fruit that falls to the ground or begins to rot on the tree. Dead or rotting fruit provides an ideal breeding site for grubs and maggots; disposing of it interrupts their breeding cycle and will reduce their numbers next season. (Other sanitary measures are discussed in detail in Chapter 3.)

Take special note if you see what appear to be small houseflies early in the spring, just about the time cherry trees start to bloom and young cabbages are set out. This is the egg-laying period, and when the maggots hatch in the soil they move from the nesting site in search of their favorite hosts. Carrot rust fly maggots burrow down to feed on the root tips of carrots, parsley and celery; cabbage maggots head for their namesake, as well as for broccoli, Brussels sprouts and other vegetables in the cabbage family. The onion maggot, which has similar habits, can destroy large portions of an onion crop by chewing up bulbs. In every case, the time to stop maggots is before they are born—when the first flies are spotted in spring (or in late summer if a second generation of adults emerges)—by destroying the flies with an appropriate insecticide (*Chapter 5*).

One variety of garden fly, however, deserves a vote of thanks: the easily spotted, brightly colored syrphid fly. Also known as the flower fly or hover fly, this insect is usually seen maneuvering above the newly opened blossoms of flowers. It is ¼ to ⅜ inch long, and can be identified by the yellow spots, stripes or hair filaments upon its shiny blue, black, green or violet back. Adults of this species help pollinate a number of plants, but their true value is in the maggot stage when they prey relentlessly upon aphids and many other kinds of soft-bodied pests.

Moths are seldom seen well enough to be clearly identified because most of them are nocturnal, flying only at night. The cutworm, which is the offspring of the noctuid moth, is often found coiled in the soil near damaged plants, but sometimes it can be detected only by the way it neatly shears off young plants as if an elf with a scythe had been in the garden overnight. Sometimes you can take a flashlight with you into the garden and nab the culprits in the act. This is advisable, though, only if your neighbors aren't the skittish type who might be alarmed at the sight of a flashlight bobbing around in your backyard in the middle of the night.

You can locate and identify many night feeders just as easily at dusk or dawn, including most moth larvae, which feed aboveground.

A LIVING THERMOMETER
To a gardener, the pulsing chirp of the snowy tree cricket signals a mixed blessing. For while tree crickets eat aphids and other small pests, they also eat fruits and foliage. Many gardeners tolerate them, however, because their chirps can be a useful warning that the temperature is dropping rapidly and plants might be endangered. A tree cricket sings more slowly as the temperature declines. If you count the number of chirps in 13 seconds and add 40 to that total, you will have an approximate reading of the outside temperature in Fahrenheit degrees for as long as the cricket continues to sing.

THE EAT-BY-NIGHTS

HOW INSECTS MATURE FROM EGG TO ADULT

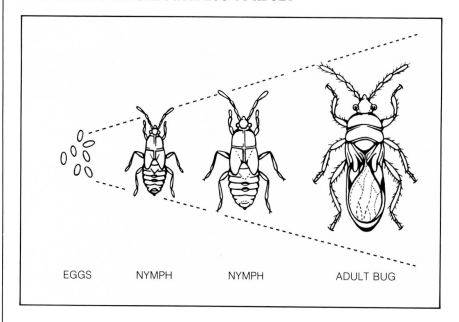

EGGS   NYMPH   NYMPH   ADULT BUG

GRADUAL METAMORPHOSIS

Insects that develop by gradual metamorphosis like the chinch bug (left) emerge from the eggs as nymphs—small versions of the adults. As a nymph grows, it sheds its rigid outer skeleton. This is called molting, and with each successive molt, the nymph grows, wings develop and its resemblance to the adult increases. Nymphs and adults eat the same plants. The chinch bug goes through five molts from egg to adult; some species need 20 molts to reach maturity.

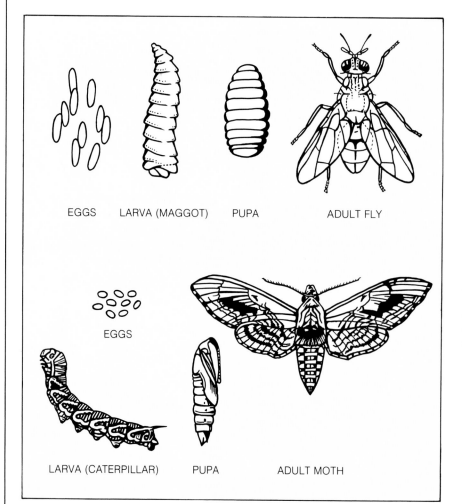

EGGS   LARVA (MAGGOT)   PUPA   ADULT FLY

EGGS

LARVA (CATERPILLAR)   PUPA   ADULT MOTH

COMPLETE METAMORPHOSIS

Most insects, including flies, moths, butterflies and beetles (opposite page), develop by a four-stage process that is called complete metamorphosis, changing their appearances dramatically at each stage. The process begins with the egg, which hatches a larva that does little but eat and get larger. (The larva of a fly is called a maggot, the larva of a moth or butterfly is a caterpillar, and that of a beetle is a grub.) When the larva reaches its maximum size, it molts into the next stage: the quiescent pupa, sometimes inside a cocoon, sometimes not. Beneath the skin of the pupa, a furious rearranging of cells takes place, and structures that characterize the adult, such as the wings and legs, are formed. In the final stage, the adult insect emerges looking nothing like the larva.

What an insect's life cycle tells us

The gardener who is familiar with the stages of life a pest goes through holds the key that will keep it under control. When he spots a harmless brown moth, he knows his attack must be against the moth's unseen offspring, the cutworm, which chews young shoots near the soil surface. Moths, beetles, flies and butterflies undergo a complete metamorphosis, eating their way through worm-like larval stages before they become adults with different appearances and eating habits. Controls that check the adults may not affect the larvae except by reducing their future numbers.

Some other pests, like the chinch bug *(above, left)*, are easier to identify and control because they develop gradually. The young, or nymphs, resemble the adults and infest the same plants. Controls that check the adult are usually also effective against the nymphs.

UPS AND DOWNS OF A JAPANESE BEETLE
Many gardeners react to a Japanese beetle invasion only after they see the beetles on their lawns and ornamental plants in midsummer. But by then a new generation has already emerged, and any relief will be a reprieve at best. The gardener who knows the beetle's life cycle can go after it when it is still below the ground, in the grub stage, and is susceptible to an effective, long-lasting natural control, milky disease. Action at this stage of the beetle's development interrupts the life cycle and eliminates the danger of attacks by future generations.

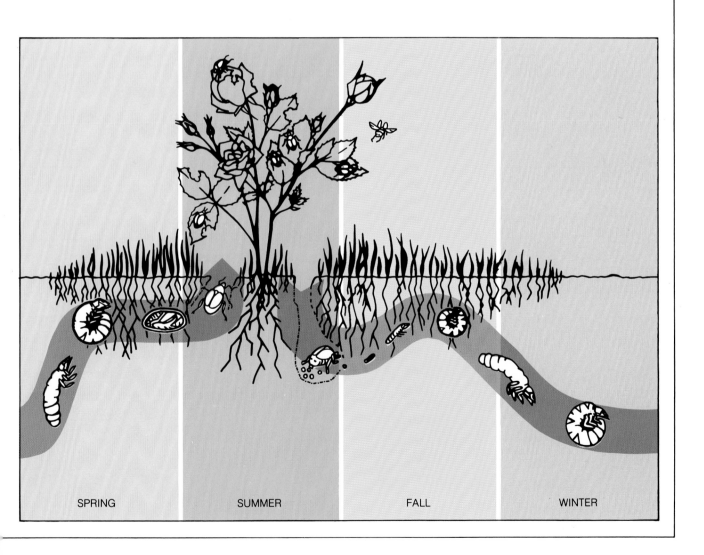

SPRING   SUMMER   FALL   WINTER

Anyone who doubts the need for tough import controls on foreign plants need only examine the devastating incursion of the gypsy moth. A native of Europe, it was brought into Massachusetts in 1869 by a French scientist who hoped to crossbreed it with the silkworm. A few escaped from his laboratory. Unchecked by natural enemies, the species was such a menace by 1906 that the federal government enacted a program of plant quarantine and inspection to keep any other foreign pests from entering this country. But it was too late to stop the gypsy moth; in the late 1970s it was defoliating up to two million acres of deciduous forest a year—as well as countless shade trees in private yards and gardens.

VORACIOUS SPEEDSTERS

The case bearers can be recognized by the tough silk pouches in which they live. These small caterpillars, which might be called nature's backpackers, drag their domiciles with them as they move along to feed on the tissues of plants. Webworms get their name from the tight, closely knit webs that they cast over leaves and in the junctures of small twigs and branches. The beet webworm is found from the Mississippi River westward and has been spotted on the East Coast, while the fall webworm defoliates fruit, shade and nut trees throughout the country. Another deadly moth offspring is the leaf roller. This caterpillar rolls a leaf up tightly, binds it in place with a web, then feeds upon it. Unchecked, leaf rollers can rapidly proliferate and defoliate a fruit tree, creating distinctly unattractive clusterings of webbed and rotting leaves.

Unlike the previously mentioned beetles, flies and moths, many pests are so small that they are barely visible to the naked eye; they make their unwelcome presence known either by their feeding habits or sheer weight of numbers. The common red spider mite, which when full grown would just about dot an "i" on this page, spins webs that cover the undersides of leaves and extend from one leaf to another. This causes rose leaves to turn colors that range from red to gray to brown, and gives the foliage of most other plants a sickly yellow hue by cutting off the supply of chlorophyll. Another common mite, the cyclamen mite, poses a different sort of threat. Though it spins no webs, this pest signals its arrival on flowering plants and vegetables by producing distorted, streaked or blotched blooms that fall early, while the leaves are left purplish and curled.

Two other minute pests, the well-armored scale insects and their soft-bodied cousins, the mealy bugs, generally stay put once they insert their mouth parts into leaves and begin drinking sap. They destroy branches as well as leaves and occasionally entire trees or shrubs. They are usually found on the undersides of leaves, but they also like stems and most fruit and vegetable surfaces as well. The advent of scales or mealy bugs is marked by gradually spreading patches or streaks of these minute specks.

These are stationary nuisances and can be fairly easily detected, but the swift flight of two other tiny pests, thrips and midges, renders them almost invisible. Thrips have two sets of fine, fringed wings. Their mouth parts are designed for rasping and for sucking, and a rasped wound is an especially hospitable setting for disease agents. The most widely distributed and destructive of these insects is the onion thrip, found wherever onions are grown, though it also attacks most other garden vegetables. The onion thrip leaves a calling card of whitish blotches, followed by blasting and distortion of leaf tips. Soon after, the plant withers, turns brown and topples over. The gladiolus thrip, which prefers flowering plants, leaves silvery patches upon foliage where it has drained sap, and the plant soon withers and turns brown. The blooms of the gladiolus and of the rose, iris, hollyhock, aster and other ornamentals upon which the thrip feeds will be deformed and flecked with small whitish streaks.

Midges, whose cousins, the biting gnats, sorely afflict human flesh, also escape detection thanks to their size and speed. But one of the worst of these minute marauders, the rose midge, makes its onset known with dramatic suddenness. Adults lay thousands of yellowish, microscopic eggs in unfolding leaves and near the bases of flower buds. Upon hatching, the larvae devour the nearby plant tissue, and overnight they can deflower an entire rose garden—sparing only the leaves—where a few hours earlier there was the promise of a many-colored summer bouquet.

Insects that attack the interiors of plants are among the most destructive and also the most difficult to find and to fight. The many varieties of borers—larvae of beetles or moths hatched from eggs laid inside a tree trunk or a thick stem—often can be destroyed only by probing with a thin wire. Upon hatching, the larvae begin feeding and tunneling through the plant, seriously disrupting the flow of water and nutrients throughout its system.

Healthy trees and shrubs usually can withstand the parent insects' efforts to implant their borer eggs, but a number of factors can weaken the plant, making it more susceptible to invasion. These include drought, sunscald, industrial pollutants, wounds inflicted by other insects and injuries from tools. The most familiar telltale sign of borer invasion is a tiny hole in the trunk or stem, surrounded by leavings of sawdust or pith that have been tunneled out. On smaller plants, the first symptom may be a bent stalk which, upon close examination, will show signs of boring within. Flat-headed apple-tree borers, common throughout the country, leave the bark discolored and slightly sunken, but without the castings left by other varieties. European corn borers, the most destructive of this type of pest, prey upon some 200 varieties of fruits and vegetables.

Just as borers work within trunks, stems and stalks, even smaller pests, known collectively as leaf miners, feed in the almost infinitesimal space between the surfaces of leaves. Leaf miners can be the larvae of beetles, moths or flies. They reveal themselves by leaving blisters upon a leaf or by causing discolored blotches; if the leaf is torn apart, microscopic veins are visible—the tunnels the miners have hollowed out.

Not every blister or blotch on a leaf is the fault of an insect,

BORING FROM WITHIN

however. Many such anomalies are caused by diseases, which are as natural in nature's master plan as the birds and the bees. Diseases help to keep millions of organisms in balance, but when they go unchecked they can become a major problem.

Plant diseases are caused by pathogens: viruses, fungi or bacteria. Some viruses may be carried from plant to plant by pests such as aphids, thrips, nematodes, leaf hoppers and whiteflies, making these pests doubly dangerous to your garden. Certain beetles, such as the cucumber beetle, transmit bacterial wilt, which can devastate cucumber, squash and pumpkin vines. And wounds that are left by virtually any pest as it feeds are open invitations to the organisms that cause disease.

Sprays, dusts or mechanical means can usually eradicate garden insects right after they are spotted, but once a disease takes hold the infected plants should be destroyed. The right time to stop a disease by spraying is before it starts, with a regular spraying program. But even when it is necessary to remove a diseased plant, you can still protect its healthy neighbors. In any spraying program, caution is the most important ingredient. If the temperature rises sharply, or humidity and moisture levels change rapidly, the applied chemical itself may harm the plant.

SIGNS THAT MISLEAD

Environmental ailments often have symptoms similar to diseases. Sunscald and leaf scorch are two common ailments, both caused by temperature and moisture changes. Most plants grow best in temperatures between 40° and 90°; they are able to withstand extremes better at the cooler end of the scale than the hotter. As summer temperatures soar, the chances of sunscald increase. And the gardener who wants to pick some tomatoes to add to a cooling salad may find that the tomatoes that looked fine in 80° temperatures have been scalded to death when the thermometer topped 90° for several days in a row.

Growing heat-susceptible plants in the shadier parts of your garden can lessen the danger of such environmental ailments as sunscald, as can proper watering. The gardener who steps outside on a bright morning and discovers that his tomatoes have turned black and rotting overnight may curse some unknown killer virus, but he probably has killed them himself by too great a variation in watering—an alternation of too much with not enough. Too little moisture, of course, stunts growth, lightens the leaf color and inhibits the development of fruit, flower or vegetable. Leaves may be scorched and wilted, simulating infectious diseases such as fusarium wilt or fungus anthracnose. Too much moisture, on the other hand, waterlogs the plant and deprives its roots of oxygen. The upper parts of the plant may begin to darken, and the collapse of root cells from the lack of oxygen invites attack by disease microorganisms that may be present in the soil.

What a gardener often fails to realize is that certain physical characteristics of his plot may naturally inhibit the distribution of moisture through no fault of his own. Slight slopes may cause water to run off before the roots of the plants can absorb it, or patches of rock or sand underlying the soil may cause moisture to build up or drain off too rapidly—and the result will be a group of unhealthy-looking plants surrounded by perfectly normal ones.

Modern industrial society has added still more environmental scourges. If you live in an area near factories or open-stack furnaces, you may observe bleaching of garden plants that is caused by any one of three common pollutants—hydrogen fluoride, sulfur dioxide or nitrogen dioxide. The same symptom could also suggest viral diseases such as mosaic.

Another major cause of ailing plants is a lack, or occasionally an excess, of soil nutrients. Plants require fairly high concentrations of three elements in particular—nitrogen, phosphorus and potassium, which are usually maintained at adequate levels in the garden by applying fertilizers. Plant health also depends on the availability of some 15 trace elements, including magnesium, iron, calcium, boron and zinc. The most common symptom of inadequate nutrition is chlorosis, resulting in leaf yellowing, but other types of discoloration, plus wilting, spotting, stunting, leaf distortion and death can also result from malnutrition.

Once you have eliminated pests and environmentally caused ailments as the reasons for your plant's distress, it is time to pinpoint the exact infectious disease. It is helpful to remember that most diseases are known by names that suggest the symptoms, such as rust, yellows, black spot, wilt or mosaic. For the most part, the home gardener need worry about only a relatively few types of diseases— most of which are readily identifiable.

For example, a gall is a swelling that is usually found near the base of the stem, though it can occur on any part of the plant. A gall usually is a plant's reaction to irritation caused by insects (as when larvae are present in a stem) or by bacteria or fungi. For example, the larvae of certain wasps are responsible for mossy rose galls and oak galls. An even greater menace are the microscopic underground nematodes, which in some instances create galls in roots and near the base of the stem. One of the most serious gall diseases, crown gall, is caused by bacteria that enter the plant through injuries—including those inflicted by tools as well as by nematodes or soil insects.

DIAGNOSING INFECTIONS

Infecting fruit and nut trees, vine fruits, flowering perennials and many kinds of vegetables, crown gall appears as a large, rough-surfaced and irregular swelling, sometimes several inches thick. It may appear near the soil or higher up on the plant and is often found at the site of a graft. Infected plants should always be promptly eliminated from the garden and destroyed.

Another common disease, anthracnose, is caused by a fungus and is characterized by a dead spot or scablike distinctive lesion on stem, leaf or fruit. A bane to melon growers everywhere, melon anthracnose first appears on leaves as small, water-soaked yellow areas that turn dark. Stems display narrow, shrunken lesions, and the unsightly black sunken spots that appear on the fruit leave it tough and bitter tasting.

TROUBLE SPOTS

A large grouping of diseases is characterized by—and named for—various spots, blights or blotches that become visible on the plant. Diseases such as black spot, which afflicts rose bushes, have clearly defined, usually round borders, often with the color of the center of the spot different from that of the periphery. The dead spot in the tissue frequently falls out, eventually killing the leaf prematurely; sometimes, if it is not controlled, black spot may defoliate an entire bush.

Unlike the clearly confined abnormalities of spot diseases,

If left unchecked, this Gulf fritillary caterpillar will make a quick meal of the passion vine on which it is perched.

blights rapidly afflict an entire leaf, branch or stem—often killing it. Fire blight, sometimes called pear blight although it infects many varieties of trees, is caused by bacteria that cause leaves to wilt suddenly, turn dark and die while remaining attached to twigs. The tree bark shrinks and sometimes develops blisters that ooze gum. Overall, large sections of the tree may look as though they have been burned by a blowtorch.

Blotch diseases fall somewhere between clearly defined spots and the general spread of blights. Purple blotch of onions, for example, begins with small white spots that enlarge to irregular purple patches, sometimes surrounded by bands of orange or yellow. Leaf tissue at the boundary of the blotch turns yellow and dies, and the stalk is killed before seeds mature.

A canker is also a more or less localized symptom of disease, which usually begins with a dead spot on a woody trunk or a thick stem. The lesion spreads rapidly, girdling the trunk and interfering with the upward flow of water from the roots. As a result, leaves and branches start dying back from the tips toward the base of the plant—a condition that duplicates the appearance of some of the blight diseases. Rose brown canker, for example, begins as a small purplish spot whose center acquires a red-ringed white spot. These spots multiply rapidly, and the leaves of the plant soon show many

Metamorphosis transposes the caterpillar opposite into this butterfly, a harmless insect.

purple or cinnamon-colored spots; the petals of the flowers also acquire cinnamon-buff blemishes.

Mildews, molds and smuts fit into other disease groups, characterized by fungus overgrowths. Powdery mildews leave soft white filament growths over sections of the plants; the most common symptom prior to the appearance of the powdery growth is a stunting and dwarfing, with leaves turning slightly red and curling as the fungus drains nutrients.

Mold is a term loosely applied to many fungus overgrowths of different colors. In damp climates, sooty mold is an almost inevitable aftermath of invasion by honeydew-producing insect pests, since it lives on the sweet secretions instead of the plant. Sooty mold is usually not fatal to plants, but because it blocks out solar rays it inhibits photosynthesis, resulting in fruits or vegetables that are small and prone to decay.

Smuts are also sooty black fungi, but they do live off the plants, attacking seeds as well as young plants, particularly different kinds of grasses. Onion smut, one of this plant's worst enemies, appears on young plants as elongated blisters or pustules; the plants either die or are severely stunted, occasionally with black or brown smut capsules on the bulbs.

Rust is a term that embraces some 4,000 different diseases, all characterized by red or rusty-brown specks or blemishes. But many other diseases, or the unwise use of chemicals, can simulate rust. The best way to determine the presence of true rust is to examine the plant closely for rust-colored spore cases in powdery pustules or with jelly-like horns. The color sometimes tends more toward yellowish than true rust color, and the plant is often stunted.

THE SCOURGE OF ROT

Another disease category, rot, is characterized by decaying tissue all over the plant. Rot is not always soft, mushy and putrid as its name implies; in some forms it is a hard, dry decay. When rot takes hold, usually as fruit or other crops ripen and are ready to be stored or processed, there is little to do but destroy the affected plants and throw the produce away. Mushroom root rot, which produces mushrooms, is a major destroyer of trees and shrubs west of the Rockies. It appears as a clump of honey-colored toadstools on the base of decaying plants. As this fungus advances through the roots, leaves turn yellow and fall, and on small fruit trees all foliage may die at the same time.

Scabs look just as their name implies: small irregular patches of overgrowth, usually on fruit and leaves. Potato scab, which also afflicts beets, carrots and turnips, produces deep warty lesions that require extra-deep peeling to remove. Apple scab is one of the world's leading destroyers of this fruit, appearing first as a dull smoky area that later changes to a raised olive-drab spot. Its lesions lead to defoliation and also to marred and split fruit.

A final fungus category, wilt, is often difficult to distinguish from environmentally caused ailments. Wilting can be caused by lack of moisture, of course, but it is also a symptom of infections that are particularly difficult to control because they are systemic, affecting the entire plant rather than being limited to certain parts. Though wilts usually invade through roots, the first symptom is often a yellowing or wilting near the topmost leaves, which then progresses downward as the disease worsens. The best-known wilt is Dutch elm disease *(page 78),* which has spread through Europe, killing the famous elms at Versailles, and has moved across the entire United States. Dutch elm disease is spread by elm bark beetles, and its first symptom is wilting, sometimes so sudden and so severe that leaves are still green when they fall to the ground. During the summer, most of the leaves turn yellow or brown and twigs curl up tightly. Once attacked, the tree is almost certain to die. Unless an extensive series of treatments is professionally applied, the diseased tree must be uprooted and disposed of to stop the disease from spreading to other elm trees.

Bacterial diseases are more difficult to diagnose than fungus diseases because the symptoms, such as wilting, rot, spotting and other characteristics, are often identical to many fungus-related infections. Indicators that bacteria may be at work are the rapid spread of the symptoms throughout the entire plant and the absence of telltale fungus growths or spores.

VENOMOUS VIRUSES

Virus diseases, too, can sometimes be identified by the rapid progress of symptoms, such as wilting, dwarfing and unproductivity. Some viral infections take distinctive paths—beginning at a leaf, spreading within a few days to the stem, and from there straight up to the top of the plant, where they gradually infiltrate all the other leaves and branches. Mosaic, which assaults many different plants, is among the most common viral diseases, and is characterized by mottled green and yellow foliage. Other symptoms may be yellow rings or a general yellowing of the plant. Once a viral disease is confirmed, destruction of the plant is almost invariably required, followed by a rigorous spraying program to protect the rest of the garden from insect carriers.

Keeping your garden totally free of pests and diseases is impossible, but you can increase the odds in your plants' favor with the proper preventive action—an ounce of prevention before trouble strikes is worth a pound of chemicals later.

Reading early signs of trouble

When disease strikes in the garden, the early symptoms are apt to be so subtle that they are all but invisible from a distance. The most common diseases, those caused by fungi, start small with spots that may blend like camouflage into the sun-dappled landscape, or with yellowing leaves that are easily mistaken for ailments caused by lack of water or nutrients. But the gardener who is alert to early symptoms such as those illustrated in these pages can diagnose many diseases with the naked eye, then take steps to check the spread of the infection to other plants and guard against its recurrence.

Unfortunately, there are no sure cures for most fungus diseases, only preventive measures. When you see the signs of infection, apply fungicides to keep it from spreading. Despite their persistence, many diseases injure but do not destroy a plant. The botrytis blight that attacks lilies *(page 38)* is usually severe only once in five years, and it does not infect the bulb from which the plant grows. If a plant infected one season is sprayed regularly with a fungicide during the next season, it may be disease-free for that year. Lily botrytis, as well as dogwood spot anthracnose *(page 36),* can also be partly controlled by disposing of debris at the end of the season, so the spores that produce the fungi will not live through the winter on the dead leaves of infected plants. Root rot of peas *(opposite)* poses a different problem. Spores of the fungus that cause this disease live in the soil, spreading infection whenever they touch vulnerable roots. If the telltale yellowing leaves appear late in the season, the gardener can still harvest a fair crop of peas from diseased plants, but the symptoms are almost sure to reappear—and may do more damage—the following year. The best defense is to plant resistant varieties and rotate crops in order to starve out the fungus, which is so specialized it can only grow on the pea plant.

The thought of millions of invisible disease spores floating in the garden air or lurking in the soil is unsettling. But good cultivation practices—keeping the plants vigorous and using preventive measures early in the season—will put the odds in the plants' favor.

This determined gardener fills his pail with peas from plants whose yellowing lower leaves warn of root rot, a soil-borne disease that could mean slim pickings next year.

A dogwood's telltale spots

The sight of a flowering dogwood's cloud of opalescent blossoms in early spring may blind the winter-weary gardener to any flaw in his garden centerpiece. But even a tree such as the one below that looks almost as healthy as the garden around it may have blossoms that are marred and deformed by fungus disease. The disease, dogwood spot anthracnose, becomes very apparent when the blossoms are viewed more closely *(right)*. This disease is a form of leaf spot that is not fatal but can spoil the appearance of a dogwood. The spores of the fungus spend the winter on infected tree twigs; they can be prevented from causing disease by applying a fungicide when the first leaf buds open and continuing into summer.

From across the garden, only an expert might notice that the blossoms on some branches of the native dogwood are abnormally far apart and not quite the luminous white so startling in the Eastern woods in spring. But anyone could detect trouble by going to the tree for a closer view.

An inspection of several blossoms reveals small circular patches on deformed and wilted petals. These are clear indications that the tree is a victim of dogwood spot anthracnose, which may also cover leaves, shoots and berries with holes or gray-yellow spots ringed with purple.

Disease from the bottom up

A slight yellowing of the lower leaves of lilies such as those in the suburban New York garden below is an early sign of lily botrytis blight, the most common fungus disease of lilies. Usually it begins with the appearance of spots near the bases of leaves on nearly full-grown plants. In a year when the botrytis attack is severe, due to a succession of cool, damp nights, the spots may increase in size, run together, spread over the leaves and then move upward until the fungus even infects the blossoms *(opposite page)*. Botrytis blight does not attack the lily bulb, but if the leaves wilt before nourishing the bulb for the next year's growth, the plant must rely on reserves of nutrients that have been stored in the bulb in previous seasons.

Although a profusion of blossoms diverts attention from the yellowing lower leaves of these Turk's-cap lilies, the discoloration is suspect, contrasting as it does with the healthy foliage of nearby annuals.

One week later (above, top) botrytis
blight has moved up the stems of the
lilies, draining most of the leaves
of their color. In only a few more
days (above) the leaves are dead and
the flowers have faded.

Mildew: the summer frost

The gardener who buys a plant from a commercial greenhouse should be wary: the high humidity and the limited air circulation around plants that are crowded together indoors are just the conditions that encourage the proliferation of fungi. When the strawberries in the hanging basket below were purchased, they were already infected with powdery mildew, a fungus that multiplies rapidly in a greenhouse with cool nights and warm days. In its early stages, the disease may appear as white, feltlike spots *(opposite)*, or as a thin, frosty coating on leaves and fruit, or as a slight darkening and curling of leaf edges. Plants bearing any of these symptoms should be rejected, lest they infect other plants.

In the sunlight that filters through a wisteria arbor, hanging baskets of early-bearing ornamental strawberry plants, bought from a greenhouse the same day they were photographed, look as healthy to the casual observer as the playful kitten chasing sow bugs on the patio.

Closer inspection reveals white spots on the lower leaves of the plants, one of the first signs of powdery mildew. This fungus disease, if unchecked, eventually will spoil the appearance of the entire plant. Its spread can be slowed with applications of a fungicide such as a sulfur spray.

Protecting your plants the natural way 3

Few gardeners have ever considered domesticating a toad—which is a shame. Though hardly suitable as a household pet, a toad is a useful resident in a garden. It will eat an estimated 10,000 insects during a normal growing season. This is a small reduction in the pest population of a garden, but it is 10,000 fewer chompers and suckers at work on your foliage, flowers, fruits and vegetables.

Only a few years ago, the idea of deliberately keeping a few toads would have seemed a bizarre way to check injurious insects. After all, a gardener could kill far more marauders with a single spraying of chlordane or DDT. But as government agencies have increasingly restricted the use of many familiar pesticides to protect the total environment, gardeners have been forced to seek alternatives. Fortunately, nature—with a little help from man and science—possesses a formidable array of defenses against both pests and diseases. Some of these involve nothing more than good gardening practices that strengthen plants and weaken their enemies. Researchers are constantly reinforcing these efforts by developing disease- and pest-resistant strains of plants and by improving understanding of the way nature itself works to keep pests in check. Some new thrusts in this battle against pests, such as the use of irradiation to destroy their breeding capacity, border on science fiction and are outside the capability of the gardener. But some checks merely call for minor mechanical skills in the construction of barriers, traps and lures to keep the intruders away from prized plants. Experimenting with various combinations of resistant plants, mechanical barricades and beneficial insects and animals will help you to protect your garden the natural way—so you can use toxic chemicals in a limited and well-managed manner.

How to attract toads and other beneficial creatures to your garden is discussed later in this chapter. All successful gardeners would agree, though, that good prevention practices are worth a

A plant with a built-in defense mechanism proves its worth. The tomato plant at left, bred to be disease resistant, shows little effect from an injection of wilt fungus that has stunted its weaker companion.

score or more of even the hungriest toads. These include those day-by-day and season-by-season practices that promote healthy, well-nourished plants and soil. In fact, many gardeners perform these tasks for the sake of a fruitful crop without ever being aware that their efforts also yield protection against pests and diseases.

For example, at some point between growing seasons most gardeners will see that the soil where they intend to plant vegetables and annuals gets a deep spading. They are aware that such tillage—turning over the earth to at least the depth of the spading fork's tines—helps increase the air supply underground, thus contributing to the development of strong, deep roots. Spading can also improve the structure of the soil and, if organic materials are added, it raises the level of soil nutrients. Last but not least, proper tillage destroys many of the insects, like grasshoppers, that winter in the ground.

LETTING FRESH AIR IN

Generous spacing and timely watering also have desirable side effects. Most gardeners know that space between plants reduces competition for nutrients and ensures that each plant gets direct sunlight. What they may not realize is that such spacing also reduces the danger of fungus disease because it improves ventilation, letting the plants shed the excess moisture in which fungi thrive. Watering should be done early enough in the day so surplus moisture on the foliage will evaporate before nightfall.

TREATING A TREE INFECTION

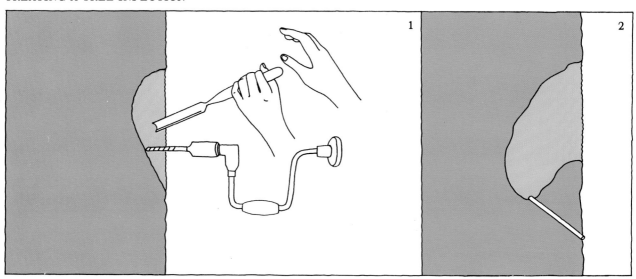

If a minor tree infection is neglected, rot will spread. Use a brace and bit as a probe to learn how deep the soft wood is. If you hit solid wood within one third of the diameter of the trunk or branch, dig out the soft patch

with a wood chisel, using the palm of your hand as a mallet. Smooth and shape the inside of the cavity so that water will drain from it. Disinfect the cavity wall with denatured alcohol and coat it with tree-wound paint.

When a cavity cannot be shaped to drain itself, drill a hole that leads downward from the lowest point. Disinfect and paint. To prevent the hole from sealing, insert copper tubing that extends beyond the bark.

Fungi can also be checked by good drainage, which lets excess water sink quickly deep beneath the surface. This stimulates the development of strong, deep roots, of course, but it also helps the soil shed stagnant water that otherwise might encourage root rot, making the weakened plants more susceptible to an onslaught of disease or pests. To avoid these problems, work enough organic matter into the soil so it will hold water in dry spells but let it drain away during downpours. This matter can consist of grass clippings, leaves, peat moss, carrot or beet tops, or any other clean plant refuse. Such a mixture, when sufficiently aged, is called compost.

A 2-inch application of compost worked into the soil each spring before planting will increase a garden's productivity. Besides promoting good drainage, composting supplies additional nutrients, which help to keep plants strong enough to outgrow pest damage.

THE CONSTANT CLEANUP

Good cultivation practices can go for nought in an untidy, unsanitary garden. During the growing season, such refuse as weeds, fallen fruit and the remains of vegetables should be removed quickly. It may not be practical to remove all the fruit beneath the trees of a large orchard, but this is a vital task in the home garden. Each removal of a dead fruit or vegetable also removes a potential feeding station for developing larvae. Similarly, elimination of weeds also eliminates possible egg depositories, as well as potential hosts for disease microorganisms. Healthy refuse, of course, can be added to your compost heap. But if you have any doubt about the cleanliness of the refuse, burn it if local laws permit, or place it in tied plastic trash bags for removal. Because disease can spread with great speed through a garden, inspection for and elimination of diseased plants should be the final chore in any day of gardening. If, despite your efforts, disease does get a firm foothold, you may need to resort to chemical controls to keep it from spreading (*Chapter 4*).

GERMFREE TOOLS

It is important to clean and disinfect your gardening tools and clothing. If they are not cleaned they can harbor disease pathogens. Clothes can be kept reasonably germfree simply by tossing them into the washing machine with a good detergent. Tools can be disinfected with a solution of 7 parts denatured alcohol to 3 parts water or in a 10 per cent solution of sodium hypochlorite—the chemical name for common chlorine-based household bleach.

Discriminating choice of seed is another vital measure in pest and disease prevention. Using resistant varieties will save you many hours of labor with chemical sprays and dusts—and many plants.

There is nothing novel about the natural, built-in resistance of plants to insect pests and diseases: nature has been evolving and elaborating such defenses for millions of years. Some plants ward off enemies by growing fine, sharp spines. Others, including several species of chrysanthemums, produce toxins that repel, sicken or kill insects. Chemical substances called terpenoids keep spider mites from damaging cucumbers.

Disease resistance, too, takes several forms. Some plants have developed, in effect, coats of armor that isolate a pathogen and keep it from spreading. Cherry trees form a corky layer of tissue around the invasion site. Another defense mechanism is a build-up of the waxy cuticle that protects exposed plant tissue.

These self-protective measures were entirely the work of nature until about the middle of the 19th Century when researchers began to search out—and breed—resistant plants. Since then, one of the most dynamic fields of horticulture has been the deliberate crossbreeding of resistant varieties and the introduction of naturally resistant strains. Some of the results are astonishing.

In 1860, for example, the grape phylloxera, a small yellow aphid, introduced to France from America, devastated French vineyards. The insect produced swellings on the leaves and roots and slowly drained nutrients from the vines, killing them in three to 10 years. Scientists eventually discovered that grape varieties in the eastern United States—where the phylloxera was indigenous—were resistant to the pest. The ensuing grafting of European vines to resistant rootstock was a success. Today, most European and American grapes are products of phylloxera-resistant grafts. And wine lovers everywhere owe a tip of the glass to these humble Yankee vines. The grafted-on European grapes, known as the scions, retained all of their own flavor characteristics, gaining only suste-

BUILT-IN DEFENSES

BIOLOGICAL BEETLE CONTROL

1. *Lawn-damaging grubs of Japanese beetles can be killed by infecting them with milky disease, which is harmless to plants, humans and other animals. Apply 1 teaspoonful of spore-bearing dust at 4-foot intervals. Since the disease is self-perpetuating, only one application is needed.*

2. *To make a dispenser, punch small holes in the bottom of a 1-pound coffee can near the center. Attach the can to a stick, about 4 inches from one end. Fill the can ¾ full and jolt spots of the dust on the lawn at 4-foot intervals.*

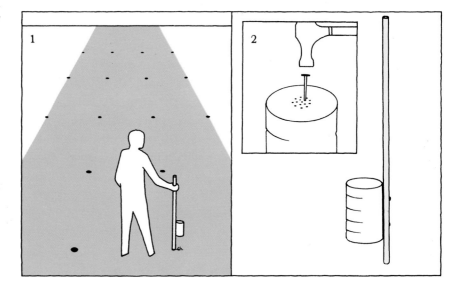

nance—and protection against phylloxera—from the foreign roots.

Not surprisingly, most resistant plant varieties have been developed for agriculturally valuable crops. But total or partial resistance also has been achieved for about 100 species favored by home gardeners. Thus, the selective choice of seeds is an easy deterrent to such pests as the European corn borer and the pea aphid.

When choosing seeds, read the catalogue or packet to determine just what safeguards you are getting. Many packagers will indicate whether the variety is immune. Resistance is signified by the prominent display of capital letters, such as "V" for virus, "F" for fungus or "N" for nematodes. Tomatoes with a bold "VFN" on the packet are resistant to certain strains of all three of these spoilers.

Unfortunately, resistant varieties are not permanently foolproof. Just as nature helps plants increase their resistance when necessary, it impartially helps insects and disease agents acquire traits to overcome the resistance mechanism. This is especially true of food plants. Plant scientists, therefore, are engaged in a continual race to develop resistant varieties that will keep them ahead of new strains of pests and diseases. The backyard gardener benefits from this research in the form of ever-improving varieties of seeds.

Ornamentals get less attention from plant breeders, but for unknown reasons the diseases of flowers and shrubs evolve less rapidly than those that prey upon other types of plants. Seeds of wilt-resistant asters and rust-resistant snapdragons are readily available.

DISINFECTING SEEDS

But the backyard gardener does not have to wait for scientists to develop resistant strains. There is an alternative. If you have harvested seed from an especially attractive plant in your own garden, or you received an envelope full of seeds from your neighbor's ribbon-winning squash, you should disinfect the seeds to destroy any possible diseases they may be harboring. Simply shake the seeds in an envelope or bag with a pinch of garden fungicide until they are uniformly coated.

If you follow good prevention measures and your garden is still infested by various scourges—as all gardens inevitably are at one time or another—you may want to try some natural remedies before you reach for the spray gun.

To add a toad to your garden's defenses, you need only catch a healthy-looking specimen and keep it penned up for a week or so to acclimate it to its new environment. An ideal shelter is made simply by knocking out one edge of a clay pot, overturning it in a shady spot and placing a shallow pan of water nearby. The toad will soon amply repay this inexpensive hospitality. Many gardeners have long encouraged the presence of toads, and one remembers a children's

Bands around trees have long been used to trap crawling insects. In 1840 Joseph Burrelle of the U.S. Department of Agriculture noted that a cloth wrapped around the trunk of an apple tree would catch caterpillars. He suggested baking the cloth in a hot oven to put a certain end to the pests. In the 1860s several strands of rope or cloth wound around a tree trunk made another kind of trap: caterpillars found the strands and folds inviting places to spend the pupation period—until the traps were collected and the pupae destroyed. Chemically treated bands—usually corrugated paper coated with beta-naphthol in oil—appeared on the market in the 1920s. Building paper, fabrics, cotton batting and sticky paper have all been tried with varying success.

BENEVOLENT BEETLES

movie matinee that was sponsored each spring by a garden club in her hometown; the price of admission: one toad per child.

Snakes have been viewed with doubt and aversion for thousands of years—as far back in Scripture as the time a serpent got Adam and Eve evicted from their own garden. But many kinds of nonlethal snakes can, nevertheless, be very helpful in a modern garden. They consume great quantities of insects and rodents.

Birds are far more welcome and attractive helpers, devouring huge quantities of beetles, caterpillars, moths, scale insects, millepedes, leaf hoppers, grasshoppers and other pests. Birds such as woodpeckers with long, strong beaks also dig inside trees for boring insects that often elude the best control measures available.

Providing a bird feeder during the winter and early spring will attract a flock of mixed birds to your garden. Nesting materials such as hair, rags, string and twine left around a tree or bush will encourage feathered visitors to set up residence. Most important during the summer is a shallow container of water placed well out of the reach of neighborhood cats.

As important as birds are, insectivorous insects—those that feed upon foraging insects—are even more important in the battle against pests. The Chinese recognized this keystone of natural control thousands of years ago—they learned to keep caterpillars from devouring their citrus crops by placing bamboo poles between the trees as bridges for a variety of ant, *Oecophylla smaragdina,* that relished caterpillars.

In fact, if it were not for predatory insects, the world would have been overrun by crop-destroying pests long ago. These beneficial insects fall into two categories: predators that kill and eat their prey and parasites that lay their eggs in the bodies of insect hosts.

You can easily recognize several beneficial insect predators by their dramatic, often beautiful appearance. Large-winged dragonflies devour mosquitoes, horseflies and garden pests near their watery habitats. And solemn, formidable praying mantises are highly efficient guardians of the plants on which they alight.

Perhaps the best known of all beneficial insects is the ladybug—which is really a beetle and not a bug at all. There are numerous varieties, all members of the insect family Coccinellidae—and virtually all of them are dedicated consumers of two of the garden's worst enemies, aphids and mealy bugs. Ladybug beetles are nearly hemispherical in shape, and most species are red, orange, brown or tan—usually with black spots. Some destructive leaf beetles, however, including the Mexican bean beetle and the squash beetle, are close look-alikes of useful ladybug beetles *(page 19).*

Another helper is the lacewing (not to be confused with the lace bug, a pest that attacks broad-leaved evergreens). The slender lacewing has shimmery green wings and red-gold eyes; it will add a touch of beauty to your garden while its more prosaic larvae attack pests. Lacewing larvae are known as aphid lions; they are flat, yellow or gray, hairy creatures with tong-shaped jaws. They eat aphids, mealy bugs, cottony-cushion scales and other pests that assault foliage and stems.

Valuable insect parasites include many species of parasitic wasps—those that lay eggs in other insects—and a large group of flies known as tachinids. The latter are gray-, brown- or black-mottled and slightly larger than the average housefly. One species, *Winthemia quadripustulata*, is one of the main enemies of the army

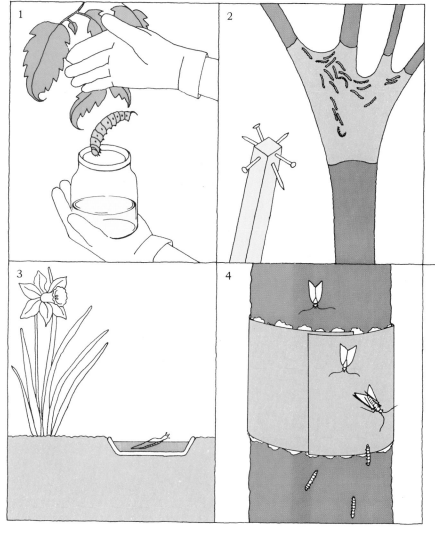

SIMPLE COUNTERMEASURES

1. *The easiest way to rid plants of caterpillars and bugs is to swipe them off with your gloved hand into a widemouthed jar containing water. Cover the jar, let it stand for a few hours, then pour the drowned pests into a hole and cover with soil.*

2. *To remove the web tents of tent caterpillars from trees, use a long strip of wood with nails driven through one end so they protrude on all sides. Poke the nails into a web and twist the pole to wind up the web with the caterpillars inside. Dispose by burning or by dunking in a pail of water.*

3. *To trap and kill slugs and snails, pour beer into a shallow pan and sink it flush with the surface of the ground near vulnerable plants. Fill the pan at dusk so the fresh smell of hops will lure the night feeders to crawl in and drown.*

4. *Adult insects and larvae that crawl up or down trees can be trapped with a 3-inch band of sticky paper wrapped around the trunk. Such bands can be purchased. Stuff absorbent cotton behind the bands so insects cannot crawl under them. When the trap is full, throw it away.*

worm. On its back they deposit their eggs, and their larvae burrow inside the insect and destroy it. Another tachinid, the *Parasetigena silvestris,* deposits its eggs on the gypsy-moth caterpillar.

Most of the approximately 90,000 species of wasps are not garden pests, and many of them are helpful in pest control. In fact, government agricultural agencies regularly introduce new species to check damaging insects. In the early 1970s, for example, a wasp from India was introduced in the eastern United States to battle the grubs of the Mexican bean beetle. Stinging wasps can seriously injure humans—or, in rare instances, even kill allergic individuals. As a general rule, though, if you don't bother a wasp it won't bother you. The parasitic wasp, which carries an egg-laying device called an ovipositor instead of a stinger, does bother many pests, drilling into

SHIELDING YOUR PLANTS

1. *To keep cutworms from severing stems of seedlings near the soil, install barriers made from plastic cups or empty tin cans. Remove the bottoms and slit the sides so the containers can be slipped around the stems. Press the barriers an inch or two into the soil.*

2. *Household aluminum foil, unrolled on the ground shiny side up and perforated with holes through which seedlings can grow, keeps moisture in the soil and repels aphids and leaf hoppers. Reflections in the foil confuse the insects. Cover the edges of the foil strip with soil to hold it down.*

3. *A simple hut protects plants by keeping flying insects from laying eggs on leaves and stems. To build one, drive four pipes, each 3 feet long and 1 inch in diameter, into the ground. Insert ¾-inch stiff plastic tubing into the pipe ends to form two arches. Cover with fine-mesh plastic netting attached to the framework with twist ties. Anchor the bottom edges with soil except on one end. Attach the edge there to a board, making an entrance. To forestall wind damage, keep the net loose. The height of the hut should be greater than the height the tallest plant will reach at maturity.*

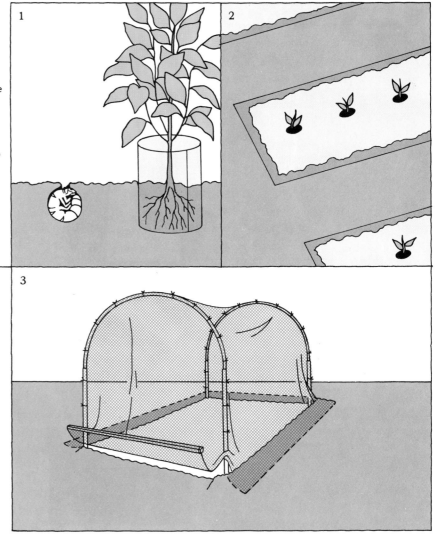

aphids, mealy bugs and caterpillars as well as minute scale insects and hard-to-reach borers. The wasp deposits eggs in these drilled holes. When the wasp eggs hatch and develop, the hosts die.

Modern science is imaginatively trying to enhance natural controls by using diseases against insect pests. Milky disease spores, mixed with a filler to achieve a uniform consistency and introduced into the soil, kill Japanese beetle grubs. One important advantage is that this disease is cumulative; the spores reproduce and spread, protecting a lawn for five to 10 years.

As scientific investigation reveals more about the ways insects communicate, navigate and select sites for feeding and breeding, the use of barriers and traps will provide increasingly effective control measures. But there are simple mechanical devices you can easily incorporate into your garden. Young vegetable seedlings, for example, can be protected from cutworms by the placement of small cardboard cylinders around them, nestled an inch or so into the soil. Paper cups with the bottoms cut out are ideal for this purpose. And there are many variations of old-fashioned flypaper. A square of sticky paper placed near crucifers will trap many cabbage maggots. A narrow band of sticky tape wrapped around the base of a tree trunk, adhesive side out, will trap climbing pests.

If gypsy moths—which are destructive defoliators—pose a problem, you can help protect your trees with a trap made by wrapping a 10-inch band of burlap around the trunk, tying it along the center with twine and folding it downward. Each day you shake out and dispose of the caterpillars caught within. A simple weapon against slugs is a saucer of beer set in the ground. Many gardeners swear that the smell of hops lures the pests to their death by drowning. Barriers and adhesive papers are the best mechanical devices to ward off crawling insects. Covers of muslin or other loose, transparent cloth are sometimes used as protection against flying pests. And a number of ingenious devices have been marketed, some using lights to attract insects and whirling fans that suck the pests into containers filled with kerosene or another liquid.

The problem with many mechanical devices is that they are indiscriminate, destroying useful as well as injurious insects. John Evelyn, in his *Gard'ner's Almanac,* published in London in 1699, offered this warning about a device intended for killing ants: "Boxes . . . pierced full of holes with a Bodkin, into which Boxes put the Powder of Arsenick mingled with a little honey: Hang these Boxes on the trees and they will certainly destroy them." Then he added: "Make not the Holes so large that a Bee may enter, lest it destroy them, too."

BLOCKING THE APPROACHES

A host of hungry helpers

For every insect that nibbles away at the plants in your garden, another insect anxiously waits to make a meal out of that pest. Without these insect allies on the side of the gardener, prolific pests would soon overrun the world.

The gardener who panics at the first sighting of a multilegged crawling or flying creature and immediately and indiscriminately blasts it with chemicals may well be doing more harm than good. For of approximately 86,000 species of insects in North America, 76,000 are considered harmless or beneficial to man.

The wise gardener avoids the unnecessary use of chemicals. Instead, he recognizes the insect and animal allies in his garden and he cultivates them as he might cultivate a prized rosebush. For instance, ladybug beetles such as those on page 54 will quickly eat most of the aphids that might otherwise decimate a rosebush. Certain other insects, such as the parasites on pages 58 and 59, deposit their eggs in aphids and other hosts, killing them more slowly but just as surely as the hungry ladybug.

But insects are not the only natural force at work controlling pests. Some birds, such as the downy woodpecker, may remain in the garden even in cold weather, feeding on insect eggs deposited on dormant twigs and brambles. And in warm weather, birds such as the wren on page 62 will catch grubs, caterpillars and other pests to feed their young.

Birdseed in winter and water in summer will help keep birds around the garden, and an aware gardener will also welcome the presence of the lizards, toads, nonpoisonous snakes and other animals such as those on pages 60 and 61 that also devour pests. But above all he will realize that, like the world at large, his garden is a delicately balanced ecological system that needs pests as well as predators to keep that balance. He seeks to control the insect pests in his garden, but not to eradicate them. For he knows that if no pests at all are left, he will lose the insect and animal allies that would help him check future invasions.

An undiscriminating praying mantis grasps a victim with the spiny front legs it uses to snatch both pests and friendly insects that cross its path.

Insects that eat insects

There are two kinds of beneficial insects in most gardens: predators, which devour insects on the spot or paralyze them to eat later; and parasites *(pages 58-59)*, which lay eggs inside the host, and whose larvae feed on it and eventually cause it to die.

Many insects, such as the ladybug *(below)* and the green lacewing *(opposite, above)*, are predators in both their mature and larval stages. The adults lay their eggs on the undersides of leaves, where many pests are found. When the larvae hatch, they have a ready source of food awaiting them. Other insects, such as the syrphid fly *(opposite, below)*, are not predators in the adult stage but are voracious insectivores as larvae.

Predators like those on pages 56 and 57 paralyze their prey and drag it back to the nest. There it lives on to provide nourishment for the waiting larvae. Sometimes a paralyzed victim is put in storage to provide fresh food when the larvae emerge.

Adult ladybug beetles converge on a broccoli flower (right); each one may eat up to 50 aphids and even more aphid larvae in a single night. A ladybug larva (above), one of the legions that emerge from eggs laid in an aphid colony, crawls over the plant seeking nourishment during its three-week larval stage.

Green lacewing adults, like the one eating aphids at left, use their tubular mouth parts like straws to draw out the body fluids of victims. The lacewing larvae often are called aphid lions. Some species hoist their victims' drained carcasses onto their backs to form "trash piles" like the one that camouflages the larva below.

An adult syrphid fly (left) alights on a plant stem long enough to deposit an egg. The adult, usually seen hovering above shrubs, eats mostly nectar and aphid honeydew. But the maggot (above) eats the aphids themselves. Using its jaws to lift a victim, the maggot drains it of fluid, then drops the aphid's carcass.

A caterpillar-hunter wasp, after paralyzing a caterpillar with a series of stings, drags it to a prepared burrow. The wasp will lay one egg on the caterpillar, which will provide food for the new wasp larva from the time it emerges until it reaches adulthood.

A yellow jacket hovers before injecting its paralyzing venom into a tobacco hornworm. The wasp will cut the caterpillar into pieces that it can transport to its papery nest to feed wasp larvae as well as some adults.

Parasites worth protecting

A parasitic insect usually needs only one host to nourish its young and uses a very direct approach to provide food: it places one or more eggs inside the body of its living victim. When the eggs hatch, the young gradually eat away inside the host, often until the larvae are full-grown and the host is dead or nearly so. When the larvae are mature, they emerge from the host by eating their way through the body wall. Then they spin cocoons in which the final stage in the transformation to adulthood takes place, often on or near the host that nourished them. Although during its lifetime a parasite takes fewer victims than does a predator, parasites are likely to produce more generations each year. Parasites attack the larvae of some highly destructive garden pests such as the tobacco hornworms that can consume tomatoes and defoliate the plant, and the cutworms that chew through the stems of such young plants as tomatoes, beans, cabbages and flowers.

An Oriental fruit fly (above, right) deposits its eggs in the rind of a citrus fruit through a hole it has made with its ovipositor, which is a specialized mechanism at the end of its abdomen. The maggots that will develop in the pulp of the fruit could do extensive damage, were it not for parasitic opius wasps. Two such wasps are shown at right, preparing to lay eggs inside the fruit-fly maggots. When the opius wasp larvae emerge from their eggs, they will devour the fruit-fly maggots.

Braconid wasps and apanteles wasps are parasites of caterpillars and the pupae of other insects. In the top picture, a braconid wasp deposits eggs through the body wall of a live gypsy-moth pupa. Above, braconid-wasp larvae have emerged from the cutworm that nourished them, and have spun cocoons beside their dead host. At left, an adult apanteles wasp emerges from a cocoon that is still attached to a caterpillar carcass and which itself is nearly hidden by a cluster of cocoons.

A motley crew of allies

In addition to insects, certain kinds of mammals, amphibians, reptiles, spiders and birds *(page 62)* help keep garden pests at bay. Some of these, such as turtles, are usually welcomed almost as pets by gardeners. Others, such as the rodent-like shrews, are received less cordially despite their prodigious appetite for insects.

Spiders lucky enough to make their homes on the property of an unsqueamish gardener are among the most valuable of predators. The web-weavers eat whatever unwary insects they catch in the sticky strands of their intricate lairs, while the hunters, such as the crab spider and the jumping spider *(below, left)* constantly scurry about the garden ready to pounce on any insect that moves. The tiny tree frog, sometimes known as a tree toad, feeds both by daylight and during the night when many other pest predators are inactive. Like the larger, more homely and even hungrier toad, it lays its eggs in water but spends most of its life on land.

A jumping spider, a roving hunter that does not spin a web, grasps a treehopper—a common pest on ornamental trees and shrubs—and prepares to suck out its body liquids.

With evident relish, a blotched and warty tree frog gulps down a cricket, one of the many garden foes it captures with flicks of its sticky tongue. When pursuing its prey, this predator can change color for camouflage and uses its feet like suction cups to cling to the underside of a leaf.

A molelike shrew pauses momentarily to devour a grasshopper. This insatiable burrowing creature, one of the most numerous of United States mammals, is usually on the move, using its long snout to ferret out three times its weight in insects daily.

Traversing a grassy plot at its measured pace, a box turtle stops to make a snack of a beetle grub, eliminating one more voracious garden enemy. Box turtles are omnivorous, eating fruit, fungi, snails, slugs and many different kinds of insects.

Birds that earn their keep

In the spring all birds, even those that prefer to eat fruits and seeds, feed their nestlings a diet consisting largely of grubs, caterpillars, worms and other soft-bodied insects. As the season progresses and the young birds seek their own food, the balance may shift; some birds will prefer plant food to insects, but insects will still comprise 20 to 50 per cent of their diet. For example, 90 to 95 per cent of a baby thrush's food consists of beetles, caterpillars, earthworms, flies, grasshoppers, snails and spiders. By fall, when berries and seeds are plentiful, plant material makes up about 75 per cent of a thrush's menu. Many birds, among them the warblers, swallows and wrens, eat only insects all year long.

Observations by ornithologists have yielded dramatic evidence of the extent to which birds can control insect pests. For example, a house wren, a relative of the Carolina wrens below, may gather 500 caterpillars and grubs for its young in one afternoon.

Perched near the edge of its nest in a cavity near the ground, a Carolina wren thrusts a beak full of caterpillars, the destructive larvae of moths, toward a ravenous nestling.

With gaping mouths, a pair of infant wood thrushes stretch eagerly from their nest in the branches of a tree toward the mixture of insects in their parent's beak.

Safe and sound chemical controls 4

Grape growers in 19th Century France had no trouble identifying a particularly troublesome pest that kept raiding their lush vines along country lanes. The marauders were two legged and highly visible—human passersby accustomed to plucking off a handful of sweet fruit as they walked beside the vineyards. To prevent these annoying losses, the vintners took to dabbing a mixture of hydrated lime and copper sulfate on their grapes. The concoction looked horrible and tasted even worse to anyone foolhardy enough to sample it, yet it was easily washed off at harvest time.

This mixture was still being plastered on roadside grapes in the 1880s when an outbreak of downy mildew threatened to destroy vineyards from Bordeaux to Beaugency. Only then did Pierre-Marie-Alexis Millardet, a French botanist, note that grapes smeared with the mixture seemed as immune to downy mildew as they were to poachers. In 1885 he published a paper on the subject, and Bordeaux mixture, named for the region where Millardet made his discovery, soon became the first widely used fungicide.

A century or so later, Bordeaux mixture is but one of a bewildering array of chemical formulations available to fight pests and diseases *(page 71)*. With such a formidable arsenal comes a compelling need to know how to use man-made controls responsibly. Choosing an insecticide or fungicide involves more than driving to your neighborhood garden center or hardware store and plucking a likely looking container off the shelf. To make an informed choice, you must understand how the various formulations work, how to employ them safely, how to store them out of harm's way and how to dispose of leftovers and empty containers.

Be guided by restraint in choosing pesticides; by reading the label carefully, you will be able to pick the least toxic one that will do the job, and one that is designed to attack only the kinds of pests you are after. The "shotgun" approach to garden defense—spraying

During World War II, a gardener was likely to react to enemies in the victory garden by immediately reaching for a spray gun. Today, however, insecticides are the last resort in the war on pests, not the first.

everything with a broad-spectrum insecticide and hoping you will hit something—kills beneficial and innocuous insects as well as the pests. Nearly all successful gardeners prefer the "rifle" technique—using controls that are precisely targeted to reduce the population of specific pests. For example, the pesticide malathion is aimed specifically at aphids, mealy bugs and other sucking insects, but it has little effect on mites (which should be controlled with a miticide). Malathion is a contact poison, one of three broad categories of pesticides classified by the way the insects are affected by them. The other categories are stomach poisons and fumigants.

THE TOXIC TOUCH

Most contact poisons enter an insect's body through its respiratory system; some do their work there, simply suffocating the pest. Other types pass into the nervous or circulatory system and fatally derange its functioning. Contact poisons may also penetrate the thick cuticle that envelops an insect's body, but only if the poison is very toxic or is applied in heavy doses. Many contact poisons are derived from plants. The most important of these are nicotine, a poison extracted from tobacco for use against such insects as aphids and thrips; pyrethrum, derived from some species of chrysanthemums for use against flies, leaf hoppers and cabbage worms; and rotenone, a poison extracted from the roots of cubé for use against Mexican bean beetles and European corn borers.

Among the contact poisons most toxic to insects are the chlorinated compounds, most of which were developed in the 1940s. They include DDT, aldrin, dieldrin and chlordane—all efficient pest killers but all restricted by federal regulations because their long-lasting residues contaminate the environment. There are, however, some other chlorinated compounds in use that do not threaten long-term chemical pollution. These include chlorobenzilate, widely used against mites, and methoxychlor, a general-purpose insecticide.

Replacements for DDT also have come from the carbamates. One of them, carbaryl, can be used on most fruits, vegetables and ornamentals because it breaks down fairly rapidly and loses its toxicity soon after it has been applied. It is very toxic to bees, however, so it should be applied only when the plants that are being treated are not in bloom.

Another group of contact poisons, the organic phosphates, work by blocking the action of an enzyme known as cholinesterase, which is involved in transmitting nerve impulses in insects and other animals. One of the most widely used of the organic phosphates is diazinon, which also breaks down fairly rapidly. It is popular with farmers and backyard gardeners alike because it can be sprayed on certain food crops within a few days of the harvest—only one day before in the case of peas or tomatoes, five days in the case of broccoli or cauliflower. Some organic phosphates, such as TEPP, are restricted because they are extremely dangerous to handle: a single drop of undiluted TEPP on exposed skin could kill a human. But for all its toxicity, TEPP's danger is short lived, and a professional applier can use it on some food crops three days before harvest.

Dormant oil spray is one contact poison that a home gardener can use without great risk. It consists of a highly refined oil mixed with water. Petroleum oil generally is used, although some dormant formulas contain fish or vegetable oils. Dormant oil spray is effective against scales and other sucking insects, moth eggs, psyllids and mites, and destroys other kinds of insect eggs as well. It is usually applied early in the spring, before leaves or flowers emerge, while the plant is still dormant but the air temperature is above 45°. This timing is important because the thin coating of oil that suffocates insects can also damage foliage. A much more dilute oil spray is sometimes applied in the growing season to control aphids, scale crawlers and mites. Dormant oil spray is available in garden-supply centers as emulsifiable concentrate ready for dilution.

INSECT FOOD POISONING

The stomach poisons comprising the second group of pesticides enter an insect through its mouth, along with its food. Most stomach poisons are applied to the surfaces of plants, where chewing and sucking insects dine. Paris green, a copper-and-arsenic mixture, was one of the first commercial stomach poisons, introduced more than 100 years ago to combat the Colorado potato beetle. The use of such arsenic compounds declined, however, because they tended to be-

SYSTEMICS: PROTECTION FROM WITHIN

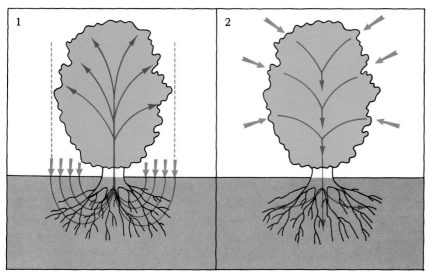

1. *A systemic insecticide sprinkled on the ground will be absorbed by a plant's roots and circulated through its vascular system, killing sucking and chewing insects as they feed. Apply a band of the chemical in granular, powder or liquid form, starting a few inches from the stem and extending just beyond the outer edge of the foliage. The insecticide will be carried to the roots by rain or watering and can be used to protect any plant, even a tall tree.*

2. *Leaves absorb a systemic applied by spraying. Wear protective clothing and avoid drifts. For safety, use such a spray only on plants shorter than you are.*

come concentrated in the soil, harming some plants. Most of the stomach poisons now used contain fluorine compounds, antimony or phosphorus. Some contemporary products are potentially more dangerous than Paris green, however. Mercuric compounds, for example, are used to treat seed that is planted in maggot-infested soil, but they are so toxic that they can be applied only by professionals.

Some newer types of stomach poisons are designed to be absorbed directly through leaves or roots as the plant ingests water and nutrients. These are called systemic poisons; they work well against both sucking insects and some chewing insects without endangering beneficial insects and other creatures. They are especially useful for protecting decorative plants, on which a film of surface spray or dust would be unsightly.

KILLED BY THE FUMES

The third group of pesticides, the fumigants, enter through the insect's breathing parts. Some are effective against disease-carrying nematodes as well as many species of insects. The fumigants work by chemical reactions that release lethal gases. They usually are injected into the soil as liquids by professionals, who use a device that resembles a large tubelike needle. One fumigant, paradichlorobenzene, familiar in the form of moth crystals, is effective against the peach-tree borer and is relatively safe for the home gardener to handle (below). But most fumigation should be done by

GAS ATTACK ON THE PEACH-TREE BORER

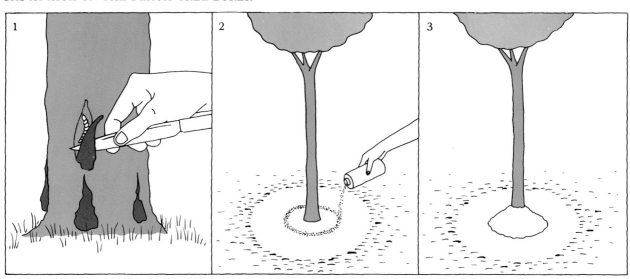

The peach-tree borer attacks all stone-fruit trees near the ground, but its holes are often covered with exuded gum. Scrape the gum away with a knife. If you can reach a borer with the knife tip, remove and destroy it.

Level the soil near the tree's trunk. Sprinkle a ring of moth crystals (paradichlorobenzene, also called PDB) 3 inches from the trunk, using ½ ounce of crystals for saplings, up to 1½ ounces for older trees.

In late summer, cover the crystals with warm soil, mounding it up and packing it tightly around the base of the tree. Gas released by PDB in the soil will destroy the borers in their burrows. Remove the mound in spring.

experts and should be undertaken at least six weeks before the planting season when the soil temperature is above 40°, or upon soil that will be left fallow, because virtually all soil fumigants will either kill or damage plants.

Identifying and controlling diseases is a trickier business than cutting down the pest population, no matter what methods you use, because most diseases live inside the plant and any fungicide strong enough to kill them is likely to injure the plant, too. In general, fungicides are employed as preventive protection: they stop disease spores from germinating and entering plants. Applied at the start of the growing season and periodically thereafter, fungicides such as thiram, maneb, ferbam and zineb, all sulfur compounds, will help to prevent such diseases as black spot on roses, cedar-apple rust and such turf diseases as dollar spot, snow mold and brown patch.

Though a fungicide works best when used to prevent infection, it is not too late to apply it after you see the first symptoms of disease. After-the-fact treatment will keep the disease from spreading to other plants. And if the invaded plant is otherwise healthy and the disease is caught early, the fungicide can keep the fungus from spreading further on the diseased plant and may even dry up the infection completely.

Most fungicides are applied by spraying or dusting and require frequent applications because, to be totally effective, they must cover the entire plant and subsequent new growth. The notion that rain will wash a fungicide away is a misconception. It does not wash off; in fact, a shower right after its application increases its effectiveness because the water helps distribute it uniformly. Systemic fungicides—like systemic pesticides—circulate inside the plant's vascular system; each application of a systemic such as benomyl on a lilac bush is effective for 10 to 14 days. Another medication is similar to streptomycin, the antibiotic doctors use to treat sore throat; it has proved effective as a systemic control for such bacterial diseases as fire blight of apples and pears.

Insect-borne diseases, such as the aster yellows spread by leaf hoppers, are particularly hard to control because the diseases are often introduced with the first insect bite. The best recourse is to attack the carriers to keep their population low.

There is no single rule that will tell you when to use insecticides or fungicides instead of depending on natural controls or mechanical devices such as barriers and traps (pages 49 and 50). Your choice must be based on the kinds of plants you are treating, last year's experience, the extent of the invasion and the results you are seeking. In general, avoid the use of insecticides until you see clear signs of an insect invasion. Then wait a few days more to see if your garden's natural defenses are keeping the pests within acceptable limits. Do not strive for an impossible goal of complete extermination. Only when other defenses fail and you are about to be inundated with pests should you resort to chemical controls, and then use the smallest quantities that will do the job. Timing is all important. If you know a pest's breeding cycle, you can catch it early, in the nymph or larval stage (*page 24*), before it can do much damage.

If you are in doubt about which pesticides to use and when to use them, consult your local agricultural agent. His office is part of your state extension service. Though extension services chiefly serve farmers and other commercial growers, many of them also maintain offices in urban centers. Extension agents, as well as local garden clubs, put out early warnings when certain diseases or infestations pose a threat in your area. Also, they can recommend specific preventive measures tailored to fit your climate and indigenous pest population.

The most important step in using any chemical as a preventive or curative measure is to read the label on the container and to follow the directions to the letter. The following information must appear on every pesticide label:

● The EPA registration number. This tells you that the product has been reviewed by the Environmental Protection Agency and is safe and effective when applied as directed.

● Directions for use. Make sure the product is approved for use on the plant you wish to treat, and also for the specific pest or disease you are trying to check. Use only the recommended amounts: increasing dosages is illegal; doing so, furthermore, will not enhance the chemical's effectiveness but may increase its toxicity until it endangers you and destroys the plant you are trying to protect.

● Precautions. The government has established three levels of toxicity. The most toxic compounds are labeled with the word "Danger." Moderately toxic compounds are labeled with the word "Warning," while those regarded as only slightly toxic and generally safe for use by home gardeners are labeled "Caution."

THE LETHAL DOSAGE These levels are determined by the pesticide's LD50; that is, the dosage of formulated pesticide that was lethal to 50 per cent of the animals, such as rats or rabbits, on which it was tested (LD stands for lethal dosage). In the case of a fumigant, the measurement is also in the lethal concentrate (LC) of a pesticide in the air. LD50 is expressed in milligrams of chemical per kilogram of body weight of the test animals, taken orally (stomach poison) or absorbed through the skin (contact poison). The LC50, as a measure of inhalation

WHERE TO GET HELP

One of the best places to get garden advice that applies specifically to your area is the office of your local extension agent, who is associated with your state's land-grant university and the U.S. Department of Agriculture. Most such offices are listed in the telephone directory as "agricultural-extension service" under the heading for your state or local government. But you may also find the office listed under county agent, extension chairman, extension advisor, USDA extension service, county agricultural agent, farm agent or farm advisor. In Canada, similar services are provided by the "district agriculture representative," usually found under provincial government listings.

Choosing and using garden chemicals

Any garden chemical should be carefully chosen for treating a specific problem that is affecting a specific plant. The encyclopedia section of this book, beginning on page 85, lists the pests and diseases that are of most concern to the home gardener and recommends means of control.

The chart on this page emphasizes special cautions that should be observed in using the suggested chemicals; handle any chemical with great care. The trade names are listed only as a guide to the gardening consumer; the list is neither all-inclusive nor an endorsement of any particular brand over others. Ultimately, you must read the fine print on any chemical's label to be sure that the treatment is safe for the intended plant and that precautions are taken to protect both you and the garden you are trying to improve.

ACEPHATE
ORTHENE. Do not use on cottonwood, crab apple, elm, maple or redbud trees; do not use on edible plants. This material is highly toxic to bees.

BACILLUS POPILLIAE
DOOM; JAPIDEMIC; MILKY SPORE DISEASE. This bacterium is toxic to grubs of Japanese beetles and some related species of scarab beetles. Do not use with insecticides on lawns.

BACILLUS THURINGIENSIS
AGRITOL; BAKTHANE; THURICIDE; BIOTROL; DIPEL. This bacterium is toxic only to caterpillars.

BENOMYL
BENLATE; TERSAN 1991. This fungicide is acutely toxic to fish. Some fungi have developed resistance.

CAPTAN
ORTHOCIDE. Do not mix with oil or with lime or other alkalies. This fungicide is acutely toxic to fish. Avoid getting any on your skin.

CARBARYL
SEVIN. This insecticide is highly toxic to bees and fish. Do not apply when foliage is wet. Do not use on Boston ivy, Virginia creeper, cantaloupes, cucumbers or melons. Since repeated use increases mite populations, carbaryl is often combined with a miticide.

CHLORPHYRIFOS
DURSBAN; LORSBAN. This insecticide is acutely toxic to bees, fish, birds and mammals.

COPPER COMPOUNDS
These compounds are not compatible with soaps and thus may reduce the efficiency of emulsified oil sprays. Bordeaux mixture leaves a residue that may dwarf plants.

DIAZINON
GARDENTOX; SPECTRACIDE. This insecticide is acutely toxic to bees, fish and birds. Do not use on pumpkins. It may burn young plants.

DICHLONE
PHYGON. Avoid skin contact.

DICOFOL
KELTHANE; ACARIN; MITIGAN. This miticide is acutely toxic to fish. Do not use on beans or eggplants. Do not mix with high concentrations of lime.

DIMETHOATE
CYGON; DE-FEND; ROGOR. This insecticide is acutely toxic to birds, bees and other wildlife. Do not use on hollies.

DINOCAP
MILDEX; KARATHANE; CROTOTHANE. Do not use above 85°.

FERBAM
FERMATE; KARBAM BLACK; COROMATE; CARBAMATE. Do not use on potatoes or sweet potatoes.

FOLPET
PHALTAN. Do not mix with alkalies.

LIME SULFUR
CALCIUM POLYSULFIDE; ORTHORIX. This chemical leaves a residue of sulfur and dulls the shine on evergreens. Use this spray only when the air temperature is below 85°.

MALATHION
CYTHION. Do not use above 80°. This product is acutely toxic to fish and to bees. Do not apply to crassulas, ferns or soft maples.

MANCOZEB
DITHANE; MANZATE 200; FORE. Do not breathe dust or spray mist.

MANEB
MANZATE D; MEB; DITHANE M-22. Do not use with copper fungicides.

METHOXYCHLOR
MARLATE. This insecticide is acutely toxic to fish. Do not apply to okra, onions or watermelons.

NALED
DIBROM; BROMEX; FLY-KILLER-D. This insecticide is acutely toxic to bees. Do not apply to beans, beets, blackberries, celery, mustard, okra, onions, peas, potatoes, raspberries or sweet corn.

NICOTINE SULFATE
BLACKLEAF 40. The insecticide is a deadly poison if swallowed.

OXYDEMETON
META-SYSTOX-R. This chemical is acutely toxic if the fumes are inhaled or the liquid contacts the skin.

PCNB
TERRACLOR. Do not use this soil fungicide as a spray. Avoid skin contact.

PHOSMET
IMIDAN. This insecticide kills bees.

PYRETHRUM
PYRETHRINS; PYREFUME SUPER 30; ORTHO INDOOR INSECT PLANT SPRAY. This insecticide is acutely toxic to fish. Do not spray on maidenhair ferns, cyclamens, roses, lantanas, poinsettias.

RESMETHRIN
CHYRSON; SYNTHRIN; SBP 1382. Use this insecticide below 80°. It kills fish.

ROTENONE
ORTHO INDOOR PLANT INSECT SPRAY. This insecticide is acutely toxic to fish. Do not spray on maidenhair ferns, cyclamens, lantanas, poinsettias, roses.

SULFUR
FLOTOX; KOLOSPRAY. Do not use this fungicide above 85°.

ZINEB
PARZATE; DITHANE Z-78; ASPOR. Do not breathe dust or spray mist.

ZIRAM
KARBAM WHITE; ZIRBERK; ZERLATE; COROZATE. Do not use on potatoes.

toxicity, is expressed in milligrams per liter. Some pesticides are given an oral LD50, a separate dermal LD50 and an inhalation LC50. Particularly hazardous irritation of eyes or skin is also considered in arriving at the ratings.

The *lower* the LD or LC value, the *more* toxic the product. A small amount of a particular pesticide with an oral LD50 of 25 milligrams or a dermal LD50 of 150 milligrams, for example, would probably be very hazardous. It would be labeled "Danger" and marked with a skull and crossbones. A product with an oral LD50 of 250 milligrams or a dermal LD50 of 1,000 milligrams might be moderately toxic. If so, it would be labeled with "Warning." A product with an oral LD50 of 750 milligrams or a dermal LD50 of 3,000 milligrams might be only slightly toxic and would require only the word "Caution."

● First-aid instructions. A mandatory "statement of practical treatment" on the label gives first-aid instructions. But do not stop with first aid: after emergency treatment, go to a doctor or hospital immediately. Take the pesticide label with you to help medical

The plight of the honey bee

Except for an occasional sting, man has coexisted peacefully with the honey bee since the dawn of history, relying on it as the principal pollinator of his crops and as a producer of honey. Today, man is making this partnership increasingly difficult for the honey bee as he expands his suburbs into fields and pastures and douses his gardens and farmlands with pesticides. These human disturbances, combined with wildly fluctuating weather, have diminished the honey-bee population in the United States about 20 per cent since 1965.

Pesticides that were introduced after DDT was restricted may be the greatest threat: in an ironic twist, carbaryl, one of the new "safe" pesticides, has killed more bees than DDT ever did. Bees that picked up DDT died before they could get back to the hives; but bees that pick up carbaryl do not die immediately—they bring the poison back to the hive in the nectar and pollen they have gathered, killing additional adults and larvae that share the common food supply.

In the mid-1970s, unusually cold weather conditions in the eastern United States killed millions of honey bees in their hives. Too cold to move, they starved to death only inches away from plentiful food supplies. During the same period, a prolonged drought in the West drastically reduced the bees' food supply, killing millions more. In California, where the drought was particularly severe, commercial production of honey dropped five million pounds during a single year.

As honey bees became scarce, the demand for their services increased. The scarcity posed a novel problem for commercial beekeepers. Besides fending off the usual four-legged honey thieves—bears, foxes and porcupines—the beekeepers now had to contend with the far more costly depredations of human thieves, who took the bees along with the honey.

To lighten the beleaguered honey bee's work load, scientists are experimenting with wild bees as pollinators, with the goal of finding species that can be programed to pollinate specific crops. In the West, for example, the alfalfa leaf-cutting bee and the alkali bee have proved to be even more efficient pollinators of alfalfa than the honey bee.

personnel determine further treatment. In many areas there are also poison-control centers that can supply emergency information.

● Storage and disposal. Directions for storing pesticides are given on the label along with instructions for the disposal of empty containers. Keep all leftover pesticides in their original containers under lock and key. Almost every hospital emergency room has treated someone who has swallowed a pesticide stored in a soft-drink bottle.

Never burn an empty pesticide container; fumes from the residue could be lethal. Instead, rinse the container thoroughly several times, sprinkling the rinse water under a plant that has been treated with the pesticide. Then wrap the container in layers of newspaper and dispose of it with the rest of your trash. Containers that held pesticides based on arsenic, mercury, lead and other metallic substances cannot be totally cleaned. They should be buried. If you cannot dispose of them at a landfill site, bury them at least 18 inches deep in your garden and at a safe distance from any well or stream. Never pour any pesticide, even the amount contained in rinse water, into your plumbing system. If you are not sure how to dispose of a particular poison, call the nearest EPA office or agricultural agent for advice.

CONTAINER DISPOSAL

All pesticides, even those that are relatively safe, are poisons. Handle them with extreme care—even more than you give iodine, disinfectants, laundry bleach, drain cleaner and other poisonous household substances you routinely use.

With the exception of systemic granules and bait traps, both usually placed on the ground, the pesticides you select will be applied as dusts or sprays. Most gardeners prefer sprays because they give more thorough coverage than dusts and are more easily directed at the undersides of leaves, where many pests feed. On the other hand, most dusts come already mixed, while most sprays must be carefully measured and mixed with water or other ingredients. Propellant sprays come ready to use but are practical only for potted plants or small areas. Many gardeners use dusts on fruits and vegetables, where appearance is not important. But even the finest film of dust may spoil the looks of roses or other flowers; their beauty will be marred less by a spray.

Most spray materials are sold as soluble powders, wettable powders or emulsifiable concentrates. Soluble powders and emulsifiable concentrates are simply mixed with water, stirred and applied. Wettable powders come mixed with ground talc and a wetting agent. To prepare a wettable powder for use, mix it with a small amount of water to make a thin paste, then add the rest of the amount of water specified on the container label; agitate this mixture frequently

MIXING SPRAY SOLUTIONS

during application because the chemicals will settle if the mixture is left standing. All mixing of sprays should be done outdoors.

Combining the various powders and concentrates in the proper proportions is vital to a successful spray program. Too much powder may kill your plants; too little powder may do no good at all. To avoid leftovers, you will often want to mix less than the full amount suggested on the label. The following equivalents will help you translate the dosages printed on pesticide containers into concentrations that will be effective for your particular requirements:

80 drops = 1 teaspoon

3 teaspoons = 1 tablespoon = ½ fluid ounce

6 teaspoons = 2 tablespoons = 1 fluid ounce

8 fluid ounces = 1 cup = ½ pint

2 cups = 1 pint

1 fluid ounce in 3 gallons of water = 2 teaspoons in 1 gallon

1 pound of wettable powder in 100 gallons = 1 level teaspoon per gallon

1 pint of liquid per 100 gallons = 1 level teaspoon per gallon

Some compounds are more effective if combined with what is known as a spreader-sticker, which helps the solution adhere to leaves. But check the label of the pesticide container to be sure it

Spraying and dusting with skill and safety

To spray or dust plants safely, first select the specific pesticide designed to do the job at hand, then read and heed the directions on the label. Dusts come ready-mixed, and they can be stored in the duster, making clean-up easier. But many home gardeners prefer sprays because they do not drift so readily and they leave no film to dim a plant's color. When using either, wear a hat, waterproof gloves and clothes that cover as much skin as possible.

To prepare a spray, measure precise amounts of concentrate or powder (no more than you need immediately) and mix with a small amount of water in a disposable container. Strain this into the sprayer, then add the full amount of water needed. Spray when plants are dry and the day is calm. Stop when a plant is wet but not dripping. Give trees, shrubs, flowers or vegetables a fine mist that evenly coats all leaf surfaces. After spraying, clean the empty equipment by pumping several times its capacity of water through it. Leave the filler cap off the tank and store it upside down so it will drain and dry completely. Wrap empty pesticide containers in several layers of newspaper and put them in the trash can.

PLUNGER SPRAYER

This easy-to-use sprayer is suitable for small indoor or outdoor plants. One type sprays only upon a thrust of the plunger; a preferable type uses air pressure to provide a continuous stream. Tank capacities vary.

HOSE-END SPRAYER

Water pressure from a garden hose operates this sprayer by drawing concentrated pesticide from a container and automatically mixing it with water. On some types the tank can be replaced with a disposable jar.

does not advise against using such an additive. Some kinds of spreader-stickers actually increase runoff, rather than retard it, thus decreasing the pesticide's efficiency. Others may injure the plant by increasing its absorption of the chemical.

Be particularly careful in opening pesticide containers. From the very moment you open a bottle or canister you risk inhaling a dust or spilling a liquid poison. Once you have prepared your spray or dust, there are some other precautions to keep in mind:

• Temperature. Certain pesticides are phytotoxic; that is, they react in extreme heat or cold to produce damage to plants that may be worse than any they are supposed to curtail. Dormant oil spray, for example, will damage evergreens if used when the temperature is below 45°. Sulfur or copper mixtures can defoliate roses if they are used when the temperature is above 85°.

• Weather. Make sure you spray on a clear day. Rain will wash some sprays and dusts away before they can do their job. Do not spray or dust on a windy day when the chemicals might be blown back in your face or into a neighbor's garden.

• Time. When using insecticides not toxic to bees, try to spray in the morning or evening when the air is calm and a slight covering of dew acts as a natural spreader-sticker. But fog-spray only at night, when

COMPRESSED-AIR SPRAYER
Ten to 15 strokes of the hand pump compress air above the liquid in this sprayer, permitting the spraying of large shrubs and small trees without interruption. Metal or plastic tanks range in capacity from 1 to 5 gallons.

SLIDE OR TROMBONE SPRAYER
As though playing a trombone, the operator uses both hands to draw pesticide mixture from a bucket and eject a continuous spray. The hose is weighted in an open bucket; the operator must avoid tipping it.

ROTARY DUSTING HOPPER
By steadily cranking a handle, the operator produces a continuous air current that propels dust onto plants. An extension tube provides a longer reach. Hoppers hold from 5 to 25 pounds of dust.

few birds or bees are foraging, and avoid spraying flowering plants when bees are active.

• Reentry time. Because pesticides are poisons, stay out of the sprayed area until the spray dries. (Some commercial applications are so potent that workers must stay out of an orchard as long as two weeks after spraying.) Warn your neighbors when you plan to spray so they can keep children and pets away from your property.

• Topography. Use only nonresidual pesticides if you live near a lake or stream where water might be polluted or fish endangered.

• Compatibility. Some insecticides can be used shortly after applying fungicides in the same general area. But others may be rendered ineffective or may combine with the fungicide to damage plants if the label indicates incompatibility. Bear in mind, too, that if you mix a liquid fertilizer with a pesticide, you may create a sludge that will clog the spray nozzle.

• Protective clothing. Whenever you handle any pesticide, cover as much of your skin as you comfortably can; wear work gloves and clothing with long sleeves. Take a shower after working with garden chemicals, and wash the gardening clothes separately from the rest of the laundry. Never smoke while you are using a pesticide; you might pass the chemical from your hands to the cigarette and thence into your mouth.

APPLICATION EQUIPMENT Hardware stores and garden centers carry a variety of spraying and dusting devices (pages 74-75), ranging from small propellant-filled cans suitable for use on house plants (always take them outdoors before spraying) to hydraulic sprayers with 100-gallon tanks suitable for dousing the acreage of a country estate. One of the easiest devices to handle is the compressed-air sprayer, which consists of a spray rod and a tank that you pump to build up the pressure that sends a fine, uniform spray toward your plants. Sprayers that can be attached to the end of a garden hose also are easy to use, but the concentrations must be carefully mixed to avoid applying more poison than is needed.

Some gardeners use specially equipped high-pressure paint guns for spraying pesticides. This is hazardous; certain types of spray guns spew out their contents under pressures as high as 3,000 pounds per square inch. That is enough force to inject a pesticide right through your skin. If any part of your body is hit by a jet from one of these sprayers, seek immediate medical treatment; if possible, go straight to a hospital emergency room.

Whatever type of sprayer you use, clean it outdoors after each use. Dusters do not need such constant attention, but they should be cleaned at least once or twice a season. Plunger-operated duster guns and bellows-action dusters are so inexpensive you can buy two or three for the different dusts you may need. In a pinch, you can put a small amount of dust into a sack made of cheesecloth and shake the sack over your plants.

Dusts and sprays work just as well on house plants as on outdoor plants. But most indoor pest problems can be solved with physical rather than chemical action. To fight a minor infestation, give your plants a sponge bath with warm, soapy water, rinsing the pests right down the drain. Or dip a cotton swab in rubbing alcohol and use it to pick off scale insects and mealy bugs. Only when these methods fail is it time to spray. Treat each plant individually outdoors. Keep it away from other plants that might be harmed by the chemical you are using; the malathion you spray on a palm, for example, might kill a nearby fern or schefflera.

Most outdoor spraying devices are too cumbersome for use on potted plants. An inexpensive hand atomizer like the kind used to mist plants is adequate, provided you are careful to cover both sides of each leaf. If the weather is too cold to spray outdoors, postpone treatment until it warms up.

If you cannot avoid treating potted plants indoors, perhaps because you live on the 34th floor, don rubber gloves and turn the pots upside down to dunk the plants in a bucket of soapy water. This will destroy many of the pests.

If any of your indoor plants become diseased, it is best to destroy them before the disease has a chance to spread to other house plants. Quarantine all newly purchased plants and the outdoor plants you bring indoors for the winter; keep them isolated for at least two weeks to make sure you are not introducing any unwelcome pests or diseases into your house.

Never rid yourself of a diseased or pest-infested plant by dumping it outdoors. Some pests and disease pathogens can survive even below-freezing temperatures, establishing themselves in a nearby garden the following spring. To protect your healthy plants, and your neighbors', put diseased plants in a securely tied plastic bag to be collected with your trash.

Of course, no one likes to throw out a plant, even a sick one, but often that is the wisest move. Experienced gardeners realize that even plants raised with the best of care can succumb to the attacks of pests or disease—but this should be the rare exception rather than the rule. With the beneficence of natural and biological controls, and with a carefully tempered use of insecticides and fungicides, you can maintain your backyard or indoor Eden with scarcely a nibble or a wilted leaf to mar its beauty.

Death and life for two native trees

In the first half of the 20th Century, disease ravaged two of the most valuable trees in the United States: the stately American chestnut of the Eastern forests and the graceful American elm, treasured in cities and towns across the nation. Although no cure was found for either chestnut blight or Dutch elm disease, fortunately neither tree was annihilated. In fact, as shown on the following pages, the outlook for both is less bleak than it once seemed.

The blight that attacked the American chestnut killed about nine million acres of towering trees that had been a source of wood, nuts and tannin essential to the livelihood of hundreds of people in small communities from Maine to Alabama and westward to Indiana. Chestnut blight was first reported in 1904 in New York, probably carried there on small trees from the Orient. In less than 40 years the blight had wiped out nearly all the chestnut trees in their natural Eastern range. The disease, a wind-borne fungus that lodged in cracks and wounds in bark, caused swollen cankers that encircled and choked the trunk and branches. However, it did not kill tree roots. Science's hope for saving the chestnut lies in old stumps that each year produce an encouraging crop of new sprouts. Occasionally some of these show an unusually high resistance to the blight.

The fungus that causes Dutch elm disease in American elms emits a toxin that clogs the tree's sap-carrying vessels, in effect strangling the tree to death. Both the fungus and the European elm bark beetle, one of two beetles that transmit it, were probably imported with a load of logs from Europe. The first infected United States tree was found in Ohio in 1930, and by the late 1970s the Dutch elm disease had marched across the nation to California and was killing American elms at a rate of up to 400,000 each year. The disease denuded whole towns of the cool, leafy canopies 50 to 60 feet high that for many were a memorable part of the hometown street scene. Although the lost elms cannot be restored, the relatively few that survived are being saved by heroic measures designed to control the beetles and protect the trees from infection.

Thin but distinctively vase-shaped crowns of four American elms at Bates College in Maine have been severely pruned to help prevent infection by Dutch elm disease.

An urgent race to save the elm

The search for a disease-resistant hybrid with the splendid height, vase shape and crown spread of the American elm began with the first onslaught of Dutch elm disease. While that search continues, those elms that have remained healthy can sometimes be saved by preventive measures. An annual pruning robs the fungus-carrying elm bark beetle of the weak wood in which it breeds. A dormant oil spray with an insecticide such as methoxychlor, applied in early spring, kills the beetles before they can feed and breed. Additional treatments, which must be administered by tree-care experts, include severing roots of adjacent trees that have grown together, using soil fumigants *(below)* to check the spread of disease and using a fungicide *(opposite)* to increase resistance to the disease.

Although disease-resistant, this pyramid-shaped Urban elm, a hybrid of Dutch and Asian trees, is hardly a match in grace and beauty for the American elm. It was developed by the U.S. Department of Agriculture in the 1950s.

A tree-care specialist injects Vapam, a chemical fumigant, into the soil to form a barrier against Dutch elm fungus. The injection will prevent the spread of the fungus from the roots of a diseased tree to those of a healthy one some 35 feet away.

In an experimental program, a worker for the National Park Service uses a complex network of tubing to inject a large limb of an elm in Washington, D.C., with multiple doses of Lignasan, a chemical fungus fighter.

The hunt for a hardier chestnut

Throughout the ancient Appalachian mountains, weathered old chestnut stumps half-buried in the debris of the forest floor send up some bright new sprouts each year. These "suckers" may live five years, grow six feet tall, even produce flowers and nuts; but eventually the chestnut blight will strike them down. Research has led to cautious optimism about the possibility of developing a less virulent strain of the chestnut fungus that might be introduced to the woods and become dominant over the present, inevitably fatal variety. Other research has focused on selecting and propagating sprouts that seem to have some degree of natural blight resistance. Also promising are hybrids that have been produced by crossing American chestnut trees with disease-resistant Asian species.

A student at the University of Tennessee checks one tree in a grove of American chestnuts grafted onto rootstock of Chinese chestnuts. The hope is that nuts from such trees will produce blight-resistant American chestnut trees.

These stately chestnuts, fortuitously transplanted in Wisconsin, survived because prevailing westerly winds generally confined the devastating blight to the tree's Eastern range.

If the blight can be eliminated, sprouts such as these, rising from a leaf-covered stump, may eventually renew the American chestnut population.

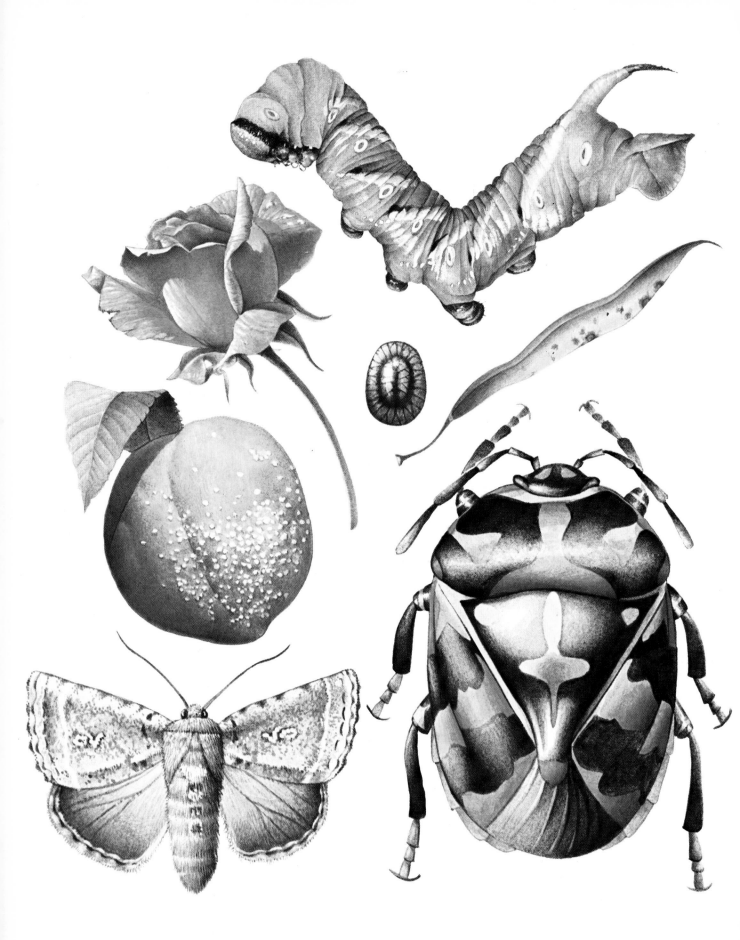

An encyclopedia of plant pests and diseases 5

The first step toward remedying any pest or disease problem is identifying its cause. Of the 1,000 different insect species that you might find in your garden, less than a tenth are likely to be harmful to the plants. The pest entries in the encyclopedia that follows describe 82 pests that do attack garden plants, give the symptoms of their damage and list the control measures available to home gardeners.

Wherever plants grow, plant diseases are sure to exist, and they are hardly less numerous or complex than human ailments. The disease portion of the encyclopedia *(pages 130-149)* gives the symptoms of 41 diseases you are most likely to find and lists the steps to take to prevent or control them. To help pinpoint the pest or malady affecting a plant, the charts on pages 150-155 list 132 plants keyed to the attackers to which they are most vulnerable.

Wherever possible, the encyclopedia gives the gardener a choice between chemical and nonchemical control measures. Nature frequently takes care of its own. Beneficial insects prey upon harmful ones. Strong plants have healing processes that enable them to survive even severe disease infections. The diligent gardener provides the best controls when he follows gardening practices that maintain plants at a peak of vigorous health. However, when an infestation or infection becomes so severe it threatens to spread faster than nature can contain it, chemicals may be necessary.

All chemical pesticides are poisons and are under the constant scrutiny of scientists for their possible damage to the environment. If you have difficulty finding any of the chemicals mentioned, it may have been removed from the market. The trade names in parentheses are intended only as shopping aids, not as product endorsements. The chart on page 71 includes cautions gardeners should observe in the use of the chemical compounds listed. But before you use any garden chemical, read all of the directions and precautions on the label of the container and follow them meticulously.

Below the tomato hornworm (top) is a terrapin scale and (clockwise) a bean with anthracnose, a harlequin bug, a cabbage looper moth, a brown-rotted peach and a chafer-damaged rose.

CORNFIELD ANT
Lasius alienus

Pests

A

ANT

Yellow, red, brown or black ants ranging from $^1/_{16}$ to $^1/_2$ inch in length are widespread throughout North America. Various species eat nearly everything humans eat, including seeds and leaves in the garden. Some ants farm, growing fungi in their nests for food. Others maintain and protect colonies of destructive aphids, scale insects and mealy bugs to get the sweet, sticky honeydew that they all exude. Some ants have poisonous stings, causing discomfort to humans and in rare cases attacking small birds and mammals.

Ants are tightly organized social insects, living in colonies containing three castes—one or more egg-laying queens that may live as long as 15 years; wingless workers, the sterile females that forage for food, build and defend the nest, look after the young and care for the queens; and winged males that swarm from the nests with new queens to mate on the wing. The males then die. A new colony is established when a queen finds a suitable nesting place, tears off her wings and lays eggs. She feeds herself on the muscles of the now-useless wings. When the eggs hatch into helpless, maggot-like larvae, they feed on the queen's saliva. After pupation, nearly all of these larvae become workers, but a small number become winged males and females that fly out and mate to begin a new cycle.

WHAT TO DO. Effective control requires the destruction of the queens in the nest. Severe infestations should be treated by a professional exterminator.

CORNFIELD ANT
Lasius alienus

Although cornfield ants build unsightly nests on lawns, the principal damage associated with them is caused by plant-destroying root aphids, especially the corn root aphid *(Aphis maidiradicis)* that the ants keep in herds. This dual infestation occurs most widely east of the Rocky Mountains and affects vegetables and fruits such as beets, carrots, corn and strawberries, and such ornamental plants as asters, browallias, buttercups, calendulas, chrysanthemums, dahlias, sweet peas and zinnias. Damage is caused by pinhead-sized, blue-green aphids that suck on roots and by the ants' tunnels.

Cornfield ants feed on honeydew secreted by the aphids. In return for this food, the ants tend the aphids from the egg to the adult stage, building their nests around the aphids' preferred food plants. During the winter the ants store aphid eggs in the nest, moving them around as soil and temperature conditions change. In early spring, the young aphids hatch and the ants carry them in their jaws to early-growing grasses and weeds where those aphids feed and reproduce for two to three generations. The ants carry succeeding generations of fully grown aphids through tunnels and deposit them on plant roots throughout the spring and summer.

SPECIAL TREATMENT. Destroy the joint infestation of ants and aphids by destroying the ants' nests. Just before planting, spade up nest areas to a depth of at least 7 inches. Repeat two or three times at three-day intervals to make sure the ants and aphids are so scattered they cannot regroup. In lawns, treat nests with diazinon (such as Spectracide) or carbaryl (such as Sevin).

APHID

Potential enemies of almost every plant in the world, tiny pear-shaped aphids, also called plant lice, are odious pests in gardens, greenhouses, orchards, fields and forests. Only $\frac{1}{16}$ to $\frac{1}{8}$ inch long, they pierce and suck sap from leaves, bark, flowers and roots. The toxic saliva of some species stunts new growth, deforms flowers and causes leaves to wilt and curl. All aphids secrete honeydew, which consists of plant sap enriched with sugars and amino acids; it attracts ants and is a growing medium for sooty mold. In a single day an aphid may produce several times its own weight of this sticky substance. Aphids also transmit fire blight, mosaic and other viral and bacterial diseases to plants they invade. Some aphids cause galls; the irritated plants encase them in structures that both protect them and supply them with food.

Aphids have a complicated life cycle. Wingless females emerge from eggs in early spring as nymphs. They mature and give birth to living young without being fertilized by males (the eggs hatch within the mothers' bodies). These young are all wingless females that reproduce in the same way for several generations until some develop wings and migrate. This process continues through the spring and summer, with winged females appearing whenever plants become overcrowded or a new food source becomes available. In the fall, winged males as well as females are born. They mate, and the fertilized females lay eggs that remain dormant through the winter. With 20 or more generations each year, aphids multiply rapidly; it has been estimated that one female could, under ideal conditions, produce a quintillion eggs a year. This does not happen because the defenseless aphid is the prey of many insects. It forms the chief diet of the ladybug beetle and the aphid lion (the larval stage of the lacewing) and is also attacked by fungi and parasitic wasps.

WHAT TO DO. Use a stream of water from a garden hose to knock aphids off outdoor plants. Indoors, wash leaves and stems with soapy water. Ladybug beetles, aphid lions and praying mantises can be purchased as natural controls. To stop a severe infestation, spray or dust with nicotine sulfate, rotenone or malathion. Repeat this treatment every week during the growing season.

GRAPE PHYLLOXERA
Daktulosphaira vitifoliae, also called *Phylloxera vitifoliae*

This gall-causing aphid is so destructive that it nearly wiped out the wine industry in France when it was accidentally introduced there in the 19th Century. Infestation is signaled by yellowing foliage covered with tiny galls that, when opened, reveal wingless yellow insects. Native American vines cultivated in the East suffer less damage from grape phylloxera than imported European vines grown in California and Arizona. Insect eggs laid on the vines in the fall hatch when the leaves come out. The nymphs move to leaves and begin feeding, causing galls to form. The nymphs mature inside these galls, giving birth to living young that form other galls on the same leaves. Every few generations some of the leaf aphids drop to the ground and burrow to the roots where they cause nodules to form. In the autumn, the root aphids produce winged females that lay eggs on the vines. These hatch into males and females that mate to produce eggs for the spring brood.

In the West, leaf aphids are rare and the root type prevalent. The latter drain sap from feeding roots as soon as the roots start to grow, starving the plants and killing them within three to 10 years. These aphids reproduce on the roots all year and occasionally produce females that are mobile enough to colonize a new area.

SPECIAL TREATMENT. Plant aphid-resistant vines such as those grafted on native rootstocks. For limited control of leaf aphids, spray with malathion at hatching time.

Cautions to observe when using chemicals, page 71.

GRAPE PHYLLOXERA
Daktulosphaira vitifoliae

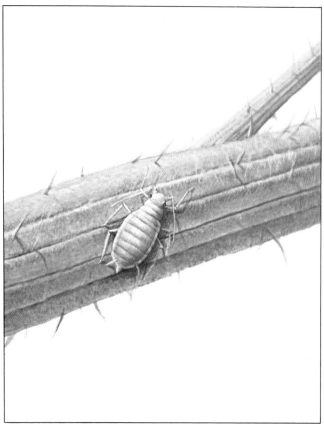

GREEN PEACH APHID
Myzus persicae

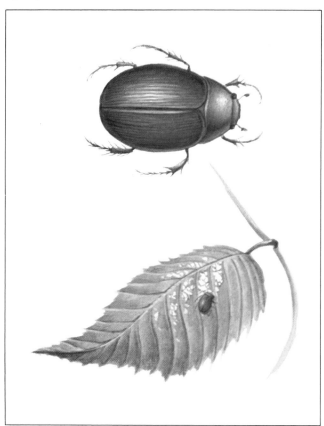

ASIATIC GARDEN BEETLE
Maladera castanea

GREEN PEACH APHID
Myzus persicae

Imported from Europe where it is known as greenfly, the green peach or spinach aphid is found throughout North America. This ½-inch light yellow or green aphid causes stunting and wilting in more than 100 plants. Vegetables affected include beets, celery, eggplants, lettuce, spinach, tomatoes, potatoes and members of the cabbage and cucumber families. Affected ornamentals include asters, carnations, English ivy, ferns, freesia, irises, lilies, nasturtiums, orchids, pansies, roses, tulips and violets. Affected fruit trees include apricot, cherry, citrus, peach and plum. This pest transmits many virus diseases, including tomato and tobacco mosaic.

The aphid lays shiny black eggs on fruit trees in fall that hatch the following spring when blossoms begin to open. Early generations feed on young twigs and flowers. Later, winged generations fly to vegetable and flower gardens. In fall, winged females fly back to fruit trees and give birth to offspring that mate and deposit their eggs on the trees.

SPECIAL TREATMENT. Control the green peach aphid with the measures indicated for aphids in general.

APPLE MAGGOT See Maggot
APPLE-TREE BORER, FLAT-HEADED See Borer
APPLE-TREE CATERPILLAR See Caterpillar, Eastern Tent
ASIATIC GARDEN BEETLE See Beetle
ASPARAGUS BEETLE See Beetle

B

BEAN BEETLE, MEXICAN See Beetle

BEETLE

The largest insect order, Coleoptera, which means "sheath wings," includes beetles, weevils and curculios. Some 28,000 of the quarter-million species live in North America.

All beetles go through a complete metamorphosis during their life cycle, from egg to larva to pupa to adult. Beetle larvae, called grubs or borers, can be distinguished from the larvae of other insects. The heads are always distinct, often a dark color, and have antennae. The bodies are stubbier than those of caterpillars, often shaped like soft half-moons. The most obvious identifying characteristic of the adults is the wing structure. Wing sheaths are hardened and opaque and when the insect is at rest, these fold neatly over the insect's back, encasing the back wings. In flight, the back wings move too rapidly to be seen and the wing sheaths are held out stiffly at the sides.

Both immature and mature beetles have chewing mechanisms. Occasionally one stage is beneficial and the other injurious, and a few beetles are beneficial at all times, like the ladybug beetles that feed on aphids both as adults and as larvae. The shape of the mouth gives a good indication of a beetle's diet. If the jaws are short and chunky, then it is most likely a plant-eater. Long, pointed mandibles with sharp cutting edges indicate that the beetle is carnivorous. If the mandibles are hairy, the beetle is a harmless pollen-feeder.

WHAT TO DO. Keep garden areas free of refuse that would shelter beetle eggs. Cultivate soil to destroy larvae in early spring. Protect special plants with cheesecloth or mosquito netting when adult beetles are active.

ASIATIC GARDEN BEETLE
Maladera castanea

All along the Atlantic coast, the Asiatic garden beetle chews irregular holes in leaf edges of almost all garden vegetables, fruits and flowers. Its grubs feed on the roots of grass, causing yellow patches in lawns. This imported pest passes the winter as a grub 6 to 10 inches deep in the soil. In spring, the ¾-inch white grub with a brown head moves close to the surface to feed. Grubs pupate and emerge as beetles in midsummer to feed and mate. Adult beetles are covered with small hairs that give a velvety appearance. The females lay eggs in cool, grassy areas, particularly those infested with weeds such as goldenrod, sorrel and wild aster. The eggs hatch into grubs that feed, then burrow into the soil for the winter. Only one generation a year is produced.

SPECIAL TREATMENT. The adult Asiatic garden beetle is strongly attracted to light, making light traps helpful. Sprays of acephate (such as Orthene), carbaryl (such as Sevin), diazinon (such as Spectracide), methoxychlor (such as Marlate) or malathion control the adult beetles. Use milky disease (such as Doom) to control grubs.

ASPARAGUS BEETLE
Crioceris asparagi

Found wherever asparagus is commonly grown, the asparagus beetle is particularly injurious in the northeast quarter of the United States and in parts of California, Colorado and Oregon. Both adults and larvae feed on new shoots and leaves. Tiny black eggs, pointing out like the teeth of a comb, cover the new shoots; tips are gnawed and stems scarred. Plants sometimes are defoliated and frequently are marred by black stains.

The slender, ¼-inch adult insect spends the winter in cracks in wood structures. As soon as asparagus appears, the beetle flies to it to eat and lays eggs on the tips. Within a week the eggs hatch into larvae that exude a dark fluid as they feed. After 10 to 14 days, they burrow into the ground to become yellow pupae. The life cycle takes three to eight weeks. There are at least two generations a year in colder climates, three to five in warmer areas.

SPECIAL TREATMENT. Ladybug beetles and other predators keep this beetle in check. During the cutting season spray asparagus with carbaryl (such as Sevin), rotenone or malathion. Be careful to follow label directions concerning the number of days between the last spraying and the harvest. Spray potential wintering spots with carbaryl in late summer or early fall. The beetle is less destructive in wet weather, and cold temperatures kill both eggs and larvae.

COLORADO POTATO BEETLE
Leptinotarsa decemlineata

The Colorado potato beetle is found across the United States and southern Canada, except in parts of Nevada, Florida and California. It originally subsisted on weeds growing in the Rocky Mountain foothills. With the introduction of the potato it became a serious pest, with both adults and larvae often denuding potato fields by stripping leaves and shoots. The beetle also feeds on eggplants, peppers and tomatoes, as well as on flowering tobacco and petunias. The ⅜-inch hemispherical adult has black spots on the front part of its yellow body and five black stripes on each wing sheath. The red larva grows to ⅗ inch in length and has rows of black spots along its sides.

From one to three generations are produced each year. The insect winters in the soil as an adult, emerging in spring to lay eggs on the undersides of leaves. The eggs hatch in four to nine days, and the larvae mature in two or three weeks. After pupating in the ground, new adults emerge.

SPECIAL TREATMENT. Spray or dust with carbaryl (such as Sevin), diazinon (such as Spectracide), malathion or rote-

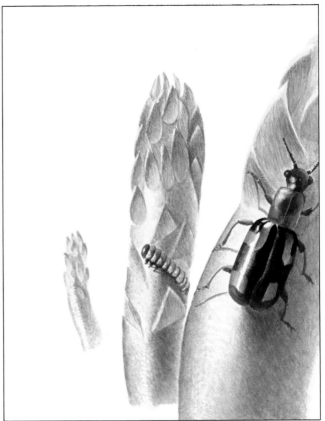

ASPARAGUS BEETLE
Crioceris asparagi

COLORADO POTATO BEETLE
Leptinotarsa decemlineata

Cautions to observe when using chemicals, page 71.

none, following label cautions concerning the number of days between the last spraying and the harvest.

ELM LEAF BEETLE
Pyrrhalta luteola

A pest all over North America, the elm leaf beetle is particularly troublesome in California. It poses an unusual problem in cities because swarms of adults are attracted to dry buildings in search of places to spend the winter. The adult beetle eats rectangular holes through elm leaves while its grub skeletonizes foliage. This pest affects all elms except the slippery, rock and winged species. (It should not be confused with the destructive native elm bark beetle that spreads Dutch elm disease.)

The ¼-inch adult beetle is yellow to dull green; the ½-inch larva is yellow and sluglike with black spots and stripes. There are usually two generations a year, though in California there are three or four. As soon as elm leaves start to unfold, the beetles come out of their sheltered places and start to feed and lay eggs on the undersides of leaves. Two or three weeks later, the larvae hatch and eat for three weeks. They then crawl down the tree, usually in a large mass, to pupate around the base.

SPECIAL TREATMENT. As soon as the leaves come out, spray with carbaryl (such as Sevin or Sevimol), acephate (such as Orthene) or methoxychlor to kill the beetles; repeat three weeks later to catch emerging grubs. When the grubs congregate at the bottom of the tree to pupate, spray them with carbaryl, malathion or diazinon. Grubs will congregate beneath boards placed at the bases of infested trees and can then be sprayed or collected and destroyed.

JAPANESE BEETLE
Popillia japonica

The Japanese beetle infests every state east of the Mississippi River. The adult is a serious garden and field pest that skeletonizes leaves, devours buds and flowers, and gouges developing fruits. It is particularly devastating to roses and corn. Adult beetles often congregate on a single blossom or fruit, especially those in sunny positions. These masses of beetles then eat until nothing is left. The beetle grubs feed on the roots of grasses, cutting them off completely. Among the few plants safe from their ravages are evergreens, chrysanthemums, gladioluses and phlox.

Japanese beetles produce one generation a year. The insect winters as a ½-inch gray grub 8 to 10 inches deep in the soil, moving up in the spring to feed on grass roots. The grub pupates in late spring and emerges as a bronze beetle a month later. The adult feeds until late autumn, growing $\frac{1}{3}$ to ½ inch long. Eggs laid in the soil hatch in 10 to 12 days, feed on roots, then burrow down for the winter.

SPECIAL TREATMENT. Shake adult beetles off plants or trees into a container of water to drown them. Sprays of diazinon (such as Spectracide), carbaryl (such as Sevin), malathion, methoxychlor or rotenone also help control the adult beetle population. To control beetle grubs, use milky disease spores (such as Doom or Japidemic). The disease spores are applied to lawns mixed with an inert powder and become established in three years. Thereafter, the disease is self-perpetuating and generally holds grub populations in control for several years.

JUNE BEETLE
Phyllophaga species

Found throughout North America, the June beetle is particularly troublesome in the South and Midwest. The brown

ELM LEAF BEETLE
Pyrrhalta luteola

JAPANESE BEETLE
Popillia japonica

adults, also called May beetles, June bugs or daw bugs, are ½ to ¾ inch long and feed on shade-tree foliage at night, and can be a household problem because they are attracted by lights. The larvae of the June beetle, called white grubs, are among the most destructive of lawn pests. Besides eating the roots of grass, these grubs also feed on the roots of beans, corn, potatoes, strawberries and such bulbous plants as hyacinths, stunting plant growth and sometimes killing plants.

The beetle's life cycle often takes three to four years, reaching a climax when female beetles lay eggs in grassy areas. These hatch in two to three weeks and the grubs feed on roots until early fall when they burrow deep into the soil to spend the winter. The following spring they move up to within a few inches of the surface to feed during the growing season. They descend again the second fall. The third year they pupate in early summer but remain in the soil as adult beetles until the fourth summer when they emerge to begin the cycle again. This cycle is shorter in warm climates.

SPECIAL TREATMENT. Major damage is caused by grubs the year after adult beetles appear. Avoid planting susceptible vegetables in these years. Control grub populations by deep spading in late spring or early summer when grubs are near the surface. During years when adult beetles are active, protect shade trees with sprays of carbaryl (such as Sevin).

MEXICAN BEAN BEETLE
Epilachna varivestis
Widespread east of the Rocky Mountains, the Mexican bean beetle resembles its relative, the ladybug beetle, but it is larger, about ¼ inch long, with 16 black dots forming lines across the wing sheaths. The yellow larva is oval in shape, with long, black-tipped spines. Feeding from the undersides of leaves, both larva and adult chew holes in the foliage of beans, especially snap and lima beans. They also feed on cowpeas and soybeans. When an infestation is severe the pest will attack pods and stems, skeletonizing entire plants.

The beetles produce one generation a year in northern states, two in central states and three or more in the South. Adults spend the winter in piles of leaves and attack plants as soon as sprouts appear. After feeding for a week or two, females lay eggs in masses underneath leaves. These hatch five to 14 days later. The larvae feed for several weeks, then attach themselves to leaves to pupate.

SPECIAL TREATMENT. Choose bean varieties that bear before the beetles are active in your area. Plant bush rather than pole beans. Remove leaves with orange egg masses and destroy them. Spray the underside of foliage with rotenone (such as derris or cubé), carbaryl (such as Sevin), diazinon (such as Spectracide) or malathion. Follow label recommendations carefully regarding the number of days between the last spraying and the harvest.

MOTTLED TORTOISE BEETLE
Deloyala guttata
Both adult and larva of this tortoise beetle, one of several species also called the gold bug, are unusual in appearance. The edges of the brown-and-gold wing sheaths of the ¹/₃-inch adult beetle are extended like the shell of a tortoise; the ³/₈-inch green larva has dark green spines along its sides and at the rear. Found throughout North America, the adults and larvae both cut holes in the leaves of sweet potatoes and morning glories.

Tortoise beetles produce only one generation each year. They spend the winter as adults in dry, sheltered places, emerging in early summer to mate and lay eggs. These hatch in 10 days and the larvae feed, then pupate in late summer.

Cautions to observe when using chemicals, page 71.

MEXICAN BEAN BEETLE
Epilachna varivestis

MOTTLED TORTOISE BEETLE
Deloyala guttata

NATIVE ELM BARK BEETLE
Hylurgopinus rufipes

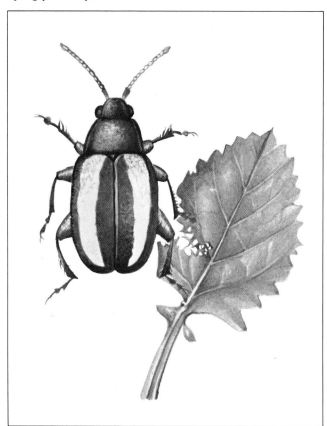

PALE-STRIPED FLEA BEETLE
Systena blanda

New beetles feed briefly in early fall, then become dormant.

SPECIAL TREATMENT. Spray infested plants with rotenone (such as derris or cubé), malathion, methoxychlor (such as Marlate) or carbaryl (such as Sevin) when the insects appear.

NATIVE ELM BARK BEETLE
Hylurgopinus rufipes

Throughout southern Canada and the United States east of the Rocky Mountains, native elm bark beetles are present wherever the American elm grows. The tiny, $1/10$-inch beetles also attack ash, basswood and wild cherry trees. Adult beetles feed in twig crotches and bore into dead or weakened branches of trees, where both they and their larvae construct broad egg galleries with many radiating tunnels. They cause infinitely more damage, however, as carriers of Dutch elm disease, which can kill an elm tree in just a few seasons. Some of the early signs of this disease are shriveled leaves and curled ends on young twigs.

One to three generations of elm bark beetles hatch each year. The insect spends the winter as either a larva or an adult beetle at the end of a breeding tunnel. It pupates under the bark, then bores out, leaving a tiny hole. The beetles fly to healthy trees to feed on foliage and young twigs. Later they return to weakened or dead wood to lay eggs and begin another cycle. Dutch elm disease is transmitted from diseased trees to healthy ones as the beetles feed.

SPECIAL TREATMENT. To help protect healthy trees, remove and dispose of all diseased trees and any dead or damaged wood in healthy trees before the beetles emerge. Methoxychlor is used to control adult beetles; many communities have spray programs. Once a tree becomes infected with Dutch elm disease, there is no known way to save it. Chemicals such as Lignasan or Arbotect show promise but treatment is costly and sometimes injures the tree. If you plant elms, choose disease-resistant types such as the Buisman elm, Groeneveld elm or Urban elm.

PALE-STRIPED FLEA BEETLE
Systena blanda

One of a large group of beetles that jump like fleas when disturbed, the pale-striped flea beetle is found throughout temperate regions of the United States. Adults eat holes in the foliage of a number of vegetables, including beans, corn, peas, potatoes and sweet potatoes. They also attack melon vines. In early spring and late fall they subsist on weeds. The beetle larvae feed on roots or seeds of germinating plants, retarding and sometimes halting growth. The larvae do most damage when germination is delayed by cool temperatures and they have more time to eat seeds.

One generation appears each year. Tiny brown adults pass the winter in sheltered places and feed on weeds in spring before going on to succulent young vegetables. They lay eggs in the soil and the thin, white, $1/4$-inch larvae hatch in time to attack germinating seeds.

SPECIAL TREATMENT. Plant late in the season if possible, after the larvae have hatched. Remove weeds and cover seedbeds with gauze to prevent the beetles from laying eggs. Spray beetles with carbaryl (such as Sevin), rotenone, diazinon (such as Spectracide), malathion or methoxychlor (such as Marlate).

PLUM CURCULIO
Conotrachelus nenuphar

In orchards everywhere east of the Rocky Mountains the plum curculio makes small, crescent-shaped cuts on young fruits of apple, cherry, pear, quince and most of the stone-fruit trees, especially plum. The adults feed on fruits, petals and buds. Depressions, scars and swellings develop on the fruits and many are totally destroyed. Larvae damage the interior of fruits.

The dark-brown, 1/3-inch adult beetles spend the winter in stone walls and garden debris, flying out when fruit trees blossom to feed on petals and buds. When the young fruit appears, females lay eggs in small holes, then cut crescent-shaped slots around them; that part of the fruit dies. The gray grubs hatch a week later and feed inside the fruit. Except for cherries and peaches, most of the damaged fruits fall to the ground where the grub moves out to pupate in the soil. After two weeks, new beetles fly to the remaining fruits to feed. There may be a second generation during a single year in warm climates.

SPECIAL TREATMENT. Pick up fallen fruit daily and remove damaged fruit from the trees. Dispose of it with your trash. Knock adult beetles off trees onto a sheet or tarpaulin and destroy them by drowning them in hot water. Sprays of methoxychlor (such as Marlate), malathion, or multi-purpose fruit tree sprays that contain methoxychlor, malathion and captan control the plum curculio. Ask your local agricultural agent for the spraying schedule recommended for your area.

ROSE CHAFER
Macrodactylus subspinosus

The adult rose chafer is particularly injurious to both the leaves and the blossoms of roses, peonies and grapes. It also attacks a number of other flowers, fruits and vegetables. The larvae feed on grass roots.

East of the Rocky Mountains, the rose chafer is primarily a pest in sandy areas. There is only one generation a year. The 3/4-inch larvae pass the winter in sandy soil, 10 to 16 inches deep, moving close to the surface in spring to feed. After pupation, the slow-moving 1/2-inch beetles emerge in early summer to feed for four to five weeks, then lay eggs in the soil. The eggs hatch and the larvae feed, then burrow down for the winter.

SPECIAL TREATMENT. Pick beetles off flowers by hand and protect valuable plants with cheesecloth fences during the short period while adult beetles are active. Methoxychlor (such as Marlate) or carbaryl (such as Sevin) controls adults. Ask your local agricultural agent for the recommended spray schedule for fruits in your area.

SPOTTED CUCUMBER BEETLE
Diabrotica undecimpunctata howardi

Ravages of the spotted cucumber beetle are particularly severe in the South, but the beetle is found everywhere east of the Rocky Mountains, and is paralleled in the West by the similar western spotted cucumber beetle. The beetle's larva, which is also known as the southern corn rootworm, tunnels through roots of cabbages, corn, cucumbers, melons, peas, potatoes and squash. Injured plants turn yellow and break off. Adult beetles chew large, irregular holes in the foliage and new shoots of these plants and a number of ornamental plants as well. Both adults and larvae spread bacteria that cause cucumber and corn wilts.

There are two or more generations each year in warm climates, one in colder areas. The 1/4-inch spotted beetles pass the winter at the bases of plants and weeds. When temperatures rise above 70° they start to feed and lay eggs at the bases of stems, just beneath the surface of the soil. The newly hatched larvae feed underground, then pupate.

SPECIAL TREATMENT. Spade the soil before planting to destroy dormant beetles. Plant wilt-resistant varieties of cu-

Cautions to observe when using chemicals, page 71.

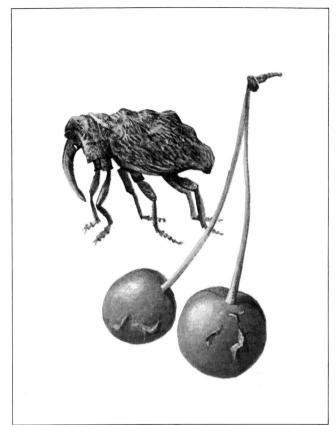

PLUM CURCULIO
Conotrachelus nenuphar

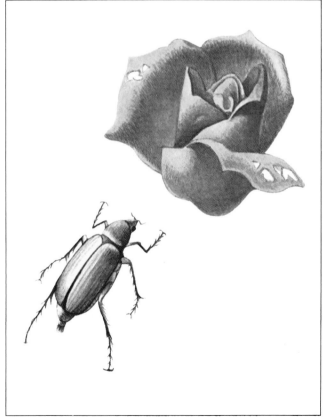

ROSE CHAFER
Macrodactylus subspinosus

SPOTTED CUCUMBER BEETLE
Diabrotica undecimpunctata howardi

STRIPED BLISTER BEETLE
Epicauta vittata

cumbers, melons and squash. Plant crops, especially corn, as late as possible. When new shoots appear, use carbaryl (such as Sevin), diazinon (such as Spectracide), malathion, methoxychlor (such as Marlate) or rotenone.

STRIPED BLISTER BEETLE
Epicauta vittata

One of a family of poisonous beetles that raise blisters on the skin if crushed, the striped blister beetle is found east of the Rocky Mountains. Only adult beetles injure plants, but these feed ravenously in swarms on the foliage and blossoms of almost any kind of vegetable. The heavy-jawed larvae are actually of some help to the garden, because they burrow through the soil to find and eat grasshopper eggs, their only food. In successive larval stages, legs and jaws grow progressively smaller. After about a month the larva enters an intermediate stage, called a pseudopupa. It can stay in this state, distinguished by a hard shell, for two years but usually does so for less than a year. In late spring, the pseudopupa molts once more, and the insect goes through another short larval stage before turning into a true pupa. The ½-inch adults reach the beetle's destructive stage in early summer, emerging to feed in swarms and lay eggs in the soil; these eggs hatch in midsummer.

SPECIAL TREATMENT. Knock adult beetles off plants into a can of water and destroy them. Cover endangered plants with cheesecloth. Control adults with sprays of carbaryl (such as Sevin), diazinon (such as Spectracide), malathion, methoxychlor (such as Marlate), or naled (such as Dibrom).

STRIPED CUCUMBER BEETLE
Acalymma vittatum

Found all over the United States east of the Rocky Mountains, the striped cucumber beetle is the most destructive pest of cucumbers, gourds, melons, pumpkins and squash. It also attacks beans, corn, peas and ornamental flower blossoms. West of the Rocky Mountains, a separate species called the western striped cucumber beetle does the same damage to western crops and is controlled in the same way. Adults feed on blossoms, leaves, shoots and vines, and chew holes in the rinds of fruits. The grubs devour roots and tunnel into the stems underground and spread cucumber-wilt bacteria and cucumber mosaic.

One generation hatches each year in the North and two or more in warm climates. The beetles pass the winter on the ground under leaves or plants, and become active in the early spring. Before the vegetables start to grow, the beetles feed on weeds or tree foliage. They lay eggs in the soil; the larvae feed for two to six weeks on roots, often destroying those plants. New adults appear in midsummer to feed on the upper parts of plants; in the fall they feed on the fruits, then return to weeds and trees.

SPECIAL TREATMENT. Plant extra seed and thin out seedlings. Cover developing plants with cheesecloth. Spray with carbaryl (such as Sevin), malathion, methoxychlor (such as Marlate) or rotenone.

WHITE-FRINGED BEETLE
Graphognathus species

A native of South America, the white-fringed beetle infests the southeastern states and is slowly migrating north. Larvae feed on the lower stem and soft outer root tissue of almost any vegetation they encounter, often severing the roots.

Grubs pass the winter 9 to 12 inches under the soil, pupate in late spring and early summer, emerging as nonflying, ½-inch beetles. They live for two to five months and travel from ¼ to ¾ of a mile before laying their eggs in the soil. There are as many as four generations a year.

SPECIAL TREATMENT. Large-scale government quarantine and eradication measures have made inroads against this pest. Deep spading in spring helps to eliminate overwintering grubs. You can trap crawling beetles in steep-sided ditches 1 foot deep around the garden, then destroy them.

BIRCH BORER, BRONZE See Borer
BLACK-BANDED SCALE See Scale, Terrapin
BLACK CRICKET See Cricket, Mormon
BLISTER BEETLE, STRIPED See Beetle
BOLLWORM, COTTON See Caterpillar, Corn-Ear Worm

BORER

Borers may be either grubs (the larvae of beetles) or caterpillars (the larvae of moths) that feed unseen inside stems and buds or beneath bark. (Borers that attack fruits, nuts and seeds are wormlike grubs that become the beetles known as weevils.) They enter either by being thrust in as eggs by the parent insects or by eating their way in after hatching. Entry holes are so minute as to be practically invisible; larger holes indicate exits. Shade and fruit trees, ornamental shrubs and garden plants all suffer from borer attacks. Some borers eat tissues of swelling buds, others attack roots or stems, still others feed on the vital cambium layer of trees, injuring the sap-carrying inner bark of branches and trunks.

Particularly vulnerable to borer attacks are newly planted trees; those weakened by drought, sunscald, fire, storm or frost; those defoliated by leaf-eating insects; and those injured by lawn mowers, by construction or by chemicals such as factory fumes or chlorides used to settle dust or melt ice.

WHAT TO DO. Since they are internal feeders, borers are hard to control during their destructive stage. The best protection is to promote vigor in plantings with deep watering during droughts, by fertilizing and by spraying to control leaf-eating insects. Trim off the ragged stumps of wind-damaged branches, making smooth, flush cuts. A year or two after transplanting, keep tree trunks wrapped to prevent sunscald and to establish a barrier that will keep borers out. Remove this wrap each year to make sure there are not mealy bugs or other insects beneath it. Brown stains on the wrap indicate that borers have penetrated the barrier. To eliminate these borers mechanically, probe into the holes with a flexible wire, or dig out each grub or caterpillar with a sharp knife. Caulk the borer holes with tree-wound dressing to prevent any invasion by bacteria or fungi.

Borer infestations of such vegetables as corn, cucumber, potato, pumpkin and squash can be slowed if all plant debris that might harbor eggs, including nearby grasses and weeds, is burned or otherwise disposed of after the harvest. Deep spading of the planting bed in the spring also helps.

BRONZE BIRCH BORER
Agrilus anxius

Found across the northern United States as far west as Idaho, Colorado and Utah, the bronze birch borer is a threat to birch trees—especially white and paper birches—as well as to poplars, cottonwoods and willows. The white grub that does the damage is slender but thickened just behind the head; it has a forceps-like appendage at the tip of its abdomen. The adult is an olive-bronze beetle with a blunt head and a slender, tapering body.

The insect winters as an inactive grub in a cell just within the sapwood under the bark. After pupating, it emerges in late spring and early summer as a beetle ¼ to ½ inch long.

Cautions to observe when using chemicals, page 71.

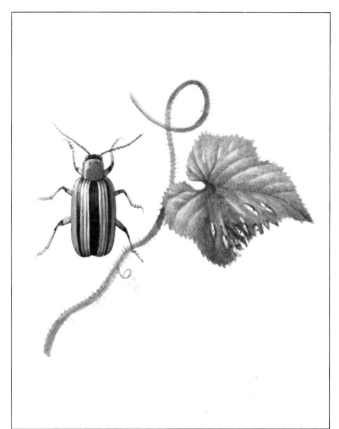

STRIPED CUCUMBER BEETLE
Acalymma vittatum

WHITE-FRINGED BEETLE
Graphognathus species

The female beetles deposit eggs singly in cracks in the bark or in crevices cut with their jaws. Tiny grubs hatch in about 10 days and chew their way into the inner bark. Full grown by fall, these larvae excavate crooked feeding galleries 4 or 5 feet long, filled with sawdust-like castings. These galleries cross and recross, sometimes completely cutting off circulation of the sap. The first indication of infestation may be the browning of tips of upper branches, which may also indicate the tree is dying. Trees that survive have swollen areas caused by the healing process.

SPECIAL TREATMENT. Infested branches, which are swollen and brown with oval holes about ⅛ inch in diameter, should be cut off and burned during the winter. Also follow the other control measures recommended for all borers.

EUROPEAN CORN BORER
Ostrinia nubilalis

One of the most destructive corn pests in the United States is the European corn borer. It was discovered on sweet corn in a Boston market in 1917, and since has spread throughout the East, to Montana, Wyoming and Utah in the West and as far south as the Florida border and Texas. This borer is a stalk pest, not only in corn but in asters, chrysanthemums, cosmos, dahlias, gladioluses, hollyhocks, zinnias and other flowers, as well as in beans, beets, celery, peppers and potatoes. It is most destructive, however, to sweet corn. Broken tassels, bent stalks and castings outside of tiny holes indicate that borers are at work.

The larva is a flesh-colored caterpillar up to an inch long with rows of round brown spots. The female moth is yellow-brown with wavy dark bands; the male is darker. They have a wingspan of 1 inch and fly mostly at night. Caterpillars winter in old stalks left in the garden and pupate in the spring. In northern states the moths emerge during the summer; in the South there may be up to three generations a year. Each female moth lays about 400 eggs on the undersides of corn leaves. Hatching in a week or less, caterpillars first eat holes in leaves, then bore into the stalks and ears.

SPECIAL TREATMENT. As soon as corn tassels are visible (or when other vulnerable plants are about half grown) spray with carbaryl (such as Sevin), repeating the application three more times at five-day intervals.

FLAT-HEADED APPLE-TREE BORER
Chrysobothris femorata

Throughout the United States, the flat-headed apple-tree borer attacks nearly all fruit, woodland and shade trees, especially newly planted shade trees in the South and Midwest. Among the plants that the grubs bore into are apple, apricot, ash, beech, box elder, cherry, chestnut, cotoneaster, cottonwood, currant, dogwood, elm, hickory, horse chestnut, linden, maple, mountain ash, oak, peach, pear, pecan, plum, poplar, prune, raspberry, rose, sycamore and willow. In the West, oak is the primary host; in the East, maples and fruit trees are most frequently victims.

Presence of the borer grubs is indicated by burrows filled with castings under the bark on the main trunk or on large branches, about 6 inches in length and sometimes going as deep as 2 inches. The overlying bark turns dark and often exudes sap. These injuries nearly always appear on the sunny sides of the trees, killing patches of bark, but they may extend completely around to kill the entire branch or tree.

A full-grown grub is about 1¼ inches long, legless and yellow to white with a body enlargement just back of the head. The body is usually curved, often U-shaped. The adult beetle, about ½ inch long, is dark olive-gray to brown, with a

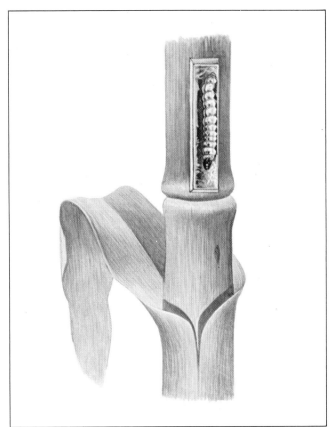

EUROPEAN CORN BORER
Ostrinia nubilalis

FLAT-HEADED APPLE-TREE BORER
Chrysobothris femorata

metallic luster on the wings. It is usually found on the sunny sides of trees and logs. The insect winters in the grub stage, changing to a yellow pupa in the spring. In summer the female beetle emerges and lays yellow, disklike, wrinkled eggs in cracks in the bark, nearly always selecting a tree that is unhealthy or injured.

SPECIAL TREATMENT. Follow the control measures recommended for all borers.

LILAC BORER
Podosesia syringae

Widely distributed east of the Rockies, the lilac borer attacks not only lilacs but white, English and mountain ashes and occasionally privet. In fact, it does more damage to ash trees than the ash borer. The larva is a white worm with a brown head, about 1½ inches long. The adult moth looks like a wasp—a ferocious resemblance that helps it survive. Its inch-wide front wings are brown; the hind wings are clear with brown borders.

Female moths deposit masses of eggs on the bases of lilac canes and on wounded tree bark. When these eggs hatch, the larvae tunnel in, weakening and sometimes girdling canes and branches. Foliage wilts, expelled castings accumulate at the borer holes and damaged canes often break off. In lilacs, infestations are found at the root crown and up to 3 feet above it. Partly grown larvae winter in the cane or tree, usually near the ground, resuming their feeding in spring.

SPECIAL TREATMENT. Cut and burn any branches containing borers. Follow the other control measures recommended for all borers.

PEACH-TREE BORER
Sanninoidea exitiosa

The peach-tree borer is the worst enemy of peach trees throughout the United States, and it also attacks apricot, cherry, nectarine and plum trees and ornamental shrubs. An attack is signaled by masses of gum and brown castings at the ground level, indicating that larvae are at work in the bark anywhere from the base of the trunk to 10 inches above. This borer also spreads plum-wilt fungus, a disease as injurious as the insect itself.

Peach-tree borer larvae are an inch or more long, with white bodies and dark brown heads. The moth is a glassy steel-blue with a 1-inch wingspan; it is active during the day, unlike most moths, and in flight resembles a large wasp.

The insect winters in the larval stage. In spring, the worms become active in bark near the ground. When grown they make cocoons of borings bound with silk at the entrances to burrows or on the soil. Moths emerge about a month later. Bark-colored eggs, 200 to 800 per female, are deposited near the ground, usually on previously infested or injured trees. They hatch in 10 days and the worms bore in.

SPECIAL TREATMENT. Spray trunks and lower branches with malathion. Fumigate soil in the fall by placing a ring of paradichlorobenzene crystals (moth crystals) 1 to 3 inches from the trunk and covering it with soil.

POTATO TUBERWORM, also called TUBER MOTH
Phthorimaea operculella

The potato tuberworm primarily destroys potatoes, especially in hot, dry years, but it also attacks eggplants, tobacco and tomatoes. It is found in the South from California to Florida and north as far as Washington, Colorado, Virginia and Maryland. The larva is a ¾-inch pink-to-white worm with a brown head; the adult is a small, narrow-winged moth, gray-brown mottled with darker brown. The potato tuber-

Cautions to observe when using chemicals, page 71.

LILAC BORER
Podosesia syringae

PEACH-TREE BORER
Sanninoidea exitiosa

worm's life cycle is completed in a month, and there may be five or six generations a year.

In spring, moths leave storage areas and lay eggs, one at a time, on the undersides of leaves or in the eyes of potato tubers. After hatching, the larvae mine the leaves and stems, causing shoots to wilt and die. They pupate in dirt-covered cocoons on the ground. Adults of late broods infest tubers directly by working through cracks in the soil to lay eggs on them or by laying eggs on exposed tubers at digging time. Larvae also migrate down stems to the tubers. After potatoes are harvested, any larvae that are left may burrow through the flesh and emerge to pupate in the storage areas.

SPECIAL TREATMENT. Plant uninfested seed pieces as early as possible; keep potato plants well cultivated and deeply hilled. Cut and destroy infested vines before digging tubers; also destroy infested potatoes. Do not leave newly dug potatoes exposed to egg-laying moths during late afternoon or night. Screen storage places and keep them clean and cool.

SQUASH-VINE BORER
Melittia cucurbitae

East of the Rocky Mountains, the squash-vine borer is especially damaging to squashes and pumpkins in home gardens and also attacks cantaloupes, cucumbers and gourds. Like the peach-tree borer, it resembles a wasp in its adult stage. It has clear copper-green forewings, 1 to 1½ inches across, and an orange-and-black abdomen. The wrinkled caterpillar is white with a brown head.

The insect winters in the soil in a tough black cocoon about ¾ inch long. When vine crops begin to produce runners, the moth emerges and darts noisily and swiftly around the plants during the day. The female glues small, oval brown eggs, one at a time, on stems and leaf stalks near the ground. In about a week the larvae hatch, bore into the stems, and begin to feed. Later the caterpillar may move into stems throughout the plant and even into the fruits.

SPECIAL TREATMENT. Dust with rotenone, malathion or methoxychlor (such as Marlate) at weekly intervals when the vines start to run; this treatment should kill larvae as they enter the stems. In the North, where only a single generation hatches each year, plant a second crop of summer squash in midsummer so that it will mature after the borers have finished feeding.

STALK BORER
Papaipema nebris

A wide-ranging feeder that moves from plant to plant, the stalk borer attacks most large, soft plants growing east of the Rocky Mountains. It favors corn and ragweed but also damages asters, chrysanthemums, cosmos, dahlias, delphiniums, hollyhocks, irises, lilies, peonies, peppers, phlox, potatoes, rhubarb, salvias, snapdragons, tomatoes and zinnias.

The young caterpillar has a cream-colored body with dark brown or purple bands that almost disappear on the full-grown caterpillar, which is gray or violet and 1 to 1½ inches long. The adult is a gray moth with a 1-inch wingspan.

The insect winters in a gray, ridged egg on grasses and weeds. Caterpillars hatch in early spring, first eating grasses, then stalks of other plants. They usually destroy the heart of the stalk while outer leaves remain green. If they enter near the top and burrow down, however, the top of the plant wilts and dies. The caterpillars rarely pupate inside the stems of their food plants but return to the ground and in two to four weeks change into moths just below the surface, emerging in late summer. Each female lays more than 2,000 eggs on ragweed, pigweed, burdock and grasses, especially bluegrass.

POTATO TUBERWORM
Phthorimaea operculella

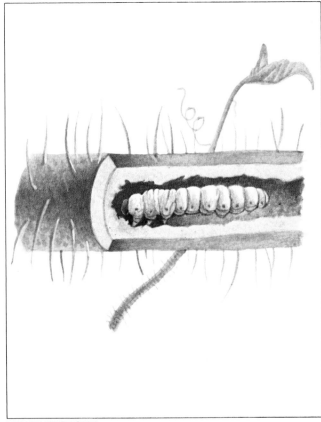

SQUASH-VINE BORER
Melittia cucurbitae

SPECIAL TREATMENT. Spray or dust with methoxychlor or carbaryl (such as Sevin) to destroy caterpillars as they move from plant to plant.

BRONZE BIRCH BORER See Borer
BROWN-TAIL MOTH See Caterpillar
BUD MOTH, EYE-SPOTTED See Caterpillar
BUDWORM, SPRUCE See Caterpillar

BUG

Most people conveniently refer to practically all insects as bugs. But to an entomologist true bugs fit into a special classification of their own, Hemiptera, and they make up a relatively minor part of the insect population. Bugs puncture plants or animals with long, slender beaks to suck sap or blood. They undergo only gradual metamorphosis between hatching and maturity, so young nymphs resemble their parents except in size. At all ages, bugs often feed together and share other traits; many have scent glands that enable them to produce strong odors when disturbed. Among plant eaters are flower bugs, leaf bugs, lace bugs, chinch bugs, squash bugs and stinkbugs.

WHAT TO DO. Maintain a clean garden, removing and destroying weeds and harvest remnants; most bugs spend the winter in or under debris. Use insecticides formulated to kill the specific bug in your garden, following label instructions on the number of days to allow between last application and the harvest of food crops.

CHINCH BUG
Blissus leucopterus leucopterus

Feeding on plants in the grass family, including all lawn grasses and corn, chinch bugs live throughout the United States but are especially injurious in the Mississippi, Ohio and Missouri River valleys and in Texas and Oklahoma. Newly hatched chinch bugs are smaller than a pinhead, red and without wings. Fully grown, they are ⅛ inch long, black with white wings. Adults hibernate in winter, then mate and lay eggs when temperatures consistently reach 70°. For three or four weeks, females deposit yellow, cylindrical eggs behind leaf sheaths, in the ground around plants or on roots. Nymphs feed first on roots, then stalks. Two to three generations are produced each year.

In northeastern states, the hairy chinch bug, which is a short-winged type, attacks lawns and golf courses, leaving brown patches of dead grass that resemble the damage done by fungus or Japanese beetles. Damage is most serious in hot, dry weather.

SPECIAL TREATMENT. To control chinch bugs around corn, choose resistant varieties. Stop migrating adults with barriers of creosote-soaked building paper set on edge in the soil or with creosote poured along a ridge around the corn plot.

For small infestations in lawns, flood the affected section with warm water and cover it with white cloth. Collect and destroy the chinch bugs that surface under the cloth. For larger areas, apply a granular formulation of diazinon (such as Spectracide) or carbaryl (such as Sevin). Treat in early summer when the bugs become active, and repeat, if necessary, in late summer. Water well after each application.

GARDEN FLEA HOPPER
Halticus bractatus

Black, long-legged, jumping flea hoppers, up to 1/10 inch long, are found throughout the United States except in the West. They attack many vegetables and ornamental plants, especially those that are grown in the shade. Some of the

Cautions to observe when using chemicals, page 71.

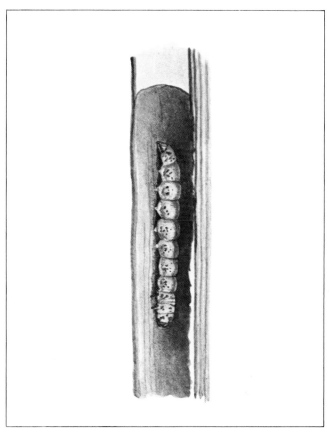

STALK BORER
Papaipema nebris

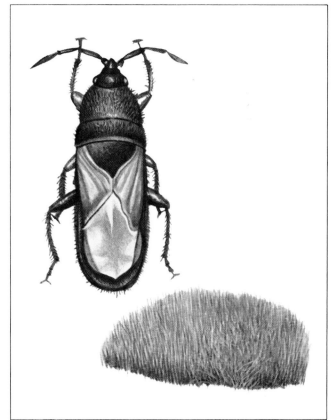

CHINCH BUG
Blissus leucopterus leucopterus

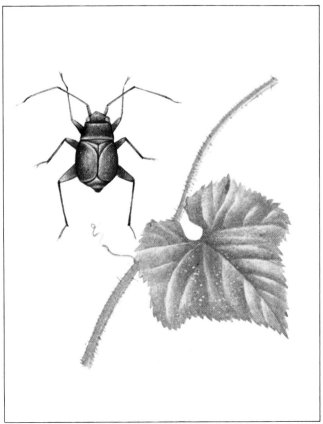

GARDEN FLEA HOPPER
Halticus bractatus

HARLEQUIN BUG
Murgantia histrionica

plants that are susceptible are beans, beets, celery, corn, cowpeas, cucumbers, eggplants, lettuce, peas, peppers, potatoes, pumpkins, squashes, sweet potatoes and tomatoes; and ageratums, chrysanthemums, gladioluses, heliopsises, marigolds, morning glories, portulacas, primroses, rudbeckias, scabiosas, sunflowers, verbenas and zinnias. The garden flea hoppers' green nymphs kill leaves by sucking out sap. In spring, females pierce leaves or stems and insert eggs. The nymphs appear on the undersides of leaves and develop rapidly. There may be five generations in a season.

SPECIAL TREATMENT. Spray infested plants with malathion or carbaryl (such as Sevin).

HARLEQUIN BUG
Murgantia histrionica

A species of the stinkbug family, the harlequin bug is the most destructive enemy of cabbage and related plants in the southern half of the United States from coast to coast. Black with bands, stripes and margins in red, orange or yellow, it is flat, broad, shield-shaped and up to ⅜ inch long. Its bizarre coloring has inspired many nicknames such as harlequin cabbage bug, calicoback, terrapin and fire bug.

The adult bug winters near old cabbage stalks. In the spring, the female lays eggs on the undersides of leaves of early garden crops. The eggs resemble tiny white barrels with black hoops standing in double rows. After hatching, the green nymphs suck out so much sap that white or yellow blotches appear where they have fed. If the bugs are abundant, leaves wilt, turn brown and die. Usually three generations appear in a season.

This pest attacks such crucifers as Brussels sprouts, cabbages, cauliflower, collards, cress, horseradishes, kohlrabi, mustard, radishes and turnips. It also eats other vegetables and fruits including asparagus, beans, corn, eggplants, lettuce, okra, potatoes, squashes, cherries, citrus, grapes and plums, and such ornamentals as chrysanthemums and roses.

SPECIAL TREATMENT. In spring, trap the bugs by placing refuse turnip or cabbage leaves in the garden, then destroy the bugs attracted to them. Search for egg masses on the undersides of leaves and crush them. Sprays containing carbaryl (such as Sevin), sabadilla, rotenone or pyrethrum (such as Pyrethrins) will control the nymphs. Consult your agricultural agent for a fruit-tree spray schedule for your area.

SQUASH BUG
Anasa tristis

Hard-shelled and ⅝ inch long, adult squash bugs are black or brown on top and yellow underneath. Distributed throughout the United States, they attack all vine crops, primarily squash and pumpkin. Among squashes, winter varieties such as Hubbard and marrow suffer most. Like stinkbugs, squash bugs give off a disagreeable odor when crushed.

Squash bugs hibernate during winter under dead leaves, vines, boards or in buildings. In spring the females lay elliptical yellow eggs on the undersides of leaves. The eggs turn dark brown before hatching. Nymphs from one mass of eggs feed close together. Bright green at birth, the nymphs turn to gray and molt five times before becoming winged adults. There is usually only one generation a year.

Stricken leaves wilt rapidly, becoming black and crisp. When bugs are numerous, no fruit will form.

SPECIAL TREATMENT. Stimulate healthy plant growth with fertilizer. Destroy squash bugs that are found under leaves and boards, where they collect at night, and leaves that are covered with eggs. Spray vines with carbaryl (such as Sevin), malathion or sabadilla.

TARNISHED PLANT BUG
Lygus lineolaris

Irregularly mottled with white, yellow and black blotches, the tarnished plant bug is found throughout the United States. The ¼-inch-long, flat, oval adults have a clear yellow triangle, marked with a black dot, on the lower third of each side. The nymphs are yellow-green with black dots.

The bug injures more than 50 crops. Vegetables that are susceptible include beans, beets, cauliflower, cabbages, celery, chard, cucumbers, potatoes and turnips. Most deciduous trees and many fruit trees are also attacked, including apples, peaches, pears, strawberries and occasionally citrus. Among flowers, dahlias and asters are frequent victims; the bug sometimes also damages calendulas, chrysanthemums, cosmos, gladioluses, impatiens, marigolds, poppies, salvias, Shasta daisies, sunflowers, verbenas and zinnias.

By injecting its poison into a plant, the bug causes a variety of injuries—deformed leaves on beets and chard; scarred, wilted and discolored stems on celery and related vegetables (called black joint); blackened tip shoots, dwarfing and pitting on beans, strawberries and peaches; and dead buds or poorly developed blooms on dahlias.

SPECIAL TREATMENT. At the first sign of blackening leaf tips, apply rotenone and repeat at weekly intervals. Or spray with malathion or carbaryl (such as Sevin) as flower buds start to form, repeating just before they open.

C

CABBAGE BUG, HARLEQUIN See Bug, Harlequin
CABBAGE BUTTERFLY See Caterpillar, Imported Cabbage Worm
CABBAGE LOOPER See Caterpillar
CABBAGE MAGGOT See Maggot
CABBAGE-ROOT FLY See Maggot, Cabbage
CALICO-BACK See Bug, Harlequin
CALIFORNIA RED SCALE See Scale
CANKERWORM, FALL See Caterpillar
CANKERWORM, SPRING See Caterpillar
CARROT RUST FLY See Maggot
CATALPA SPHINX See Caterpillar

CATERPILLAR (MOTH or BUTTERFLY)

Caterpillars, the larvae of moths or butterflies, undergo a complete metamorphosis in four stages—egg, larva, pupa and adult. After hatching from eggs, caterpillars feed on vegetables, ornamental plants and trees almost continuously until they enter a dormant pupal stage, usually but not always spent in a cocoon. When the adult moths and butterflies emerge, all of the males and some of the females have wings that enable them to fly great distances—the Monarch is an intercontinental traveler. Wingspans range from less than $^1/_{10}$ of an inch up to 12 inches. The name of the order, Lepidoptera, means scaly wings. Minute, powdery, often colorful scales cover the wings and bodies of butterflies and moths in an overlapping pattern like that of a shingled roof. Although their eggs hatch into plant-eating caterpillars, nearly all moths and butterflies are themselves harmless to plants and delightful to have in a garden. Some are able to taste flowers with the soles of their feet, triggering the proboscises, coiled tubes beneath their heads, to lash out for water and nectar. A few ingest carrion and excrement or cloth and paper. Some moths are not equipped to eat anything.

WHAT TO DO. Destructive caterpillars are best controlled by keeping a garden sanitary and cultivating it frequently. Many species that pupate underground can be destroyed in early spring by deep spading. Dispose of all visible cocoons.

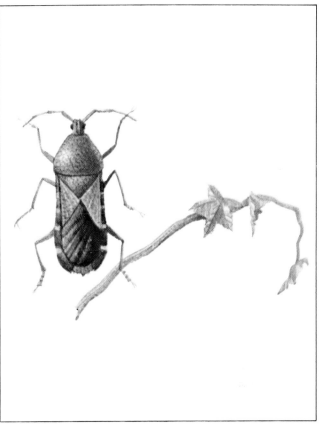

SQUASH BUG
Anasa tristis

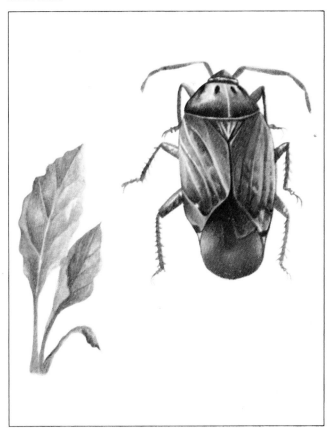

TARNISHED PLANT BUG
Lygus lineolaris

Cautions to observe when using chemicals, page 71.

BAGWORM
Thyridopteryx ephemeraeformis

BROWN-TAIL MOTH
Nygmia phaeorrhoea

Attract birds by providing water, feeders and bird houses. Destroy caterpillars by knocking them into a can of water with a stick. An effective biological control that attacks caterpillars but is harmless to all else is a spore-forming bacterium called *Bacillus thuringiensis.* Available in liquid or powder form under such trade names as Biotrol, Dipel and Thuricide, it is mixed with water and applied as a spray.

BAGWORM
Thyridopteryx ephemeraeformis

Found east of the Rocky Mountains, bagworms prefer to feed on such evergreens as arborvitae, cedar, hemlock, juniper, larch and pine. But they are also general feeders that will eat leaves and sometimes even completely defoliate box elder, citrus, linden, locust, Norway and soft maples, plane and poplar trees. Similar insects are distributed throughout the United States and Canada.

Immediately upon hatching in spring or early summer, the tiny brown caterpillars begin to construct tentlike bags of silken threads, which may become 2 inches long; they live within these bags and carry them around like mobile homes, tethering them to leaves or branches during pupation. After pupation inside the bag, black or gray winged male moths emerge in fall. They mate with tiny, wingless female moths that remain in the bag. Females have no mouths and do not eat. They mate in the bag, lay their eggs there, then die.

SPECIAL TREATMENT. Hand-pick bags during winter and early spring before eggs hatch. Destroy the occupants by crushing the bags or burning them. *Bacillus thuringiensis* is effective against bagworms. Spray heavy infestations in early summer with acephate (such as Orthene), malathion, diazinon (such as Spectracide), dimethoate (such as Cygon or De-Fend), or carbaryl (such as Sevin).

BROWN-TAIL MOTH
Nygmia phaeorrhoea

Found mainly in New England, Nova Scotia and New Brunswick, the brown-tail moth's caterpillars attack deciduous shade and fruit trees such as oak, willow, apple, cherry and pear. They also damage some shrubs but do not attack evergreens. The eggs hatch in late summer or early fall, and the tiny caterpillars live through the winter as a group in webs made of silken thread and bits of leaves attached to a twig. When leaves bud in the spring, the hairy brown-to-black caterpillars, striped and spotted with red and white, leave the nest to feed. The caterpillars have barbed hairs that can cause a skin rash if touched. About 1½ inches long when full grown, they pupate in early summer in webbed cocoons spun among leaves. Pure white moths, active flyers with wingspans of nearly 2 inches, emerge from the cocoons in midsummer. Each female deposits 200 to 400 eggs, usually on the undersides of leaves.

SPECIAL TREATMENT. Remove webs from bare branches during the winter. When leaves first come out in the spring and the caterpillars begin to feed, spray trees with carbaryl (such as Sevin) or methoxychlor.

CABBAGE LOOPER
Trichoplusia ni

A native species, the cabbage looper is found throughout the United States and in those parts of Canada where cabbage is grown. Besides cabbage, it feeds on beets, broccoli, Brussels sprouts, cauliflower, celery, collards, kale, lettuce, peas, potatoes, radishes, tomatoes and turnips. It also chews irregular holes in the leaves of many ornamental plants, among them carnations, chrysanthemums and geraniums.

The pale green 1½-inch caterpillar is sometimes referred to as a measuring worm because it doubles up into a loop and then stretches to its full length as it crawls along. It winters as a pupa wrapped in a cocoon attached to a leaf of the plant on which it feeds. The cocoon is so thin that the outline of the pupa can be seen inside. Moths, about 1 inch long with a wingspan of 1½ inches, emerge in early spring. They are brown and gray with distinctive silver spots on their upper pairs of wings. The females lay many small, round white eggs singly on the upper surfaces of leaves. The eggs hatch in about two weeks and the young loopers feed for three or four weeks. Four or more generations may appear in a year.

SPECIAL TREATMENT. Clean up and dispose of all crop remnants each fall and remove weeds, especially mustard, shepherd's-purse and peppergrass, that are near the garden. If worms appear, knock them off into a jar of water to drown them. Malathion or carbaryl (such as Sevin) are effective when the worms are small. Cabbage loopers are also susceptible to *Bacillus thuringiensis*.

CATALPA SPHINX
Ceratomia catalpae

In the United States the catalpa sphinx is found most abundantly east and south of the Mississippi and Ohio rivers and in parts of Ohio, Indiana and Illinois. The large, dark caterpillar, 1 to 3 inches long with green or yellow stripes, has a prominent black horn at the rear of its body. Doubly justifying their name, these pests feed on the leaves of catalpa trees, and crouch sphinxlike when they are disturbed. A heavy infestation can defoliate a catalpa tree in a single day. The brown naked pupae winter 2 or 3 inches below the soil surface, emerging as gray-to-brown adult moths in spring. The moths attain a wingspan of up to 3 inches and fly mainly at night, so they are seldom seen. Female moths lay as many as 1,000 eggs at a time, usually on the undersides of leaves. The eggs hatch in about two weeks.

SPECIAL TREATMENT. If eggs or small caterpillars are discovered, hundreds can be killed by plucking and destroying single leaves. Young caterpillars are susceptible to attack by parasitic wasps that help control their numbers for two or three years before infestations become heavy enough to defoliate trees again. Catalpa caterpillars make good fish bait, especially for catfish.

CODLING MOTH
Laspeyresia pomonella

A scourge throughout the apple-growing regions of the world, the inch-long caterpillar of the codling moth is the most destructive of all apple pests. It also damages almonds, crabapples, English walnuts, peaches and pears. During the winter, the caterpillars, pink to white with brown heads, hibernate in tough-skinned cocoons underneath loose bark, in crevices of trees, fences and buildings, and even in cracks in the ground. The gray-to-brown moth that emerges in the spring has a ¾-inch double wingspan, dark brown marks on its upper wings and darker brown edges along both pairs of wings. The female lays flat white eggs, one at a time, on the upper sides of leaves or on twigs. Hatching in six to 20 days, the caterpillars head for young apples or other fruit, tunnel to the core, then burrow out, leaving brown castings behind them. Several generations appear each summer, the later ones damaging ripe apples.

SPECIAL TREATMENT. Band trunks and large branches of fruit trees in early summer with 6-inch strips of burlap or chemically treated commercial tree wraps. Destroy the caterpillars that crawl behind the wraps and spin cocoons there.

Cautions to observe when using chemicals, page 71.

CABBAGE LOOPER
Trichoplusia ni

CODLING MOTH
Laspeyresia pomonella

Scrape loose bark from the trees and remove debris that might provide shelter. Sprays of diazinon (such as Spectracide), carbaryl (such as Sevin) or malathion plus methoxychlor are effective against codling moths if applied at the right time. Consult your agricultural agent for a spray schedule tailored to your locality.

CORN-EAR WORM
Heliothis zea

One of the worst menaces to crops of field corn and sweet corn, the corn-ear worm is most prevalent in the South but lives throughout the United States and Canada in corn-growing areas. Also called the tomato fruitworm, cotton bollworm, tobacco budworm and vetchworm, the pest attacks beans, lettuce, potatoes, tomatoes and other food plants as well as cotton, tobacco and many flowers. On corn, the full-grown 2-inch caterpillars, green to brown and marked with lengthwise light and dark stripes, feed first on leaves and silks which wilt and turn brown. Boring into the ear, they then feed on the kernels and eventually eat their way into the corn cob. After feeding for a month, the caterpillars crawl down the stalk or drop to the ground where they tunnel 3 to 5 inches under the soil to pupate. They emerge in about two weeks as green-to-brown moths with 1½-inch wingspans. Each female moth lays from 500 to as many as 3,000 eggs. Two or three generations may emerge each year in warm climates. Though pupae may not survive Northern winters, infestations continue to persist because the adult moths migrate from warmer regions.

SPECIAL TREATMENT. Plant corn varieties with long, tight husks (such as Dixie 18, Country Gentleman, Golden Security and Silver Cross Bantam). Apply a few drops of mineral oil to the silks, just inside the tip of each ear, when the silks first appear, or dust with carbaryl (such as Sevin) every two or three days until the silks turn brown. To check for caterpillars, carefully pull back the husk; pick off and destroy any pests you find. On plants other than corn, malathion or carbaryl are effective against the egg-laying moths.

EASTERN TENT CATERPILLAR
Malacosoma americanum

In early spring the silken webs of the eastern tent caterpillar can be seen in the forks and crotches of susceptible trees in the eastern United States and Canada as far west as the Rocky Mountains. Also known as the apple-tree caterpillar, this pest favors apple and wild cherry trees but will also feed on hawthorn, peach, pear, plum and other deciduous trees and shrubs. A heavy infestation will completely defoliate the trees. In early spring the caterpillars hatch from egg masses and the young stay together to spin their tent. They emerge from the tent to strip nearby leaves from the branches. As the hairy, striped and spotted caterpillars grow to their full 2-inch length, they enlarge the tent. After four to six weeks, they leave it to spin cocoons attached to bark, fences, brush, piles of debris or nearby buildings. After pupating, the moths emerge and the females deposit masses of several hundred eggs in bands around twigs, covering them with a secretion that hardens to a dark brown, varnish-like finish. The eggs hatch the following spring.

SPECIAL TREATMENT. Inspect trees for egg masses during the winter. Prune and burn any twigs that are banded with egg masses. In the spring, tear out any tents you can reach, winding them on a pole if necessary, before the caterpillars leave the nests to feed. After they have begun to feed, sprays of Bacillus thuringiensis (such as Thuricide), carbaryl (such as Sevin), diazinon (such as Spectracide),

CORN-EAR WORM
Heliothis zea

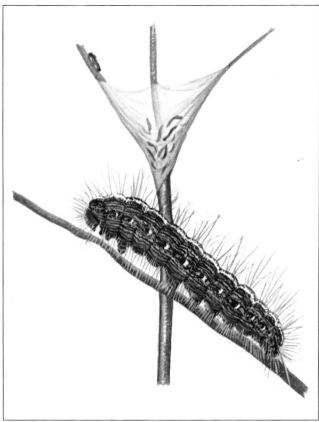

EASTERN TENT CATERPILLAR
Malacosoma americanum

acephate (such as Orthene), malathion or methoxychlor (such as Marlate) are effective.

EYE-SPOTTED BUD MOTH
Spilonota ocellana

Apple, cherry and pear trees in the northern United States and southern Canada are principal targets of the eye-spotted bud moth. It also attacks hawthorn, laurel, oak and plum trees. The ½-inch caterpillars, brown with black heads, feed on buds and unfolding leaves during the early spring months, weaving small shelters of silk that also damage fruits. In early summer they pupate inside these shelters, and small brown or gray moths with wing spots emerge in midsummer. Eggs, which the females lay singly or in clusters on the undersides of leaves, hatch in a few days and the new caterpillars feed until early fall. They then spin shelters in the forks of twigs or in bark crevices where they hibernate through the winter, emerging again in the spring.

SPECIAL TREATMENT. Malathion, diazinon (such as Spectracide) and *Bacillus thuringiensis* (such as Biotrol) are effective sprays. Good apple production requires a program tailored for a specific climate. Consult your local agricultural agent for the best spray dates in your area.

FALL CANKERWORM
Alsophila pometaria

Despite its name, the fall cankerworm does its damage in early spring in parts of California, Colorado and Utah, in most of the northern United States and in southern Canada. A small caterpillar less than an inch long, it feeds on the young leaves of apple, cherry, elm, oak and other fruit and shade trees. It suspends itself from a twig on a fine strand of silk and waits for a breeze to carry it to a neighboring tree. When ready to enter the pupal stage, it crawls or drops to the ground and burrows into the soil to spin its small cocoon. The gray-to-brown male moths that emerge have wings, but the females are wingless and must crawl up a tree to lay eggs on the trunk or branches. The gray eggs, shaped like flower pots, do not hatch until the following spring.

SPECIAL TREATMENT. Band tree trunks in fall with a sticky tree wrap to trap migrating female moths before they lay eggs. Sprays of carbaryl (such as Sevin), acephate (such as Orthene) or *Bacillus thuringiensis* (such as Dipel) applied in spring according to your local agricultural agent's guidelines are effective against young caterpillars.

FALL WEBWORM
Hyphantria cunea

More than 100 species of fruit and shade trees throughout the United States and Canada are attacked by the fall webworm. Its preferences vary from region to region: it infests alder, cottonwood, willow and fruit trees in the western United States, American elm, hickory and maple in western Appalachia and the Ohio valley. The caterpillars grow to a length of 1¼ inches as they feed in groups under protective webs spun on the ends of branches. When full grown, the caterpillar crawls down the trunk to the ground and forms a cocoon, often under rubbish piles or in crevices in bark or fence posts. In late summer, white moths with wings spotted black or brown emerge and lay eggs for a second generation of webworms in fall. After the new generation feeds for four to six weeks, the worms return to the ground to spin cocoons and winter in the pupal stage. The moths reappear in spring to deposit white egg masses on the undersides of leaves.

SPECIAL TREATMENT. Destroy branches with webs. Pick and destroy leaves on which the moths have laid eggs. When

Cautions to observe when using chemicals, page 71.

EYE-SPOTTED BUD MOTH
Spilonota ocellana

FALL CANKERWORM
Alsophila pometaria

FALL WEBWORM
Hyphantria cunea

new webs first appear, spray with diazinon (such as Spectracide), naled (such as Dibrom) or carbaryl (such as Sevin). *Bacillus thuringiensis* (such as Dipel or Biotrol) is also effective.

FRUIT-TREE LEAF ROLLER
Archips argyrospilus

Though particularly damaging to apple trees in the northern United States and southern Canada, the fruit-tree leaf roller is found coast to coast, and in California it attacks buds, leaves and fruit on most deciduous fruit and citrus trees. It may also infest ash, box elder, elm, English walnut, hickory, horse chestnut, locust, oak, osage orange, poplar, sassafras and willow trees, as well as roses. It winters in clusters of 30 to 100 eggs deposited on branches and tree trunks and covered with protective coatings that camouflage them. Small green caterpillars emerge in the early spring and feed for about a month as they grow to a length of ¾ inch. They spin webs, tying several leaves together and sometimes enclosing small fruit. They then pupate within rolled leaves or in flimsy cocoons attached to branches. Light-brown moths come out in late June or July. The female moths lay eggs that hatch the following spring, completing the year-long life cycle that produces a single generation.

SPECIAL TREATMENT. Apply a dormant oil spray, heavy enough to cover the egg masses, just before buds break open in the spring. Destroy larvae by spraying with *Bacillus thuringiensis* (such as Dipel or Thuricide), carbaryl (such as Sevin), diazinon (such as Spectracide) or malathion. A regular spray schedule suited to climate and other conditions in your area is necessary for good fruit production. Consult your local agricultural agent for the schedule and insecticides he recommends.

GARDEN WEBWORM
Loxostege rantalis

Working under the protection of its own silken covering, the garden webworm feeds on the stems, leaves and fruits of castor beans, corn, cowpeas, peas, soybeans and other plants throughout the United States and southern Canada. Webworms spend the winter in the pupal stage in the soil. When the small buff-colored moths emerge in the spring, females lay clusters of about 50 eggs on leaves. Caterpillars hatch in about a week, spin web shelters and feed for a month, growing an inch long before pupating. Several generations are possible each season. When disturbed, garden webworms drop to the ground or hide in their tubular shelters.

SPECIAL TREATMENT. Knock caterpillars off leaves into a can of water. Cut out and destroy the protective webs. Malathion, diazinon (such as Gardentox), rotenone (such as derris) or pyrethrum are effective insecticides.

GRAPE BERRY MOTH
Paralobesia viteana

Few grape vines in the East entirely escape the grape berry moth; the "berry" in the name indicates that it attacks young grapes. Under webs attached to leaves, the ½-inch caterpillars feed in the northeastern United States, southeastern Canada, westward to Wisconsin and Nebraska and south to Louisiana and Alabama. Webbed together, young grapes turn dark purple and drop from the stems when only the size of garden peas. The pests pupate in the winter in cocoons attached to fallen leaves, bark scales or other rubbish. In late spring, moths emerge and lay flat, circular, cream-colored eggs on stems, flower clusters or new grapes. There are two generations a season in the eastern United States, three in southern states.

FRUIT-TREE LEAF ROLLER
Archips argyrospilus

SPECIAL TREATMENT. In late summer, approximately a month before harvest, hoe the soil around vines, making a flat, wide ridge that can be seeded with a winter cover crop. Moth cocoons that accumulate on the surface can be turned under the soil in the spring. Compacting and watering the soil helps to seal the cocoons in. Carbaryl (such as Sevin), captan or malathion used as part of a regular spray schedule are also effective. Consult your local agricultural agent for the insecticides and spray schedule best for your area.

GYPSY MOTH
Porthetria dispar (illustrated overleaf)

Imported for crossbreeding experiments in the vain hope of producing a silkworm that would thrive in the United States, the gypsy moth escaped from a scientist's laboratory in 1869 to cause untold millions of dollars of damage. It is now well established in all the New England states and southeastern Canada, has spread to New York, New Jersey, Maryland and Pennsylvania and has been reported in several other states. It feeds on all deciduous and evergreen trees and shrubs, the foliage of some garden plants and cranberries. Heavy infestations quickly defoliate trees.

The female moths deposit inch-long, light-brown oval egg masses on branches, fences, buildings or vehicles, covering the eggs with hairs. The pest spends the winter in this egg stage. The caterpillars hatch in early to late spring. As they begin to feed, caterpillars sometimes suspend themselves from leaves on silken threads and are blown by the wind to other trees. When fully grown, the dark, hairy caterpillars, 2½ inches long, find a sheltered place to pupate in either a brown-to-black cocoon or by securing themselves to a limb or trunk with a few strands of silk wound loosely around their bodies. Adult moths emerge in 10 to 14 days. Females are too heavy for flight so they lay their eggs in clusters of 300 to 500 near the places where they have pupated. The adults usually live less than two weeks. Gypsy moths frequently hitchhike from one region to another in cocoons attached to camping equipment, cars, trucks and mobile homes. Several states have inspection and quarantine programs aimed at detecting hitchhiking moths before they emerge from their cocoons to infest new areas.

SPECIAL TREATMENT. Destroy egg clusters in fall and winter by painting them with creosote. During spring, bands of burlap tied to the trunks of trees will capture some caterpillars, which should be destroyed daily. Carbaryl (such as Sevin), methoxychlor (such as Marlate), acephate, (such as Orthene) and *Bacillus thuringiensis* (such as Dipel or Thuricide) are used against the gypsy moth but no completely effective chemical controls are known.

IMPORTED CABBAGE WORM
Pieris rapae

All members of the cabbage family are attacked by the imported cabbage worm, including Brussels sprouts, cabbage, cauliflower, collards, kale and radishes, as well as lettuce and such annual plants as mignonette, nasturtium and sweet alyssum. Found throughout the United States and Canada, it chews outer leaves and tunnels inside cabbage and cauliflower heads. About 1 inch long when full grown, the green caterpillars pupate in cocoons suspended by silken threads from plants or other objects. The white cabbage butterflies emerge in early spring with black-spotted wings nearly 2 inches from tip to tip. Each female lays several hundred bullet-shaped eggs singly underneath leaves. These hatch in less than a week, making as many as six generations possible during the growing season.

Cautions to observe when using chemicals, page 71.

GARDEN WEBWORM
Loxostege rantalis

GRAPE BERRY MOTH
Paralobesia viteana

GYPSY MOTH
Porthetria dispar

SPECIAL TREATMENT. *Bacillus thuringiensis* (such as Dipel, Biotrol or Thuricide) is effective against the imported cabbage worm. Also use rotenone, malathion or carbaryl (such as Sevin) when larvae first appear. Destroy all plant remnants and weeds after harvest.

ORIENTAL FRUIT MOTH
Grapholitha molesta

Well established in the East where peaches are grown, the Oriental fruit moth has become a serious pest in some western states. Besides peaches, it attacks apple, pear, plum, quince and other fruit trees. The ½-inch white caterpillars with brown heads first bore into twigs and new shoots, killing them. The pests then bore into the stem ends of fruit to eat the pulp; the outside of the fruit may show no damage but the fruit is ruined. The caterpillars pupate in silken cocoons attached to tree trunks, rubbish or weeds or set on the ground. They emerge as gray moths with ½-inch wingspans. The female moths lay white eggs on leaves or twigs. As many as seven generations may occur in one year.

SPECIAL TREATMENT. Plant early varieties of peach and apricot that can be harvested before the pest enters the fruit. Before trees bloom, cultivate soil to a depth of 4 inches to kill larvae there. Spray schedules using diazinon (such as Spectracide), malathion or carbaryl (such as Sevin) are effective. Consult your agricultural agent for the spray schedule recommended in your area.

SPRING CANKERWORM
Paleacrita vernata

Found east of the Rocky Mountains and also in Colorado and California, the spring cankerworm attacks apple, cherry, elm, hickory, maple, oak and other fruit and shade trees, causing defoliation and crop loss. With leaves eaten just at the time of fullest foliage, trees look as if they had been scorched by fire. In winter, naked brown caterpillars pupate 1 to 4 inches under the soil surface near trees. The moths appear during the first warm weather in early spring and continue to emerge until late spring. Dull-gray males have strong wings but females are wingless with spidery gray bodies. The females crawl up tree trunks to mate and deposit masses of dark-brown oval eggs under loose bark. In about a month, the small brown or green worms hatch, feed on foliage for three or four weeks, then crawl down the trunk or spin down on silken threads to spend the remainder of the summer and the following winter in the pupal stage.

SPECIAL TREATMENT. Cultivate the soil around trees to a depth of 4 inches in fall. Before the first warm weather in early spring, band trees 2 to 4 feet above the ground with a sticky substance to trap migrating females. *Bacillus thuringiensis* (such as Biotrol or Thuricide) is effective. Sprays of carbaryl (such as Sevin), or malathion with methoxychlor also control this pest. For fruit trees, consult your local agricultural agent for the schedule recommended in your area.

SPRUCE BUDWORM
Choristoneura fumiferana

After the cotton boll weevil and the corn-ear worm, the spruce budworm ranks as the third most destructive insect in North America. This coniferous forest pest consumes the needles of fir, hemlock, larch, pine and spruce trees in the northern United States and Canada. Damaged trees look as if they have been scorched by fire and are slowly dying.

When buds open in spring, the caterpillars emerge from cocoons attached to twigs near buds and feed for three or four weeks. They are full grown by midsummer, about 1

Cautions to observe when using chemicals, page 71.

IMPORTED CABBAGE WORM
Pieris rapae

ORIENTAL FRUIT MOTH
Grapholitha molesta

SPRING CANKERWORM
Paleacrita vernata

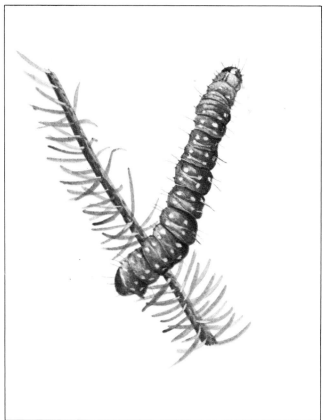

SPRUCE BUDWORM
Choristoneura fumiferana

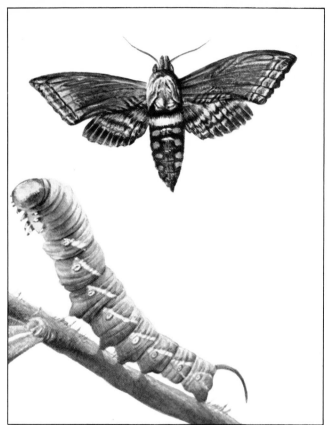

TOMATO HORNWORM
Manduca quinquemaculata

VARIEGATED CUTWORM
Peridroma saucia

inch long with thick, dark-brown bodies. They spin threads over young shoots, tying them together to form shelters where they pupate for a week or 10 days before emerging as moths. The females lay oval green eggs in small clusters and the young caterpillars hatch about 10 days later to feed for several weeks before spinning the cocoons where they will spend the winter.

SPECIAL TREATMENT. Sprays of malathion, carbaryl (such as Sevin) and *Bacillus thuringiensis* (such as Dipel or Biotrol) are partially effective against this difficult-to-control pest.

TOMATO HORNWORM
Manduca quinquemaculata

The ferocious-looking tomato hornworm is found throughout most of the United States and southern Canada, where it strips the foliage of eggplant, pepper, potato, tomato and related plants. A similar species feeds on tobacco plants. The 3- to 4-inch green caterpillar with white bars has a slender horn projecting near its hind end. It cannot sting, however, and is harmless to humans except for the damage it does to plants. The pest spends the winter underground in a brown, hard-shelled, spindle-shaped case about 2 inches long. Large moths called hawk or hummingbird moths, with wingspans of 5 inches, emerge in early summer and can be seen flying at dusk. The females lay spherical, yellow-green eggs singly on the undersides of leaves. Caterpillars hatch in a week and begin feeding. When full grown, they use their mouths to dig 3 or 4 inches into the soil where they pupate and remain for the winter. In warm climates, there may be two generations during the growing season.

SPECIAL TREATMENT. Hand-pick and destroy caterpillars except those carrying the small white cocoons of the parasitic braconid wasps on their backs. These wasps help control the hornworm. Spade deeply in the fall to destroy pupae. Spray with carbaryl (such as Sevin) to control large infestations. *Bacillus thuringiensis* (such as Thuricide) is also effective.

VARIEGATED CUTWORM
Peridroma saucia

Found worldwide, cutworms feed on nearly all plants including ornamentals and greenhouse plants. In home gardens, the variegated cutworm favors beans, cabbages, corn and tomatoes. It cuts through stems at ground level or climbs stems, vines and trees to eat buds, leaves and fruits of vegetable, orchard and vineyard crops. It spends the winter as a naked brown pupa in the soil. When adult moths emerge in early spring, females lay 60 or more eggs in patches on leaves, tree trunks, fences or buildings. In two to 10 days the eggs hatch into plump, smooth caterpillars—the cutworms. These caterpillars feed for several weeks, growing 1½ inches long, before burrowing into the soil to pupate. Three or four generations are possible each growing season.

SPECIAL TREATMENT. Many worms can be trapped under boards laid down between rows in the garden, then picked up and destroyed. Protect young plants with collars made from plastic cups or tin cans with the bottoms cut out. Place collars around the stems and push them an inch into the soil. Diazinon (such as Spectracide) or carbaryl (such as Sevin) will also control cutworms.

WHITE-MARKED TUSSOCK MOTH
Orgyia leucostigma

A pest destructive to all shade trees except evergreens, the white-marked tussock moth is found in the eastern United States and Canada. It also feeds on apple, pear, plum, quince and other fruit trees. The eggs survive the winter in conspicuous masses of 50 to 100 covered with a stiff white substance that looks like meringue attached to tree trunks, branches or dead leaves, usually on the remnants of the female moth's cocoon. Hatching in the spring, distinctive hairy, light-brown caterpillars skeletonize leaves and scar fruit. They reach their full 1½-inch length in midsummer when they spin cocoons and pupate. In less than four weeks, adult moths emerge. The brown males have gray-striped wings and white hairs on their legs. The gray females cannot fly and hardly move from their cocoons. They mate immediately and lay eggs for another generation. In warm climates there are three generations each year.

SPECIAL TREATMENT. Paint egg masses in winter with creosote. Spray with acephate (such as Orthene) or carbaryl (such as Sevin) to control caterpillars.

CENTIPEDE

Often called hundred-legged worms, centipedes are neither true insects nor true worms. True centipedes are harmless to humans and beneficial as predators of insect pests. Unlike insects, they have no thorax or wings and up to 15, rather than three, body segments. Centipedes are 1 to 8 inches long, flatter than worms, usually darker in color, with jointed legs on each body segment and long antennae. They paralyze earthworms, snails and many insects with a pair of poisoned claws located just behind their heads. Gray or tan house centipedes grow up to 3 inches in length on a diet of roaches, moths, flies and other insects.

WHAT TO DO. Learn to distinguish true centipedes from the much smaller garden centipedes (or symphylans), which are harmful and require control measures.

GARDEN CENTIPEDE or SYMPHYLAN
Scutigerella immaculata

The symphylan, which looks much like a tiny centipede, is a serious pest in 25 states with warm climates. The adult is only ¼ inch long, white, and has a pair of legs on each of 12 body segments. It attacks asparagus, cucumbers, lettuce, radishes, tomatoes, and ornamentals such as asters, snapdragons and sweet peas, eating fine roots and root hairs so plants are stunted, grow slowly or die. An underground creature adverse to light, it thrives in damp soil, leaf mold and manure piles. After harvests, it burrows down a foot or more to moist subsoil where the females lay clusters of spherical white eggs. In the spring, the newly hatched young ascend to nibble at the roots again. New generations hatch every few months until cold weather.

SPECIAL TREATMENT. Before planting, examine several shovelfuls of soil. If you see more than two small, white centipede-like insects per shovelful, you can expect damage to plants. Avoid planting there or treat the top 6 inches of soil with malathion.

CHIGGER See Mite
CHINCH BUG See Bug

CICADA

Often incorrectly called locusts, cicadas are wedge-shaped insects, ½ inch to 4 inches long with irregular green, yellow or white spots covering their bodies. Females weaken trees by inserting their eggs in branches. Males make a high-pitched, pulsating sound by vibrating drumlike membranes on their abdomens. Most common in the United States are the periodical cicada (17-year or 13-year locust) and the annual cicada, which is larger than the periodical.

WHAT TO DO. Soon after the pulsating buzz of the male is

Cautions to observe when using chemicals, page 71.

WHITE-MARKED TUSSOCK MOTH
Orgyia leucostigma

GARDEN CENTIPEDE
Scutigerella immaculata

first heard, cover young trees with mosquito netting to protect them, or spray them with carbaryl (such as Sevin).

PERIODICAL CICADA
Magicicada septendecim

Notable for a very long life cycle of either 13 or 17 years, periodical cicadas damage the branches of such trees as apple, dogwood, hickory, oak and peach. The females puncture the bark to lay eggs, leaving deep cuts 1 to 4 inches long. The 13-year cicada is concentrated in the South, from Virginia to Oklahoma. The 17-year species, often called the 17-year locust, is found mainly in the Northeast. Since there are multiple overlapping broods, the young may emerge from the ground more often than the 13- or 17-year cycles. Entomologists keep records that enable them to predict when a new brood can be expected.

Underground, the young feed on sap from small roots. Although as many as 40,000 may live under a single tree, their feeding has no discernible effect on it. The young nymphs emerge at night and crawl up the trunks of trees to attach themselves firmly to branches or twigs. Their skin splits and adult insects emerge. The adults live only five or six weeks after emerging from the ground, and during that time each female lays 400 to 600 eggs. Upon hatching, the antlike young drop and move into cracks in the soil.

SPECIAL TREATMENT. Ask your local agricultural agent when a new brood of periodical cicadas may be expected. Avoid planting orchard seedlings, which are very vulnerable to damage, for two years before the arrival of the pests, and do not prune young trees within one year before that date. During years when new broods are hatching, band trees with a sticky adhesive material and remove trapped nymphs daily. Protect young trees with mosquito netting to prevent egg laying. Adult cicadas can be controlled with a spray of carbaryl (such as Sevin).

CITRUS MEALYBUG See Mealybug
CLICK BEETLE See Wireworm
CORN BORER, EUROPEAN See Borer
CORN-EAR WORM See Caterpillar
CORN WIREWORM See Wireworm
COLORADO POTATO BEETLE See Beetle
COTTON BOLLWORM See Caterpillar, Corn-Ear Worm

CRICKET

Relatives of grasshoppers, crickets are short, dark-colored insects with wiry antennae and wings that look like shield-shaped jackets. They are distributed throughout the United States and southern Canada. Powerful hind legs enable some species to jump many times their length. Others can neither jump nor fly but move forward by crawling and flutter-hopping. Males of the species common in the United States make a loud, chirping sound by rubbing together parts of their front wings. Some families of crickets live in fields and trees, while others live underground. Females deposit clusters of eggs in the soil or in stems of plants. Tree crickets weaken twigs and branches by inserting eggs in them. Crickets feed on plants or on other insects; some kinds eat both. Among the plants that are damaged by field crickets are beans, peas, tomatoes and strawberries. Crickets also eat holes in paper, cotton, linen or fur.

WHAT TO DO. Destroy any crickets that are found indoors. Encourage natural predators such as birds. If the cricket infestation is heavy, use insecticide sprays or poison baits that are specifically formulated to kill the kinds of crickets you have in your garden.

PERIODICAL CICADA
Magicicada septendecim

MORMON CRICKET
Anabrus simplex

The Mormon cricket, also called western Great Plains, Idaho or black cricket, is found in most states west of the Rocky Mountains from Colorado to California, north into Canada, and in some midwestern states. Mormon crickets become a scourge when they migrate in enormous hordes, sometimes covering several square miles, from their breeding grounds in the mountains to feed in the productive valleys. Crawling like a great sea at a rate of ⅛ to 1 mile a day, they feed on everything in their path including grasses, garden crops, fruits, grains and flowers. The adult male is 1 inch long, the female 1½ inches. Both have thick, clumsy bodies divided into four segments and wings too short for flight.

In 1848, when Mormon crops were being devastated by crickets, flocks of sea gulls came and devoured them. In Salt Lake City, the Mormons erected a monument to the gulls and Mormon crickets thus were given their common name.

SPECIAL TREATMENT. Government agencies annually survey the possible cricket menace in affected areas and determine the need for aerial spreading of poison bait. Since the insects cannot fly, they can be kept from small gardens by a fence of 10-inch strips of sheet metal set on edge.

CUCUMBER BEETLE, SPOTTED See Beetle
CUCUMBER BEETLE, STRIPED See Beetle
CURCULIO, PLUM See Beetle, Plum Curculio
CUTWORM, VARIEGATED See Caterpillar
CYCLAMEN MITE See Mite

D

DOORYARD SOW BUG See Sowbug

E

EAR WORM, CORN See Caterpillar
EASTERN TENT CATERPILLAR See Caterpillar
ELM BARK BEETLE, NATIVE See Beetle
ELM LEAF BEETLE See Beetle
EUROPEAN CORN BORER See Borer
EYE-SPOTTED BUD MOTH See Caterpillar

F

FALL CANKERWORM See Caterpillar
FALL WEBWORM See Caterpillar
FIRE BUG See Bug, Harlequin
FLAT-HEADED APPLE-TREE BORER See Borer
FLEA HOPPER, GARDEN See Bug
FLY See Maggot
FRUIT-TREE LEAF ROLLER See Caterpillar
FUNGUS GNAT See Maggot, Mushroom Fly

G

GARDEN BEETLE, ASIATIC See Beetle
GARDEN FLEA HOPPER See Bug
GARDEN SLUG See Slug
GARDEN SYMPHYLAN See Centipede
GARDEN WEBWORM See Caterpillar
GLADIOLUS THRIPS See Thrips
GOLD BUG See Beetle
GRAPE BERRY MOTH See Caterpillar
GRAPE PHYLLOXERA See Aphid

GRASSHOPPER
Often called locusts when they migrate in swarms, grasshoppers are among the world's most destructive insects. They are found throughout the United States and Canada, but

MORMON CRICKET
Anabrus simplex

Cautions to observe when using chemicals, page 71.

serious outbreaks occur most often in the northern Great Plains. Hordes of grasshoppers can consume thousands of acres of productive grasslands. A swarm of them can defoliate an orchard in a few hours, even chewing off small branches. If they find their way inside a house, they will eat any kind of fabric. Among the 600 species that are found in North America, the two-striped, differential, clear-winged, red-legged and migratory grasshoppers cause at least 90 per cent of grasshopper damage to plants.

Grasshoppers are 1 to 2½ inches in length, usually dark gray, green, brown or black. Strong hind legs enable them to jump 20 to 30 inches. Most species have four wings and some species fly long distances. The female grasshopper uses flexible prongs at the end of the abdomen to bury eggs about an inch below the soil line. The eggs are enveloped in a gummy substance that hardens to form a protective pod. The eggs hatch in early spring and the young nymphs molt five or six times while feeding. Most species of grasshoppers produce only one generation a year, but in warm climates there may be two or more.

WHAT TO DO. Broad-scale control of grasshoppers is usually done under the direction of government agencies. Home gardeners can turn soil under in the fall to bury the eggs so deeply the young cannot make their way to the surface. Quart jars partly filled with a solution of 1 part molasses and 9 parts water and scattered about a garden will trap some grasshoppers. Spray or dust plants with rotenone, carbaryl (such as Sevin), malathion or diazinon (such as Spectracide).

MIGRATORY GRASSHOPPER
Melanoplus sanguinipes

The migratory grasshopper is the most widely distributed and destructive of all grasshopper species. Swarms frequently ravage the western United States and Canada, moving from the Dakotas northwest into Montana and Saskatchewan. When a swarm stops to feed, it devours every plant in an area as large as several square miles. In summer or fall, each inch-long adult female deposits in the soil about 20 pods, each containing about 20 cream-colored eggs. The eggs hatch in the spring. One generation a year is common, but in warm climates two may occur.

SPECIAL TREATMENT. Follow the control measures recommended for all grasshoppers.

GREEN PEACH APHID See Aphid
GREENFLY See Aphid, Green Peach
GREENHOUSE WHITEFLY See Whitefly
GYPSY MOTH See Caterpillar

H

HARLEQUIN BUG See Bug
HAWK MOTH See Caterpillar, Tomato Hornworm
HORNWORM, TOMATO See Caterpillar
HUMMINGBIRD MOTH See Caterpillar, Tomato Hornworm
HUNDRED-LEGGED WORM See Centipede

I

IDAHO CRICKET See Cricket
IMPORTED CABBAGE WORM See Caterpillar

J

JAPANESE BEETLE See Beetle
JUMPING PLANT LOUSE See Psylla
JUNE BEETLE See Beetle
JUNE BUG See Beetle, June

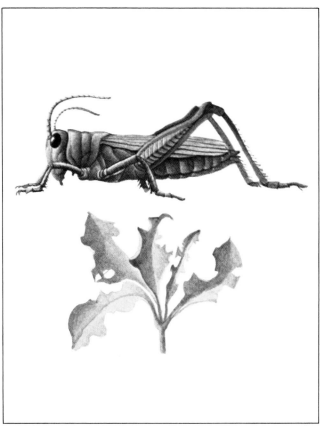

MIGRATORY GRASSHOPPER
Melanoplus sanguinipes

L

LEAF HOPPER

More than 2,000 species of leaf hoppers live on trees, shrubs and other plants and grasses throughout North America. Several million may invade a single acre of fruit trees or vegetables. Most often affected are apples, beans, beets, celery, eggplants, grapes, lettuce, peppers, potatoes and tomatoes. Most species favor a particular plant but some move from one to another. Leaf hoppers are slender wedge-shaped insects up to ½ inch long, usually pale green or yellow. When disturbed, adults take flight while the wingless young scamper to the other side of leaves. They damage plants by piercing them and sucking sap, by injecting a toxin and by depositing eggs in stems and leaves. Infested leaves become stippled with white dots, then turn yellow. Grasses lose chlorophyll, become white speckled, then yellow and die. Infested lawns appear scorched and wilted. Leaf hoppers transmit viruses such as aster and peach yellows that cause malformed leaves and dwarfed flowers. They excrete honeydew, a sticky, sugary substance that attracts ants and bees.

From one to five generations hatch each year. Eggs laid in fall hatch in the spring. Some species hibernate in the North during winter; others migrate to the South.

WHAT TO DO. Because leaf hoppers migrate extensively and continuously, spraying provides only temporary relief. Your local agricultural agent can provide spray schedules recommended for fruit trees in your area. Carbaryl (such as Sevin), acephate (such as Orthene), malathion or methoxychlor (such as Marlate) can be used.

POTATO LEAF HOPPER
Empoasca fabae

Feeding first on apple foliage, the potato leaf hopper then moves on to beans and potatoes when these plants are 4 to 8 inches tall. It also attacks ornamental plants, birch trees and citrus. It ranges throughout the eastern United States and southern Canada, and it occasionally appears in the West. Damage includes discolored leaves, short stalks, no blooms and crinkled, curled and wilted leaves. The insect's feeding and egg laying also cause hopperburn, also called tipburn, a condition that slows growth, reduces yield and may kill eggplants, potatoes and rhubarb, as well as dahlias and roses.

The ⅛-inch, green female leaf hopper lays eggs in plant tissue. These hatch in 10 days, become full-grown, non-flying nymphs in about two weeks, and molt several times before they become flying adults. Two to four generations appear each year. Adult leaf hoppers migrate south in winter and return north in the spring.

SPECIAL TREATMENT. Follow a regular spray program using the insecticides recommended for all leaf hoppers. Consult labels for the number of days to wait between the last spray date and the harvest of various food crops.

LEAF MINER, SPINACH See Maggot
LEAF ROLLER, FRUIT-TREE See Caterpillar
LILAC BORER See Borer
LOCUST See Cicada; Grasshopper
LOOPER, CABBAGE See Caterpillar

M

MAGGOT (FLY)

Maggots, the destructive larvae of flies worldwide, are usually white or yellow, legless, soft, grublike creatures. After a period of feeding, they bury themselves under 1 to 6 inches of soil, pass through the pupal stage, then emerge as adult flies. Flies belong to the order Diptera, which includes nearly

Cautions to observe when using chemicals, page 71.

POTATO LEAF HOPPER
Empoasca fabae

APPLE MAGGOT
Rhagoletis pomonella

all insects with only one pair of wings. Flies have large eyes compared to the size of their bodies, and their mouths are equipped to pierce, suck and lap. Some flies carry plant and human diseases, but others are useful as scavengers or predators of harmful insects.

WHAT TO DO. Since most flies breed in damp, unsanitary places and are attracted by organic waste, the best control is to drain or clean up their breeding grounds.

APPLE MAGGOT
Rhagoletis pomonella

The apple maggot, prevalent in southeastern Canada and the northeastern United States west to the Dakotas and south to Arkansas and Georgia, ravages apples, blueberries and huckleberries. Its coming is signaled by small black flies with zigzag black markings on their wings and white stripes on their bodies. Female flies puncture apples or other fruit to lay eggs that hatch in mid- to late summer. Infested apples have winding brown tunnels excavated by the 3/8-inch maggots that hatch from the eggs. Brown streaks show on apple skins. Hard winter-apple varieties develop an uneven, pitted surface and corky streaks through the pulp. When infested apples drop, usually before ripening, the larvae enter the ground to pupate and later emerge as flies.

SPECIAL TREATMENT. Dispose of the dropped fruit before maggots leave the apples. To destroy maggots in picked fruit, place apples in cold storage for four or five weeks. Healthy apple production is difficult without spraying. Ask your local agricultural agent for a spray schedule appropriate in your area. Multipurpose sprays combining a fungicide for disease protection with an insecticide such as carbaryl, captan, malathion or diazinon are often used.

CABBAGE MAGGOT
Hylemya brassicae

The cabbage maggot is the wedge-shaped larva of the cabbage-root fly. Although found throughout North America, it causes the most severe damage in the northern United States and southern Canada. About 1/3 inch long with no legs or head, this underground pest eats the roots and stems of broccoli, Brussels sprouts, cabbages, cauliflower, radishes and turnips. It also feeds on beets, celery and cress. Roots under attack show brown scars, and stunted, off-color plants may be honeycombed with slimy, curving tunnels. This maggot also transmits spores of blackleg disease.

The adult cabbage-root fly emerges from an underground cocoon in spring, early summer or autumn. Half the size of a housefly, it is dark gray with black stripes and bristly hairs. The female deposits tiny white eggs on stems of plants near the soil or in cracks in the soil's surface. The cabbage maggot thrives in cool, moist weather. A third generation in autumn infests fall radishes and turnips.

SPECIAL TREATMENT. Cover plants with fine gauze to prevent flies from laying eggs on them. To prevent maggots from reaching roots, slit 3-inch squares of tar paper and slip them around the stems at ground level. After the harvest, dispose of damaged plants. Diazinon (such as Spectracide) mixed into the top 3 or 4 inches of soil before planting and again seven days later will reduce the maggot population.

CARROT RUST FLY
Psila rosae

The carrot rust fly is a 1/5-inch shiny green insect with black eyes and a yellow head, legs and hair. Originally from Europe, it is now common in eastern Canada and the northern United States, especially the Pacific Northwest. Its life

CABBAGE MAGGOT
Hylemya brassicae

CARROT RUST FLY
Psila rosae

span is only a few weeks, with three generations during the growing season. In late spring the females lay eggs on or near the crowns of carrots, caraway, celery, coriander, dill, fennel and parsnips. Upon hatching, the yellowish, legless maggots work their way down to the roots where they grow to ⅓ inch in length as they feed before hibernating in cocoons in the soil. If the infestation is severe, entire roots are destroyed. Leaves wilt and turn yellow. The maggots also make way for soft-rot bacteria that cause vegetables to decompose.

SPECIAL TREATMENT. Delay planting susceptible vegetables until late spring or early summer and harvest before the flies lay eggs. Rotate susceptible crops with nonsusceptible ones. Screen plants with fine gauze tacked to a frame. The soil may be treated with diazinon (such as Spectracide).

MUSHROOM FLY
Sciara species

The slender, dusty gray or black mushroom fly (fungus gnat), ¹/₁₀ to ⅛ inch long, resembles a mosquito. Its maggots burrow through mushroom caps and stems; they also attack many species of indoor and greenhouse plants. The gnawing maggots consume tender roots and root hairs, causing plants to turn pale and droop. The infestation may lead to root rot, further damaging the plant. The mushroom fly breeds in moist soil rich in humus, manure and decaying plant debris. Threadlike, legless maggots hatch from eggs that are deposited in clusters in the soil around plants and feed on root tissue.

SPECIAL TREATMENT. Spray the soil, benches and floor of an infested greenhouse or the soil around infested house plants with a weak solution of malathion or diazinon (such as Spectracide); applications every three or four weeks may be necessary. Keep soil as dry as possible during treatment. Avoid overwatering house plants.

ONION MAGGOT
Hylemya antiqua

Onion maggots are the larvae of the onion fly, a ¼-inch insect that looks much like the common housefly. Onions grown in the northern United States and Canada may be severely damaged by this pest, but those grown in the South are rarely affected. This fly, with a brown, hairy body, appears in late spring and lays eggs inside onion bulbs at the bases of leaves, or in the soil of the onion patch. When the yellow maggots hatch, they invade stems and bulbs to feed on plant tissue. One maggot can destroy a seedling; several maggots tunneling through a large bulb will destroy it or cause it to rot later. Leaves become flabby and faded. Two or three generations hatch each year. The most severe damage is done to early plantings by the first brood; the third generation attacks at harvest time and causes storage rot.

SPECIAL TREATMENT. Purchase clean onion sets that show no signs of injury. Since maggots spend the winter in the soil or garden refuse, destroy cull onions after harvest and remove all trash. To destroy flies, spray with malathion during the growing season; to control maggots spray diazinon (such as Spectracide) or carbophenothion (such as Trithion) on the soil at planting time.

ROSE MIDGE
Dasineura rhodophaga

A minute yellow-to-brown fly, the rose midge can devastate a rose garden within a few weeks. Although the rose midge is scattered throughout the United States, its greatest concentration is in the East. The female fly deposits small yellow eggs in buds, behind flower sheaths or in unfolding

Cautions to observe when using chemicals, page 71.

MUSHROOM FLY
Sciara species

ONION MAGGOT
Hylemya antiqua

ROSE MIDGE
Dasineura rhodophaga

SPINACH LEAF MINER
Pegomya hyoscyami

leaves. In two days the eggs hatch and white-to-orange maggots begin feeding on plant tissues. As many as 20 or 30 maggots may feed on one bud. Distorted leaves and buds turn brown and die. After a week maggots fall to the ground, burrow into the soil and spin white cocoons. A week later they emerge as adults and the egg laying resumes. A new life cycle starts every 12 to 16 days in a greenhouse, every 20 days outdoors, producing several broods in one season.

SPECIAL TREATMENT. Select and plant only guaranteed midge-free plants. An infestation can be checked somewhat by pruning and destroying affected buds and shoots daily.

SPINACH LEAF MINER
Pegomya hyoscyami

Throughout the United States and Canada, the spinach leaf miner attacks the leaves of spinach, beets and chard. The thin, gray, ¼-inch adult fly lays up to five white, oval eggs side by side on the underside of a leaf. Pale green maggots eat threadlike tunnels inside the leaves, giving them a blistered appearance. An infestation hinders seed and root development. Leaves drop and seedlings die if the attack is severe. Moving from leaf to leaf, the maggots eat for one to three weeks before dropping from the plant to spin cocoons in the soil. Adult flies emerge in two to four weeks, so three life cycles are possible in a single season.

SPECIAL TREATMENT. Deep spading before planting helps to control maggots. Remove weeds and destroy all infested leaves. Spinach that matures in late fall is most likely to escape attack. Screen plants with cheesecloth to protect them from egg-laying adults. Adult flies can be controlled with diazinon (such as Spectracide) or malathion. Follow label instructions regarding the number of days between the last application and harvest.

MAY BEETLE See Beetle, June

MEALY BUG
Found throughout the United States, mealy bugs are serious pests in warm climates, especially when they have been transported on plants to areas devoid of their natural parasitic and predatory enemies. Indoors and in the garden, mealy bugs infest all parts of trees, shrubs and ornamental plants. They extract plant juices with their piercing-sucking beaks, causing dwarfing, wilting and early dropping of fruit. They also excrete a sweet, sticky honeydew that encourages the growth of black sooty mold, a fungus disease that hinders photosynthesis (the process by which plants convert light into food). The honeydew also attracts ants that carry mealy bugs from plant to plant, somewhat like farmers moving their cows to different pastures.

The white powdery secretion that covers its oval ⅛- to ¼-inch body and projects in thin white tufts makes the insect look like a speck of cotton.

There are two groups of mealy bugs: the short-tailed type lays eggs and the long-tailed type bears live young. Both the eggs and the smooth, yellow young bugs can be found where leaves meet stems. The life cycle takes about a month, with one generation following another the year round indoors.

WHAT TO DO. Outdoors, encourage the spread of ladybug beetle larvae and adults: they devour mealy bugs. Destroy the ants that defend mealy bugs from their natural enemies. Clean debris from crotches and crevices of trees and plants. Spray with acephate (such as Orthene), diazinon (such as Spectracide), malathion or carbaryl (such as Sevin). Indoors, syringe leaves frequently with water, using as much force as the leaves will tolerate. Pick mealy bugs off plants with a toothpick or kill them by dabbing them with rubbing alcohol on a cotton swab. Use insecticides labeled for indoor use on heavy infestations. Consult your local agricultural agent for fruit-tree spray schedules in your area.

CITRUS MEALY BUG
Planococcus citri

In addition to citrus trees, the citrus mealy bug feeds on a large number of soft-stemmed house plants—African violets, cacti, coleuses, crotons, ferns, fuchsias, gardenias and many others. It is a pest in greenhouses and homes throughout North America and in outdoor gardens in subtropical areas. This species has a short tail and, outdoors, lays egg clusters in cottony masses in crevices in bark and in the sheltered spots between leaves and stems. It feeds by piercing leaves and sucking plant juices.

SPECIAL TREATMENT. Follow the control measures recommended for all mealy bugs. An Australian ladybug beetle known as the mealy bug destroyer has been used successfully in California citrus orchards to control this pest.

MEXICAN BEAN BEETLE See Beetle
MIDGE, ROSE See Maggot
MIGRATORY GRASSHOPPER See Grasshopper

MILLEPEDE

Common throughout North America, only a small number of millepede species are serious garden pests. Some even benefit garden greenery by eating insects that are more destructive. Most millepedes feed at night on decaying vegetable matter such as leaf mold or rotting wood; some larger species eat dead animal matter. When decaying matter is scarce, however, they will feed on living plant tissue such as the seeds of beans, corn and peas or the roots of underground vegetables such as beets, carrots, parsnips, potatoes and turnips. They also eat melons, strawberries and tomatoes lying on moist ground, and some millepedes may further injure plants by transmitting diseases.

Most millepedes are ½ to 2 inches long with hard-shelled bodies divided into many segments, each with two pairs of legs. Sometimes called "thousand-legged worms," they may have from 30 to 400 legs but usually no more than 100. Unlike speedy centipedes, millepedes glide slowly by contracting and stretching.

Millepedes produce young only once a year. Females deposit sticky sacs of about 300 translucent eggs on or in soil during the summer. The new adults live through the winter and produce a new brood the following year. The life span of a millepede is usually one to two years, but some species live as long as seven years.

WHAT TO DO. Keep the garden free of debris. A piece of old window-screen wire, slit and placed on the ground under tomato plants, will protect the plants from millepedes. Mulch will deter invasion of strawberries and other fruits that grow close to the ground. Treat severe infestations with carbaryl (such as Sevin), diazinon (such as Spectracide) or malathion.

MILLEPEDE
Oxidus gracilis, also called *Orthomorpha gracilis*

This millepede species is an outdoor pest found throughout the United States. It is especially damaging in the South and along the West Coast, where it attacks philodendrons and roses. The flat, 1-inch pest chews ragged holes in leaves. Its behavior and life cycle are similar to those of all millepedes.

SPECIAL TREATMENT. Use the control measures recommended for all millepedes.

Cautions to observe when using chemicals, page 71.

CITRUS MEALY BUG
Planococcus citri

MILLEPEDE
Oxidus gracilis

MITE

The minute, almost microscopic creatures that are called mites are related to spiders. They are common throughout North America, thriving in dry, warm climates, and are most destructive during hot summer months. Many species of mites affect a variety of plants, both indoors and out. Among the most destructive kinds are broad, bulb, cyclamen and spider mites. They injure ornamental plants, trees, shrubs, vegetables and fruits. Other mites such as chiggers and ticks annoy or harm humans and animal pets. Some mites infest food stored in sacks or boxes. Yet many species are beneficial because they destroy other garden pests.

The plant-damaging mites feed by sucking juices from the undersurfaces of leaves. Yellow mottling may show on upper surfaces before the leaves turn brown and drop prematurely. Plants lose vigor and show poor growth. Infestation is often severe before the damage is noticed. To detect mites, place a piece of white paper under a tree branch or small plant, then shake the branch or plant sharply. If mites are present, some will fall onto the paper and you will see specks moving.

WHAT TO DO. As soon as damage is apparent, spray or wash valuable plants with soapy water, being sure to wash the undersurfaces of leaves. If garden infestations are heavy, buy and release tiny black lady beetles (*Stethorus* species). Both *Stethorus* larvae and adults eat mites. Acephate (such as Orthene), diazinon (such as Spectracide or Gardentox), dicofol (such as Kelthane), chlorophyrifos (such as Dursban), dimethoate (such as Cygon) or malathion kills mites. To keep mites from becoming resistant to any one chemical, switch insecticides from time to time.

CYCLAMEN MITE, also called PALLID MITE, STRAWBERRY CROWN MITE
Steneotarsonemus pallidus

Found throughout North America, cyclamen mites are especially damaging to strawberries in the northern states and southern Canada. These mites damage plants by sucking juice from stalks and leaves. Indoors, the mites infest African violets, cyclamens and other plants. Outdoors they attack delphiniums, monkshoods and snapdragons as well as peppers, strawberries and tomatoes.

Cyclamen mites, abundant in dry, warm weather, are so minute that they can be seen only with a magnifying glass in buds and furled leaves where they cluster. They rarely appear on exposed areas of a plant. A cyclamen will not flower if it is attacked early in the growing season; if attacked later, blooms will be distorted, streaked and blotched; foliage turns purple, wrinkles and curls. Infested African violets develop twisted stems and their growth is stunted; delphiniums show thick and puckered leaves, dark, twisted stalks and black buds, caused by a mite-borne fungus or bacterium; strawberry plants are shriveled and fruitless.

SPECIAL TREATMENT. Discard plants that are severely infested. Avoid working among infested plants: hands or garden tools can spread mites and disease. Water abundantly in dry weather. For heavy infestations, use the chemicals recommended for use against all mites. When growing strawberries, buy certified mite-free plants. Immerse infested house plants in 110° water for 15 to 30 minutes.

TWO-SPOTTED SPIDER MITE, also called RED SPIDER MITE
Tetranychus urticae

The most common spider mite in home gardens is the two-spotted species. It appears everywhere in North America and affects almonds, English ivy, fruit trees, hollyhocks, phlox, primroses, roses, violets and vegetables. It multiplies most

CYCLAMEN MITE
Steneotarsonemus pallidus

rapidly in dry, warm weather, reaching a peak in midsummer when it often infests evergreens, shrubs and deciduous ornamental plants.

With its piercing-sucking mouth parts, the pest destroys leaf tissue and lowers the vitality of plants by extracting nutrients. Affected leaves turn pale green and may show blisters on the upper sides. The mites construct dusty-looking webs over flower buds, leaves or between leaf stalks and stems. The tiny, oval invaders are about as big as specks of paprika. Although often called the red spider mite, this pest is more often green, yellow or brown.

Female mites lay about 100 eggs attached to delicate webs on the undersides of leaves. Mites hatching in late summer pass the winter in the soil and emerge in spring. Their life cycle is only one or two weeks, however, and as many as 17 overlapping generations develop each year. In fact, it is possible to find all stages of growth—from egg to adult—on the underside of a single leaf at the same time.

SPECIAL TREATMENT. Keep plants clean. A forceful spray of water will wash away many mites. For serious infestations use diazinon (such as Spectracide), dicofol (such as Kelthane), malathion, acephate (such as Orthene), dimethoate (such as Cygon) or tetradifon (such as Tedion). Consult your local agricultural agent about specific fruit-tree spray schedules recommended in your area.

MORMON CRICKET See Cricket
MOTH See Caterpillar
MOTH, POTATO See Borer, Potato Tuberworm
MOTTLED TORTOISE BEETLE See Beetle
MUSHROOM FLY See Maggot

N

NATIVE ELM BARK BEETLE See Beetle

NEMATODE
Ranging from $\frac{1}{50}$ to $\frac{1}{10}$ of an inch in length, nematodes are plant parasites, abundant in most soil and dreaded by gardeners everywhere. Although minuscule, they are complex. They feed by means of a stylet, much like a hypodermic needle, with which they puncture plants and inject a secretion to predigest tissue before they suck it up. As many as 500 different plants are known to be susceptible to nematodes. Among their favorite hosts are tomatoes, cucumbers, potatoes and cyclamens. They also attack begonias, chrysanthemums, dahlias, ferns and many other ornamental plants. Nematodes that cause root decay are often found on boxwoods, pin oaks, irises and peonies.

Several hundred nematode species have been classified according to their eating habits. Some feed inside the host plant, some on the outside, some on roots, bulbs or stems. Others distort or stunt plants or make wounds through which various bacteria and fungi enter. Some nematodes themselves spread ring spot or other viruses. Wilt, yellowing, root rot, and some kinds of galls result from nematode infestation. Sometimes the roots of infested plants become heavily swollen and knotted with galls.

Not all nematodes are garden pests. Many are beneficial because they help convert organic material in the soil into a form plants can use. Others feed on the bodies of beetles, cockroaches, grasshoppers, moths and other damaging insects. The species of nematodes that attack the grubs of Japanese beetles and striped cucumber beetles are important natural controls of those pests.

WHAT TO DO. Mulch established plants in the spring with peat moss to create a barrier between infested soil and new

TWO-SPOTTED SPIDER MITE
Tetranychus urticae

Cautions to observe when using chemicals, page 71.

leaves. Always take cuttings from healthy, uninfested plants; destroy plants that you know are infested. In a vegetable garden, practice crop rotation. Avoid wetting foliage when watering; this will prevent nematodes from swimming up the stems in a film of water.

If you suspect nematodes are attacking your plants, dig up the roots and some soil surrounding a sample plant, place the material in a plastic bag, keep it moist and mail it as soon as possible to the nearest agricultural experiment station. Ask your local agricultural agent for the address. Usually only an expert can tell what kind of nematode problem you have. Heavily infested soil can be fumigated by professionals.

ROOT-KNOT NEMATODE
Meloidogyne species

Various species of root-knot nematodes attack more than 2,000 species of plants in nearly every state in the United States and throughout Canada, with some surviving even the extreme cold of far northern winters. These nematodes produce swellings on roots of infested plants, giving them a gouty appearance. The swellings may be globular, or elongated and gnarled, and they become parts of the root. Infested plants are more vulnerable to fusarium and bacterial wilts and to crown gall. They wilt, turn yellow and die.

Female nematodes usually lay 300 to 500 eggs each but may lay as many as 3,000 in a yellow-brown gelatinous mass outside the root on which they are feeding. Larvae develop almost fully inside the eggs and are able to begin searching for roots to feed upon immediately upon hatching. They swell rapidly into sausage shapes as they eat. The females later become pear shaped and large enough to be visible without magnification. The life cycle is completed in a month or less, depending upon the temperature. Higher temperatures speed the process; lower ones slow it down. Both eggs and larvae pass the winter either inside galls or simply mixed into the soil.

SPECIAL TREATMENT. Rotate crops and plant nematode-resistant varieties whenever possible. Asparagus and French marigold roots produce chemicals that help reduce the nematode population. Where soil is heavily infested, fumigation by professional pesticide applicators may be necessary.

O

ONION MAGGOT See Maggot
ONION THRIPS See Thrips
ORIENTAL FRUIT MOTH See Caterpillar
OYSTER-SHELL SCALE See Scale

P

PALE-STRIPED FLEA BEETLE See Beetle
PALLID MITE See Mite, Cyclamen
PEACH APHID, GREEN See Aphid
PEACH-TREE BORER See Borer
PEAR PSYLLA See Psyllid
PERIODICAL CICADA See Cicada
PHYLLOXERA, GRAPE See Aphid
PILL BUG See Sow Bug
PLANT LOUSE See Aphid
PLANT LOUSE, JUMPING See Psyllid
PLUM CURCULIO See Beetle
POTATO LEAF HOPPER See Leaf Hopper
POTATO TUBERWORM See Borer

PSYLLID

Psyllids, also known as jumping plant lice, are small, active insects with enlarged hind legs that enable them to spring off

NEMATODE
Meloidogyne species

leaves into flight. They usually measure less than ¼ inch and have long antennae and piercing-sucking mouths. Psyllids attack apples, blackberries, boxwoods, figs, laurels, magnolias, pears, potatoes, quinces and other plants. Some feed on mature leaves, others on new leaves and developing buds, often causing the growth of galls. Foliage turns brown, blackens and dries by midsummer. Their honeydew excretions cover both foliage and fruit. Adult psyllids occasionally bite humans, but the bites are of little consequence. Many species of psyllids do not damage plants directly but are nuisances because their honeydew attracts troublesome insects and supports viruses and molds—especially a sooty black mold and a western type called psyllid yellows.

Some psyllid species develop into nymphs inside eggs laid in the fall but do not hatch until spring. Others pass the winter as adults, in cracks in tree bark or among fallen leaves on the ground, then lay eggs in the spring. Many kinds of psyllid nymphs produce white waxy filaments that form a protective web. Sometimes this material is so plentiful it looks like a ball of cotton.

WHAT TO DO. Use waterborne oil sprays to help control psyllids. When applied to hardy shrubs or trees during winter or early spring, these sprays are called dormant oil sprays and contain a heavier oil than those applied later in the season. To increase the effectiveness of oil sprays, add diazinon (such as Spectracide).

PEAR PSYLLA
Psylla pyricola

In its final nymph form, the pear psylla is a light-brown insect about 1/10 inch in length. The damage nymphs cause comes principally from diseases they transmit and the honeydew they excrete, supplying food for a fungus that scars and blackens pear fruits and foliage. Bartlett and d'Anjou pears are the varieties most susceptible to this psyllid; it may also damage quinces. The pest occurs in most states where pears are grown, ranging as far south as South Carolina.

In early spring, the female lays pear-shaped yellow or orange eggs in cracks in tree bark or around buds, each attached by a slender tube. Eggs laid in summer are attached to leaves and stems. Extremely small (1/80-inch), wingless, translucent yellow, green or light-brown nymphs hatch in two to four weeks. Nymphs molt five times, gradually broadening and darkening, to become dark brown adults in about a month. Three to five generations appear each season.

SPECIAL TREATMENT. Use a dormant oil spray in spring as buds swell, adding diazinon (such as Spectracide) when infestation is heavy. Follow with a spray of malathion, carbaryl (such as Sevin), or rotenone in summer oil. Your agricultural agent can tell you the best times to spray in your area.

R

RED SPIDER MITE See Mite, Two-Spotted Spider
ROLY-POLY See Sow Bug
ROOT-KNOT NEMATODE See Nematode
ROOTWORM, SOUTHERN CORN See Beetle, Spotted
  Cucumber
ROSE CHAFER See Beetle
ROSE MIDGE See Maggot

S

SAN JOSE SCALE See Scale

SCALE
Scale insects on plants sometimes look like bumpy bark, sometimes like fine dusty ash. They may not be noticed until

PEAR PSYLLA
Psylla pyricola

Cautions to observe when using chemicals, page 71.

the infestation is severe. Heavily infested plants lose vigor and often drop some of their leaves; those retained become yellow and spotted. Fruit may be spotted too, especially at stems and blossom ends. In extreme cases scale insects kill the infested plant.

The 200 species of scales are divided into two categories: armored scales, those with hard, separate scales that can be lifted off the body of the insect; and soft or tortoise scales, whose scales are a part of the body and cannot be separated. Most armored scales mate and lay eggs, but some species give birth to live young. Both the crawlers that are born live and those that hatch from eggs have legs and antennae. Threadlike mouth parts enable them to suck sap from leaves and bark. After feeding for a short time, crawlers molt and lose their legs and antennae. The skin they shed becomes part of the scale they construct of fine waxy threads.

Females molt twice but always stay beneath their scales. Males, after their second molt, pass through a pupal stage and emerge as minute, yellow-winged adults. They move around until they find a female and fertilize her, then die. After the female has mated, she feeds as she produces eggs or live offspring, then she too dies. Both kinds of scales attack a wide variety of plants, often invading greenhouses.

WHAT TO DO. Minor infestations can be removed by hand with a tweezers or knife, or by swabbing with rubbing alcohol. To treat heavy infestations on woody plants, prune and dispose of all badly encrusted branches. Apply dormant oil spray in spring before buds open when the temperature is above 40°. To increase the efficiency of the spray, add carbaryl (such as Sevin), diazinon (such as Spectracide), malathion or methoxychlor (such as Marlate). To be effective, insecticide sprays must be used when the insects are in the crawler stage. Spray soft-stemmed plants with malathion or acephate (such as Orthene) or scrub the leaves gently with a soft brush and warm, soapy water, then rinse thoroughly. Indoors, wash plants with soapy water, remove scales by hand, or spray with pyrethrum or rotenone.

CALIFORNIA RED SCALE
Aonidiella aurantii

California red scales are most damaging to citrus trees in California and seriously afflict citrus in Arizona and Texas. Other vulnerable plants are acacias, aloes, apples, avocados, box elders, boxwoods, chinaberries, eucalyptuses, figs, fuchsias, grapes, hibiscuses, hollies, mulberries, oaks, olives, palms, privets, walnuts, willows, yews and yuccas. Damage is caused by a toxic substance the insects inject during feeding. Leaves and fruit become yellow and spotted, and sometimes all the foliage turns yellow. This scale is reddish brown and hard to see without a magnifying glass. The round armored female measures up to $1/12$ inch across. She produces two or three live crawlers daily for two or three months. In the South, four generations appear each year.

SPECIAL TREATMENT. Use the control measures recommended for all scales.

OYSTER-SHELL SCALE
Lepidosaphes ulmi

About $1/8$ inch long and $1/16$ inch wide, oblong and slightly broader at one end, the oyster-shell scale attacks deciduous fruit trees, shrubs and shade trees everywhere except in arctic and tropical regions. Although known to gardeners and fruit growers all over North America, they are most common in northern states. They often cluster together in such great numbers that they entirely cover tree bark.

Oyster-shell scale occurs in two forms that differ in appear-

CALIFORNIA RED SCALE
Aonidiella aurantii

OYSTER-SHELL SCALE
Lepidosaphes ulmi

ance and development. A gray form, common on lilacs, has bands across the shell and is larger than a brown form. It produces one generation a year and most commonly infests ash, beech, maple and willow trees as well as lilacs. The brown form, which becomes nearly black as it ages, produces one generation annually in colder areas and two generations in warmer ones. Fruits commonly infested are apples, apricots, currants, figs, grapes, pears, plums, quinces and raspberries. It is also a pest of almonds, beeches, birches, boxwoods, dogwoods, elms, horse chestnuts, lindens, mountain ashes, pachysandras, plane trees, tulip trees, viburnums and Virginia creepers.

SPECIAL TREATMENT. Use control measures recommended for all scales.

SAN JOSE SCALE
Quadraspidiotus perniciosus

When San Jose scale attacks a tree in large numbers, the branches look as if they are coated with gray ashes. If you lift up the loose, separate shell of one of these scales, you will see the soft, pinhead-sized, bright-yellow scale insect underneath. Found in every state of the United States, this scale is especially injurious to deciduous fruit trees, but numerous other plants are also susceptible. Infested parts of the plants appear inflamed due to the toxins released by the scales, and foliage becomes yellow and spotted.

The nearly black scales become full grown about the time buds bloom and produce from two to five generations of live crawlers each year.

SPECIAL TREATMENT. Use the control measures recommended for all scales.

SCURFY SCALE
Chionaspis furfura

A heavy infestation of scurfy scale, which can be found throughout much of the United States on deciduous fruit and ornamental trees and shrubs, gives a flaky look to the bark. Common victims are apples, ashes, black walnuts, cherries, currants, dogwoods, elms, gooseberries, hawthorns, hickories, horse chestnuts, maples, mountain ashes, peaches, pears, quinces, raspberries and willows. It generally attacks the shaded parts of trees, appearing often in neglected orchards.

The female scurfy scale is gray, rather pear shaped and about ⅛ inch across. The male is only about one quarter as large. Females live through the winter on tree bark with about 40 eggs under their shells; the eggs hatch after the tree is in leaf. Two generations occur annually in warm areas, only one generation where winter cold is severe.

SPECIAL TREATMENT. Use the controls that are recommended for all scales.

TERRAPIN SCALE
Lecanium nigrofasciatum

Terrapin scale is a common pest of fruit trees, shrubs and shade trees throughout the eastern United States and Canada. Clustered on branches and twigs, the male insects look like myriads of minute turtles. Terrapin scale is also called black-banded scale because a number of dark bands radiate from the center of the back. When the infestation is heavy, it has a putrid odor. Excretions of honeydew cover trunks and branches, on which a sooty black mold grows. Smaller branches die, causing thin foliage. Among the victims of this scale are ashes, bays, blueberries, box elders, cherry laurels, gums, hawthorns, hollies, jasmines, limes, lindens, live oaks, maples, mulberries, plane trees and poplars. The adult female terrapin scales are unarmored and almost hemispheri-

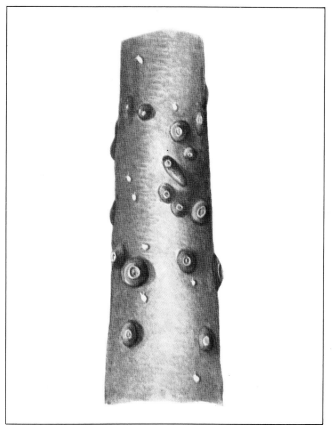

SAN JOSE SCALE
Quadraspidiotus perniciosus

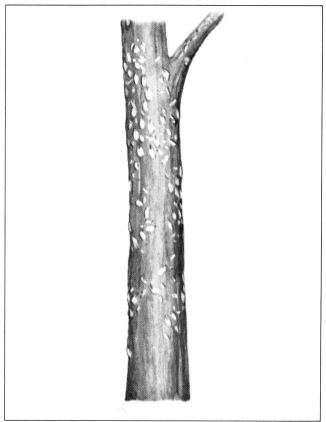

SCURFY SCALE
Chionaspis furfura

Cautions to observe when using chemicals, page 71.

TERRAPIN SCALE
Lecanium nigrofasciatum

SPOTTED GARDEN SLUG
Limax maximus

cal. They measure about ⅛ inch across and are dark brown or reddish-brown, smooth and shiny.

SPECIAL TREATMENT. Use the controls that are recommended for all scales.

SCURFY SCALE See Scale
SEVENTEEN-YEAR LOCUST See Cicada, Periodic
SILKWORM See Caterpillar, Gypsy Moth

SLUG

Slugs are pests in almost all home gardens where there is moisture enough for them to survive. It is easy to determine whether they are present in your garden because each has a gland that produces a mucous-like secretion and leaves a shiny trail. There are more than 30 kinds of these slimy, legless, soft-bodied creatures, all with mouths equipped with horny files with which to rasp leaves. They make large round holes, especially in leaves that are near the ground, and often devour entire young shoots and seedlings. Slugs feed from early spring through late fall. They attack many different kinds of plants, including coleuses, cinerarias, dahlias, geraniums, hollyhocks, irises, lilies, marigolds, primroses, snapdragons and violets.

Slugs are not insects but mollusks. Unlike most other mollusks—clams, oysters and snails—slugs have no outer shells to protect them, so they spend much of their lives hiding under flowerpots, boards or garden trash, feeding at night. Slugs vary in color from white to gray and brown, usually mottled with long dark spots. They range from ¼ inch to 10 inches in length. The females lay masses of 25 or more oval eggs in damp soil; they hatch in about a month. Though smaller and lighter in color, the young look like the adults. They develop slowly and live a year or longer.

WHAT TO DO. Reduce hiding places for slugs by keeping your garden free of debris. Remove old iris leaves after the first frost because slugs often winter under them. Spading in the spring destroys dormant slugs and eggs. Slugs are easy to trap. Scatter slices of raw potato or lettuce or cabbage leaves. Early next morning, collect them in a can and pour boiling water in it. A shallow dish of beer or grape juice left in the garden overnight with the lip of the dish at ground level will lure slugs to death by drowning. To prevent slugs from reaching a plant, set a barrier of fly screening 4 inches wide into the soil, or spread a ring of sand, lime or cinders around valuable plants.

SPOTTED GARDEN SLUG
Limax maximus

Newly hatched spotted garden slugs are dull white and unspotted until they are about 1 inch long and a month old. Adults are yellow-gray or brown, with elongated black spots; they grow to a length of 7 inches.

SPECIAL TREATMENT. Use the methods of control recommended for all slugs.

SOUTHERN CORN ROOTWORM See Beetle, Spotted
  Cucumber

SOW BUG

Sow bugs are not insects but small crustaceans related to the crab, crayfish and lobster. They breathe through gills and prefer moist surroundings in rotting wood, decaying plant material and manure. Although they may invade outdoor gardens, they are primarily pests of greenhouses, appearing where they find both shelter and decaying vegetable matter to feed on. They feed mainly at night, cutting into roots, stems and occasionally foliage. Sow bugs have flat, oval, slate-colored bodies about ½ inch long, distinctly segmented, with seven pairs of legs. The female has a pouch called a marsupium in which she lays 25 to 75 eggs. After hatching, the brood remains in the pouch, kangaroo-style, until the offspring are able to feed on plants. One species, the pill bug, is called roly-poly because, when disturbed, it rolls up into a tight ball like a tiny armadillo.

WHAT TO DO. A bait that is attractive to sow bugs is half of a potato placed cut side down on the surface of the soil. The next morning those sow bugs attracted to it can be disposed of in a can of boiling water. Commercial sow bug bait is also available, and tobacco dust is effective as a repellent.

DOORYARD SOW BUG
Porcellio laevis

A pest in greenhouses and some outdoor gardens, the dooryard sow bug attacks roots and tender growth of nearly all greenhouse plants. It hides in cracks, decaying wood and under plant refuse.

SPECIAL TREATMENT. Protect wood surfaces near plants with paint or wood preservative. Remove all plant refuse. Spray soil and greenhouse benches with diazinon (such as Spectracide), malathion or methoxychlor (such as Marlate).

SPINACH APHID See Aphid, Green Peach
SPINACH LEAF MINER See Maggot
SPOTTED CUCUMBER BEETLE See Beetle
SPOTTED GARDEN SLUG See Slug
SPRING CANKERWORM See Caterpillar
SPRUCE BUDWORM See Caterpillar
SQUASH BUG See Bug
SQUASH VINE BORER See Borer
STALK BORER See Borer
STINKBUG See Bug, Harlequin
STRAWBERRY CROWN MITE See Mite, Cyclamen
STRIPED BLISTER BEETLE See Beetle
STRIPED CUCUMBER BEETLE See Beetle
SYMPHYLAN, GARDEN See Centipede

T

TARNISHED PLANT BUG See Bug
TERRAPIN See Bug, Harlequin
TERRAPIN SCALE See Scale
THOUSAND-LEGGED WORM See Millepede

THRIPS

Thrips are active, needle-thin insects that look like black or straw-colored wood slivers moving about on plants. They are easily identified by their two pairs of slender wings, edged with long hairs. Thrips appear wherever the plants they feed upon are grown, and species are commonly named for their feeding specialties. There are cotton thrips, tobacco thrips, flower thrips, onion thrips, citrus thrips, bean thrips, pear thrips, oat thrips and greenhouse thrips, among many others. Thrips attack a variety of ornamental plants, among them chrysanthemums, daisies, peonies and roses. Their mouths are equipped for rasping plant tissue such as flower petals, leaves and stems and then sucking the plant juices. They feed between leaves, where they are often sheltered from insecticide sprays.

Female thrips insert their eggs in leaves and stems. Minute, pale nymphs hatch in about a week and begin to feed. There are five to eight generations each year, but thrips are most numerous in late spring and midsummer.

WHAT TO DO. Some thrips are repelled by sheets of alumi-

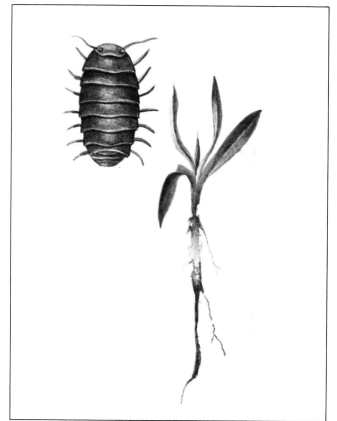

DOORYARD SOW BUG
Porcellio laevis

Cautions to observe when using chemicals, page 71.

num foil spread between rows of plants. Among their natural enemies are ladybug beetles, toads and aphid lions, the larvae of lacewings. For chemical protection, spray growing plants every two weeks with diazinon (such as Spectracide), dimethoate (such as Cygon or De-Fend), malathion or acephate (such as Orthene).

GLADIOLUS THRIPS
Taeniothrips simplex

Gladiolus thrips are found wherever gladioluses are grown and cause severe damage to gladioluses and irises. They also feed on amaryllises, asters, carnations, delphiniums, freesias, hollyhocks, narcissuses, lilies and red-hot pokers. Leaves that have been damaged by thrips first appear silvery, then turn brown and die. Blooms are deformed and frequently have whitish spots or streaks. Infested stems become corklike, rough, sticky and brown.

Although gladiolus thrips are larger than most other species, the adult is only about $1/16$ inch long. It is black or dark brown with a white band across the base of its wings.

SPECIAL TREATMENT. Examine every gladiolus corm you plant to make certain it is not thrip infested. Avoid planting them where thrips were a pest the preceding year. To control thrips on plants, begin to spray or dust with acephate (such as Orthene), diazinon (such as Spectracide), malathion or naled (such as Dibrom) when leaves are about 6 inches tall. Repeat every 10 days. At the end of the growing season, when dug-up corms have dried, dust them with malathion and store in a cool place.

ONION THRIPS
Thrips tabaci

Onion thrips, only about $1/25$ of an inch long, are difficult to see. The males are wingless and rare; the females can reproduce without them. Onion thrips are found in all onion-growing regions of the world. Besides onions, they damage many other vegetables, among them beans, beets, carrots, cabbages, cauliflower, celery, cucumbers, melons, squashes, tomatoes and turnips. They also transmit the spotted wilt virus to tomatoes and to dahlias and other flowers. Ornamental plants attacked by onion thrips include roses and carnations. Other victims are asparagus ferns, callas, Canterbury bells, chrysanthemums, dahlias, foxgloves, gaillardias, gloxinias, Jerusalem cherries, mignonettes and sweet peas.

Damage to onions appears first as white blotches. Leaf tips then become distorted; the plant withers, turns brown and falls over. The onion bulbs that develop are misshapen and small. Onion thrips gather in large numbers at the bases of leaves of other vegetables, causing them to have wrinkled, dwarfed foliage.

SPECIAL TREATMENT. Do not allow weeds to flourish in or around your garden, since thrips thrive among them. Do not grow onions from sets, which may carry the pest, near those that are grown from seeds. After the vegetables have been harvested, rake up any remaining tops and dispose of them. If thrips are numerous enough to scar leaves, treat them with two or three applications of diazinon (such as Spectracide) or malathion, as a spray or dust, at one- to two-week intervals.

TICKS See Mites
TOBACCO BUDWORM See Caterpillar, Corn-Ear Worm
TOMATO FRUITWORM See Caterpillar, Corn-Ear Worm
TOMATO HORNWORM See Caterpillar
TORTOISE BEETLE, MOTTLED See Beetle
TUBER MOTH See Borer, Potato Tuberworm
TWO-SPOTTED SPIDER MITE See Mite

GLADIOLUS THRIPS
Taeniothrips simplex

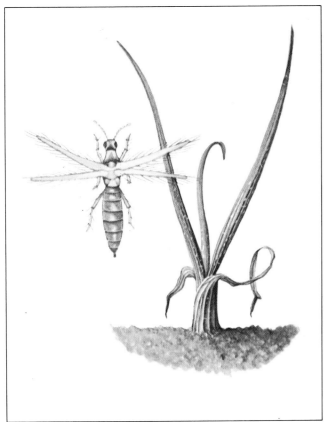

ONION THRIPS
Thrips tabaci

V

VARIEGATED CUTWORM See Caterpillar
VETCHWORM See Caterpillar, Corn-Ear Worm

W

WEBWORM, FALL See Caterpillar
WEBWORM, GARDEN See Caterpillar
WEEVIL See Borer
WESTERN GREAT PLAINS CRICKET See Cricket,
  Mormon
WHITE GRUB See Beetle, June

WHITEFLY

Although they are primarily tropical insects and citrus pests, whiteflies are found throughout the world. They often appear in greenhouses and on house plants and infest some garden plants, especially in warm climates.

Whiteflies are minute, about $^1/_{30}$ inch long, with two pairs of wings covered with white waxy powder. They can be present in large numbers on the undersides of leaves, unnoticed until the plant is disturbed when they fly out in a cloudlike swarm. Whiteflies are sucking insects that pierce leaves or stems and attach themselves while they draw out sap. The leaves become coated with their sticky secretion, honeydew, which makes a growing surface for sooty black fungus. Infested plants become covered with this unsightly substance; fruits produced are undersized and of poor color; foliage yellows and dries out.

The female whitefly lays 20 to 25 pinhead-sized eggs at a time, generally in a circle around her feeding spot. They hatch into almost invisible green or yellow nymphs called crawlers. Soon after beginning to feed, the nymphs shed their skins and lose their legs; left with oval scalelike bodies, they feed through a second molting, then enter a pupal stage from which they emerge as adult whiteflies.

WHAT TO DO. Scrutinize new cuttings or plants for evidence of whiteflies, especially those you purchase from a greenhouse. If your plants become infested, spray the undersides of the leaves with resmethrin (such as SBP 1382), malathion or acephate (such as Orthene), making two or three applications at weekly intervals. Consult your local agricultural agent for the proper times recommended for spraying fruit trees in your area.

GREENHOUSE WHITEFLY
Trialeurodes vaporariorum

This is the whitefly most often found in greenhouses; it may also appear on indoor plants and in outdoor gardens. It attacks a wide variety of plants. Often infested are ageratums, asters, azaleas, barberries, begonias, bignonias, calceolarias, calendulas, chrysanthemums, cinerarias, coleuses, ferns, fuchsias, geraniums, heliotropes, hibiscuses, honey locusts, lantanas, lupines, morning glories, primroses, privets, redbuds, rhododendrons, roses and salvias. Some fruits and vegetables commonly infested are avocados, blackberries, cantaloupes, cucumbers, grapes, lettuce, peas, peppers, potatoes, soybeans, strawberries, tomatoes and watermelons.

SPECIAL TREATMENT. Follow the control measures recommended for all whiteflies.

WHITE-FRINGED BEETLE See Beetle
WHITE-MARKED TUSSOCK MOTH See Caterpillar

WIREWORM

Wireworms are the larvae of click beetles, so named because when they are placed on their backs, they are able to snap

GREENHOUSE WHITEFLY
Trialeurodes vaporariorum

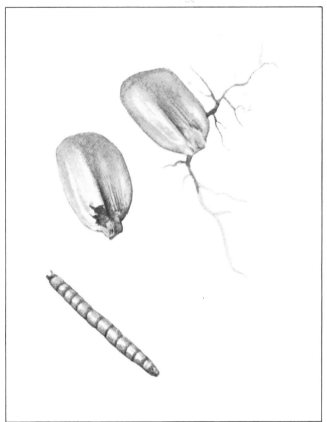

CORN WIREWORM
Melanotus cribulosus

Cautions to observe when using chemicals, page 71.

BEAN ANTHRACNOSE
Colletotrichum lindemuthianum

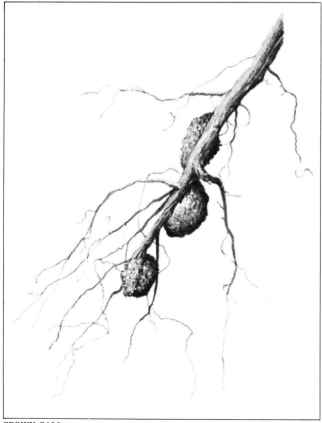

CROWN GALL
Agrobacterium tumefaciens

back onto their feet with a clicking sound. They are found throughout North America. The wireworms spend their lives burrowing in the soil or in rotten wood and are therefore seldom seen. Some species of wireworms remain in the larval stage for three to six years. They are ½ to 1½ inches long, blunt at the head, tapered at the tail, with three pairs of legs. They bore into bulbs, roots and germinating seeds, doing great damage to corn and various grasses as well as to potatoes and other kinds of underground vegetables. Sometimes a crop may come up, then it will become thin and patchy as wireworms bore into the roots.

WHAT TO DO. Because of their long life cycle, all ages and sizes of click beetles are present in the soil at any particular time. In hot, dry weather they burrow deep into the soil, making them hard to control even in heavily infested areas. Seeds that have been treated with lindane will kill most of the wireworms that are attracted to them. Diazinon (such as Spectracide) is an effective deterrent; it should be applied as a dust and spaded into the garden soil to a depth of 6 to 8 inches before planting.

CORN WIREWORM
Melanotus cribulosus

These wireworms consume the insides of corn seed, thus preventing its germination. They also feed upon developing young corn plants.

SPECIAL TREATMENT. Every three years or so, spade an area intended for corn, but let it lie fallow that season. When you plant the following year, spade between rows in the early part of summer.

WORM, HUNDRED-LEGGED See Centipede
WORM, THOUSAND-LEGGED See Millepede

Diseases

A
ANTHRACNOSE
BEAN ANTHRACNOSE
Collectotrichum lindemuthianum

Anthracnose is a fungus disease that appears when growing conditions are wet. The bean anthracnose infects all kinds of beans grown in the eastern and central United States but rarely occurs west of the Rocky Mountains. Cowpeas are also susceptible. This anthracnose starts as tiny, rusty-brown dots along the pod; these gradually expand into deep, black cankers. Pink spore slime oozing from this dead tissue forms a thin red rim. In young pods, the beans turn yellow, then brown or black. Dark spots develop along the veins on the undersides of the leaves and sometimes on the stems. Rain, or merely handling plants when they are wet, spreads the fungus.

WHAT TO DO. Plant certified disease-free western-grown bean seeds in soil that has not been used for bean crops during the previous two years. Do not touch the plants when they are wet. Beginning when plants flower, spray weekly with a solution of maneb (such as MEB or Dithane M-22), zineb (such as Parzate or Dithane Z-78), ferbam (such as Fermate or Karbam Black), or thiram (such as Arasan or Tersan). Follow label instructions concerning the number of days between the last spraying and the bean harvest. Pull up and dispose of infected plants.

APPLE BLOTCH, SOOTY See Blotch
APPLE TRUNK CANKER See Canker, Bleeding
ARMILLARIA ROOT ROT See Rot, Mushroom
AZALEA LEAF GALL See Gall

B

BACTERIAL DISEASE

Bacteria can infect most plants, entering through wounds that are caused by weather, insects or careless gardening. The microscopic organisms survive for years in the soil. After attacking a plant, they remain dormant through the winter and renew their activity in the spring. Bacterial diseases are grouped according to their symptoms: bacteria that stimulate growths at the plant's base are called crown galls, those that penetrate a plant's water-conducting system are known as wilts, and those that kill plant tissue are called blights.

WHAT TO DO. Avoid injuring plants. Keep the soil as acid as the plants will tolerate, since acidity inhibits bacterial growth. Dispose of small diseased plants or prune away infected parts of woody plants and trees, cutting well below the diseased part and sterilizing the shears with rubbing alcohol. Choose disease-resistant plants or seeds if they are available. Rotate annual crops and spray to control the population of disease-carrying insects.

CROWN GALL
Agrobacterium tumefaciens

Crown galls are swollen growths, sometimes several inches in diameter, that occur near the soil at the base of many different plants throughout the United States. The rough-textured galls may be hard or spongy. As the gall grows, it weakens the plant and may kill it. Among susceptible plants are brambles (blackberry, raspberry, grape, rose); fruit trees (apple, cherry, fig, nectarine, peach, plum); nut trees (almond, pecan, walnut); shade trees, shrubs and vines (euonymus, flowering quince, forsythia, honeysuckle and weigela); and beets, tomatoes and turnips.

SPECIAL TREATMENT. Do not buy plants with bumps at the soil line. Be careful not to wound plants when you cultivate them. Dispose of diseased plants.

CUCUMBER WILT
Erwinia tracheiphila

Cucumber wilt strikes the vascular systems of such vines as cantaloupes, cucumbers, pumpkins and squashes. Prevalent east of the Rocky Mountains, the disease is spread by cucumber beetles that carry the bacteria in their digestive tracts. In spring, bacteria excreted by the beetles on leaves enter wounds or leaf pores and cause dull green splotches on the foliage. Leaves and stems wilt and shrivel; the infected vines ultimately die.

SPECIAL TREATMENT. Reduce the beetle population by spraying weekly with carbaryl (such as Sevin), rotenone, methoxychlor (such as Marlate), malathion or diazinon (such as Spectracide), from the time vines sprout until they flower. Remove and destroy plants showing signs of the disease.

FIRE BLIGHT
Erwinia amylovora

Fire blight causes blossoms and leaves of young fruit trees, especially pear and apple, to shrivel and turn brown or black as if seared by fire. Bacteria carried by insects, rain, wind or garden tools attack plant shoots in the spring, working their way into the bark and causing dark cracks or cankers of dead tissue that ooze clear or amber-colored droplets laden with bacteria. The infection spreads most rapidly in wet weather

Cautions to observe when using chemicals, page 71.

CUCUMBER WILT
Erwinia tracheiphila

FIRE BLIGHT
Erwinia amylovora

BLACK KNOT OF CHERRY
Diobotryon morbosum

ROSE BLACKSPOT
Diplocarpon rosae

and also strikes young fruits which, like the leaves, shrivel and darken. From late summer through winter, the bacteria remain dormant inside the cankers, becoming active again the following spring.

SPECIAL TREATMENT. Plant disease-resistant varieties and avoid the high-nitrogen fertilizers or the heavy pruning that stimulate rapid twig growth. As a preventive, spray with an antibiotic solution of streptomycin sulfate (such as Agrimycin 17) at five- to seven-day intervals during the blossoming season. Prune off diseased branches during winter and apply an asphalt-based tree-wound dressing to the cut surfaces. Disinfect tools by dipping them in 70 per cent alcohol or household bleach. Your local agricultural agent can recommend the best time to spray fruit trees in your area.

BEAN ANTHRACNOSE See Anthracnose

BLACK KNOT
BLACK KNOT OF PLUM AND CHERRY, also called PRUNUS BLACK KNOT and PLUM WART
Dibotryon morbosum

A fungus disease of apricot, sweet and sour cherry, plum, and prune trees, black knot causes rough, cylindrical, black swellings on small branches. Widespread east of the Mississippi River, the infection occurs in the spring but cannot be detected until a year later when olive-green growths appear on the ruptured bark. These growths can be as much as two to four times the thickness of the branch and several inches long. In fall these swellings harden and darken; they finish their two-year growth cycle the following spring. The gnarled limbs weaken, growth halts and the tree gradually dies.

WHAT TO DO. When buds first appear, spray infected trees with zineb (such as Dithane Z-78), Bordeaux mixture or liquid lime-sulfur. Spray again when trees are in bloom, a third time in the fall. Consult your agricultural agent for spray dates for your area. During winter, prune and destroy infected branches, cutting 4 to 6 inches below the knot.

BLACKLEG
BLACKLEG OF GERANIUM, also called STEM or CUTTING ROT
Pythium species

Disease organisms of the *Pythium* species are in almost all soils, ready to attack plants when temperature and moisture conditions become favorable. When they infect geranium cuttings the stems first turn black, then the disease rapidly progresses upward. It can kill cuttings within a week.

WHAT TO DO. Take cuttings from healthy plants and use a sterile rooting medium. Do not overwater.

BLACKSPOT
ROSE BLACKSPOT
Diplocarpon rosae

Rose bushes grown in humid regions are susceptible to blackspot, a fungus disease that disfigures and kills leaves. Hybrid tea, hybrid perpetual, polyantha and tea roses are among the most vulnerable. Blackspot creates black circles up to ½ inch in diameter on either side of the leaf. The circles have indistinct, fuzzy edges, with centers that are speckled with tiny, pimple-like dots. Soon after infection the tissue around the spots turns yellow and the leaves drop off. Rain, water from a garden sprinkler, or a gardener's hands can transport fungus spores to neighboring plants. In cold climates where shrubs drop their leaves in the fall, the dormant fungus spends the winter in the dead leaves; in warm regions and in greenhouses it is active year round.

WHAT TO DO. Before purchasing plants inspect them carefully for signs of disease. When planting, space them to allow good ventilation. Water early in the day so leaves will be dry by evening. Do not work among roses when the foliage is wet. Remove dead leaves and cut off infected canes in the fall; mulch in spring to keep fungus spores from splashing from the ground up to leaves. During the growing season and into the fall, spray roses weekly with benomyl (such as Benlate), captan (such as Orthocide), ferbam (such as Fermate), folpet (such as Phaltan), maneb (such as Dithane M-22 or Manzate) or zineb (such as Dithane Z-78).

BLEEDING CANKER See Canker

BLIGHT
A large number of fungus diseases that suddenly damage leaves, blossoms and fruit are called blight. Plants wither and growth stops but, unlike the leaf-spotting diseases, the area of infection is not clearly defined. Blight often, but not always, causes plants to rot. Like most fungi, blight usually flourishes in humid or wet weather.

WHAT TO DO. Prevent infection by setting plants in well-drained, sunny locations. Space plants for good air circulation to reduce humidity. Apply sprays of fungicides or antibiotics as necessary; consult your local agricultural agent for the spray schedule suited to your area.

BOTRYTIS BLIGHT or GRAY MOLD BLIGHT
Botrytis species
The gray mold sometimes seen on boxed strawberries, raspberries or other soft, ripe fruit is Botrytis blight, one of the most common fungus diseases of fruits, vegetables and flowers. It is most common during the cool, damp summer weather in temperate regions but occurs in warm climates during the winter. At first, small yellow, orange or brown splotches spot the leaves, flowers, ripening fruit or roots and bulbs. These spots soon blend together into a fuzzy, gray mold. Enveloped in slime, the infected part becomes mushy and quickly rots. The blight can survive the winter in hard black blisters on plant stems. Botrytis blight affects more than 80 species of plants. Berries are susceptible, as are asparagus, endive, escarole, globe artichokes, kidney beans, lettuce, lima beans, snap beans and tomatoes. Susceptible flowers are African violets, begonias, chrysanthemums, dahlias, gladioluses, hyacinths, lilies, marigolds, peonies, roses, snapdragons and zinnias.

SPECIAL TREATMENT. Spray perennials or vegetables during cool, wet weather with benomyl (such as Benlate), captan (such as Orthocide), ferbam (such as Coromate), thiram (such as Thylate) or zineb (such as Dithane Z-78). Remove fading flowers and yellowed foliage from ornamentals. Propagate new plants only from healthy cuttings and bulbs, using a sterile growing medium when possible. Do not plant bulbs that have brown spots.

EARLY BLIGHT OF TOMATO AND POTATO
Alternaria solani
Tomato and potato yields can be severely reduced if early blight hits plants at the beginning of the growing season. At the start of summer, brown spots with concentric rings appear on leaves. These leaves gradually turn yellow, then they become brown before they drop off. Older leaves at the base of the plant are usually affected first, and the disease progresses upward. Seedlings may sometimes develop brown, sunken cankers on their stems near the ground; these are called collar rot. Dark sunken circles form at the stem ends of ripening tomatoes.

Cautions to observe when using chemicals, page 71.

BOTRYTIS BLIGHT
Botrytis paeoniae

EARLY BLIGHT OF TOMATO
Alternaria solani

LATE BLIGHT OF POTATO
Phytophthora infestans

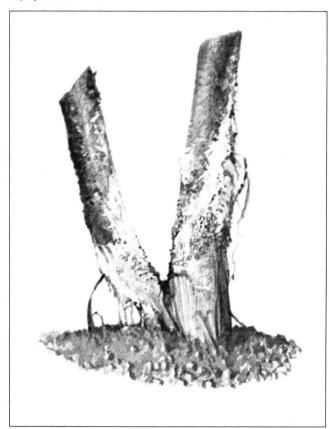

SOUTHERN BLIGHT
Pellicularia rolfsii

SPECIAL TREATMENT. Choose resistant varieties, use treated seed and rotate crops on a three-year cycle. Spray plants with maneb (such as Dithane M-22 or Manzate), chlorothalonil (such as Bravo or Daconil), mancozeb (such as Dithane M-45) or zineb (such as Dithane Z-78 or Panzate). Spray tomatoes when the fruit first appears and at weekly intervals through the growing season. Spray potatoes every seven to 10 days once plants are 4 to 6 inches tall.

LATE BLIGHT OF TOMATO AND POTATO
Phytophthora infestans

A million people starved during the famine of 1845 when late blight hit the potato crop in Ireland. Despite its name, late blight attacks tomato and potato plants quite early in the growing season, during cool, wet weather, and develops rapidly as the weather becomes warmer. The blight endangers potato crops in the Northeastern, Middle Atlantic and North Central states and occasionally affects crops along the West and Gulf coasts. Tomato plants are vulnerable in all humid areas during wet seasons.

The first symptom is the appearance of dark, watery spots on the undersides of leaves. The dark centers quickly shrivel and dry as a soft, white mildew-like growth blankets the leaves. On potato leaves, dead spots reach ½ to 1 inch in diameter in less than a week; tomato seedlings die within three or four days. Once potato leaves are infected, rain carries the disease spores underground to the tubers, which develop small brown or purple spots on their skins. When the potato is exposed to air, these blemishes deepen into dark pits and if the potato is sliced, the interior is full of red-brown dry rot. In mature tomato plants, late blight quickly moves from the leaves to the fruit, covering it with dark spots. The tomatoes rot and drop to the ground.

SPECIAL TREATMENT. Choose resistant varieties, plant certified disease-free seeds and rotate crops on a three-year cycle. Spray tomatoes when fruit becomes pea-sized and at weekly intervals through the growing season. Once potato plants are 4 to 6 inches tall, spray them every seven to 10 days. Use maneb (such as Dithane M-22 or Manzate), chlorothalonil (such as Bravo), mancozeb (such as Dithane M-45) or zineb (such as Dithane Z-78 or Parzate).

SOUTHERN BLIGHT or CROWN ROT
Pellicularia rolfsii, also called *Sclerotium rolfsii*

White fibrous fans of fungus near the bases of plants are the most obvious symptoms of southern blight. This rotting disease affects nearly all ornamentals and vegetables and is prevalent in the South where warm soil and moisture favor its growth. As the fungus develops, small white-to-dark bodies the size and shape of mustard seeds appear. The white fungus changes and hardens into a red or light-brown crust, sometimes extending several inches over the soil. As the rot spreads, it cuts off the plant's water supply; the plant yellows, wilts and dies. The fungus survives the winter 2 or 3 inches below the soil line, resuming growth with the return of warmth and moisture in spring.

SPECIAL TREATMENT. Rotate vegetable crops on a three-year cycle. Water seedlings weekly with a solution of captan, ferbam (such as Coromate), folpet (such as Phaltan) or thiram (such as Thylate). If the fungus appears, dig up infected plants and burn them.

BLIGHT, FIRE See Bacterial Disease
BLIGHT, LILAC SHOOT See Canker, Bleeding
BLIGHT, TYPHULA See Snow Mold
BLOSSOM BLIGHT See Blight

BLOTCH DISEASE

SOOTY APPLE BLOTCH, also called SOOTY BLOTCH OF FRUIT
Gloeodes pomigena

Common in the eastern and central United States as far south as the Gulf Coast, sooty apple blotch is a disfiguring fungus disease that afflicts the skin of apples, blackberries, citrus fruits, crabapples and pears without affecting the fruit inside. During rainy weather in summer, the fruit becomes mottled with irregularly shaped brown or black spots, up to ¼ inch in diameter. When these splotches run together the condition is called cloudy fruit. Although marred, infected apples and pears are still edible. The harder rind of citrus fruits, unpierced by the fungus, is easily rubbed clean.

WHAT TO DO. Space and prune fruit trees to permit air to circulate. Spray with benomyl (such as Benlate), captan plus zineb (such as Dithane Z-78); consult your local agricultural agent for the spray schedule recommended in your area. Do not plant vulnerable fruit trees near such trees as persimmon, prickly or white ash, hawthorn, maple, sycamore or willow; spores of this fungus pass the winter in cankers on twigs of these trees. Prune and burn cankered twigs.

BLUEGRASS LEAF SPOT See Leaf Spot
BOTRYTIS BLIGHT See Blight
BROWN PATCH OF TURF See Rot
BROWN ROT OF STONE FRUITS See Rot

 C

CANKER

Sores on the trunks, stems or branches of trees and other plants are known as cankers. Oval or irregularly shaped dead patches, they range from an inch to more than a foot in length. Often the canker-crack opens, oozing dark, watery sap. It may form a deep, sunken area, edged with raised callous tissue or a flat discoloration. Sometimes the canker is merely a bump on the bark. The infection is caused by fungi or bacteria from the soil that enter trees and plants through wounds or insect holes. The disease kills water-conducting tissues, and eventually it causes leaves to turn yellow and branches or shoots to wilt and die from the tips down. This condition is called dieback. Moist weather conditions in the spring and early fall stimulate fast growth of the pathogens, but they also grow in dry periods.

WHAT TO DO. Avoid wounding tree trunks or plant stems; protect trunks with stone or wire guards. Cut the infected branches off trees and shrubs well below the diseased part. Gouge out small cankers with a sharp knife. Disinfect tools between cuts with 70 per cent denatured alcohol or a 10 per cent solution of household bleach. Coat wounds with tree paint or Bordeaux paste. Pull up and burn all diseased plants and rotate annual crops.

BLEEDING CANKER
Phytophthora cactorum

The fungus that causes bleeding canker on beech, birch, elm, horse chestnut, linden, maple and oak trees also causes crown canker or collar rot on dogwoods, dieback on rhododendrons, foot rot on lilies, shoot blight on lilacs, stem rot on ornamental flowers and trunk canker on almond, apple, apricot, cherry and peach trees. The disease occurs throughout North America.

Bleeding canker is characterized by red sap that drips from open wounds on the branches or trunks of trees. When dry, the sap forms hard red crusts. The inner bark develops brown areas with green edges. The fungus secretes a toxin that causes leaves and branches to yellow, wilt and die.

Cautions to observe when using chemicals, page 71.

SOOTY APPLE BLOTCH
Gloeodes pomigena

BLEEDING CANKER
Phytophthora cactorum

Crown canker or collar rot of dogwoods begins with cankers that form near the soil on the trunks of trees. At first leaves appear smaller and lighter in color than usual, then turn prematurely red in late summer. In dry weather the leaves may curl and the branches die. In advanced stages, the canker causes an infected area to become dark and sunken. The bark dries out and peels off, exposing discolored inner wood. The canker eventually encircles the entire trunk base or roots and kills the tree. Transplanted dogwoods are particularly susceptible.

Rhododendrons afflicted with rhododendron dieback look as if they have been killed by the cold; leaves and buds turn brown, curl up and wither. If plants are in the shade, the leaves sometimes develop watery spots. Eventually the canker girdles and kills twigs. When these symptoms occur on lilacs, the disease is called lilac shoot blight.

Trunk canker in mature fruit and nut trees starts as a watery area on the bark that gradually grows into a large canker, encircling the trunk or lower branches.

Ornamental flowers afflicted with the cankers known as stem rot develop dead areas at the bases of their stems. These eventually encircle the stems, and the plants wilt, topple over and die. Susceptible flowers include calceolarias, clarkias, cornflowers, golden seals, snapdragons, sweet peas and double tulip varieties. When the symptoms appear on lily stems just below the soil, the disease is called foot rot.

SPECIAL TREATMENT. Bleeding canker is difficult to cure, but mildly diseased trees may heal themselves. Avoid heavy feeding. Prune and burn infected parts. Spray diseased rhododendrons with Bordeaux mixture. To eliminate stem rot and foot rot, destroy infected plants. Rotate crops.

CANKER DIEBACK
Botryosphaeria ribis chromogena

This canker afflicts many woody-stemmed plants. It occurs throughout North America in regions where apples, avocados, currants, figs, forsythias, hickories, pecans, pyracanthas, quinces, redbuds, rhododendrons, roses, sweet gums, willows and other susceptible plants are grown. The bark of infected apple trees develops watery blisters. Infected redbuds have deep oval cankers that encircle their branches. On currants, forsythia and roses, brown, dead leaves dangle from diseased branches. Rhododendrons are marked with watery patches on leaves and twigs. Trunk cankers rupture the bark of willows, killing a tree in a few years.

SPECIAL TREATMENT. Follow the measures given for canker and dieback. A spray of a copper-based fungicide can be used except on apples and roses.

CHERRY BLACK KNOT See Black Knot

CLUBROOT
CLUBROOT OF CABBAGE
Plasmodiophora brassicae

Brussels sprouts, cabbages, garden cress, mustard, radishes, rutabagas, turnips and some annual flowers are subject to clubroot, which attacks the underground parts of the plants. It is especially prevalent in the northern states.

WHAT TO DO. Reject diseased seedlings. Plant in alkaline soil. Pull up and burn diseased plants. Rotate crops.

COLLAR ROT See Canker, Bleeding
CROWN CANKER See Canker, Bleeding
CROWN GALL See Bacterial Disease
CROWN ROT See Blight
CUCUMBER WILT See Bacterial Disease

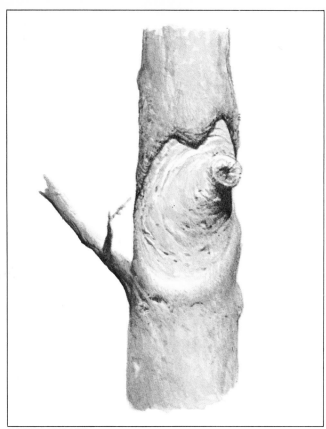
CANKER DIEBACK
Botryosphaeria ribis chromogena

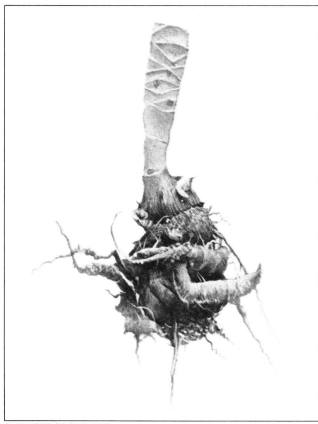
CLUBROOT OF CABBAGE
Plasmodiophora brassicae

D

DAMPING-OFF

PRE-EMERGENCE AND POSTEMERGENCE DAMPING-OFF
Rhizoctonia solani and *Pythium debaryanum*

A variety of organisms cause damping-off, which is one of the most common of the diseases that afflict seeds and seedlings. Fungi from the soil destroy either the seed or the newly emerged plant. If the seeds rot before sprouting, leaving empty spaces in a row of plants, the condition is called pre-emergence damping-off. When seedlings rot or wither and topple shortly after they have pushed through the soil, it is called postemergence damping-off. Hollow stems become water soaked, and dead areas develop near the stem bases, followed by decaying of the roots. Pre-emergence damping-off strikes plants when germination is slow because the soil is wet and cold. Postemergence damping-off affects overcrowded seedlings, particularly perennial flowers and trees, during humid, warm weather.

WHAT TO DO. Start plants in a sterile planting medium, such as packaged potting soil, sand, vermiculite, perlite or sphagnum moss. To protect seeds during germination, dust them before planting with captan (such as Orthocide 75 Seed Protectant), chloranil (such as Spergon), dichlone (such as Phygon Seed Protectant), or thiram (such as Arasan). To coat the seeds, open the corner of a packet, insert a tiny amount of fungicide on a knife or toothpick, fold the corner down and shake the packet. Larger seeds can be treated in a jar. Keep the soil barely moist and thin seedlings to prevent overcrowding. Spray young plants weekly with captan (such as Orthocide), ferbam (such as Coromate), zineb (such as Dithane Z-78) or ziram (such as Zerlate or Karbam White). Destroy diseased plants and remove the adjacent soil.

DIEBACK OF RHODODENDRON See Canker, Bleeding
DOGWOOD CROWN CANKER See Canker, Bleeding
DOLLAR SPOT See Rot

DOWNY MILDEW

DOWNY MILDEW OF LIMA BEAN
Phytophthora phaseoli

A number of plants are infected by a fungus disease called downy mildew, but lima beans, grown extensively in the East, are the most vulnerable. A white, cottony down develops on the pod in irregular splotches, wrapping around the pod until it blackens and curls. Occasionally, pale yellow or green spots appear on the leaves, flowers and shoots and the white covering is less evident. Spores of these fungi can survive in pods through the winter. Insects carry the infection to other plants in the spring. Damage is greatest during wet periods when nights are cool and days warm.

WHAT TO DO. Plant disease-free, western-grown seeds and do not crowd the plants. When cool weather is predicted or you notice mildew, spray at five-day intervals with maneb (such as Manzate or Dithane M-22) or zineb (such as Dithane Z-78). Pick beans only when pods are dry. To eradicate the disease, dispose of infected plants and do not plant lima beans in the same soil for three consecutive years.

E

EARLY BLIGHT OF TOMATO AND POTATO See Blight

F

FIRE BLIGHT See Bacterial Disease
FOOT ROT See Canker, Bleeding; Leaf Spot, Bluegrass
FUNGUS, HONEY MUSHROOM See Rot, Mushroom Root
FUNGUS, OAK ROOT See Rot, Mushroom Root

Cautions to observe when using chemicals, page 71.

POSTEMERGENCE DAMPING-OFF
Pythium debaryanum

DOWNY MILDEW OF LIMA BEAN
Phytophthora phaseoli

AZALEA LEAF GALL
Exobasidium vaccinii

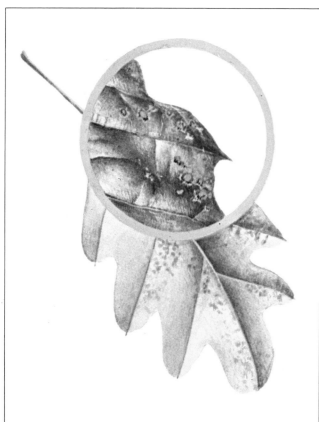

OAK LEAF BLISTER
Taphrina coerulescens

G

GALL

AZALEA LEAF GALL
Exobasidium vaccinii

Galls are abnormal growths or tumors that appear on most plant species. They vary from the size of a wart to swellings several inches thick. They may be hemispherical or irregular and usually appear on only one part of a plant, often near the soil line. Insects, mites and nematodes feeding on plant tissue cause many galls. Others result from infection from fungi, viruses or bacteria that enter plant tissue through wounds. The presence of a gall or two does not cause serious damage, but rampant growths may interfere with food and water distribution and stunt, weaken or kill a plant.

Azaleas, rhododendrons and other ornamental plants are sometimes attacked by the azalea leaf gall, as are blueberry and huckleberry bushes. This fungus disease appears wherever susceptible plants are grown, most frequently in shady gardens during periods of warm, wet weather. Leaves, usually those on the lowest branches, thicken, then turn pale green. Blossoms may also become fleshy, turn waxy, then become covered with powdery white fungus spores.

WHAT TO DO. Preventive measures through cultivation of the soil and control of insect pests, fungi and weeds are the gardener's best defense against galls. Buy disease-resistant plant varieties. Inspect new plants carefully and reject those with bumps near the soil line. Avoid wounding plants. Spray with zineb (such as Dithane Z-78) or ferbam (such as Fermate) just before leaves unfold.

Remove and burn or otherwise dispose of galls whenever possible. Prune infected branches from woody plants, cutting them off 4 to 6 inches below the gall. Dip shears in a 70 per cent solution of denatured alcohol or a 10 per cent solution of household bleach between cuts. Paint cut ends with tree-wound dressing. Dig up and destroy severely infected plants.

GALL, CROWN See Bacterial Disease
GRAPE BLACK ROT See Rot
GRAY MOLD BLIGHT See Blight
GRAY SNOWMOLD See Snowmold

L

LEAF BLISTER and LEAF CURL

A single species of fungi causes most kinds of leaf blister and leaf curl, springtime diseases that affect birch, elm, maple, oak and poplar trees, as well as almond, cherry, nectarine, peach and plum trees throughout the United States except where dry conditions do not favor fungus growth. Other fruit and nut trees, bush fruits and ornamentals are also susceptible. Leaves develop curled edges and blisters. In severe cases the thickened, puckered leaves fall prematurely, and successive defoliations can kill the tree. Fruits fail to develop, or they may be misshapen, cracked or swollen.

WHAT TO DO. Plant disease-resistant varieties if they are available. Water and feed trees to keep them growing vigorously and remove dead branches that might harbor insects or disease. Prune trees to permit good ventilation. Control insects that weaken trees and carry disease. Keep garden areas free of weeds and debris. For fruit trees, consult your local agricultural agent to obtain a spray schedule for your area.

OAK LEAF BLISTER
Taphrina coerulescens

The severe damage caused by oak leaf blister can occur on cherrybark, laurel, live, red, southern red, water and willow oaks. Black, blackjack and southern oaks are also sometimes affected. The disease is found throughout the United States but is especially rampant in the South. Leaf surfaces are scarred with circular blisters that turn yellow, red or brown and run together, causing leaves to curl or pucker. Leaves usually remain attached, but in severe cases they may drop prematurely. Spores that form on blisters blow onto bark and branches, where they remain during the winter. The spores become active during cool, wet weather in the early spring when wind-blown rain carries them to new leaves.

SPECIAL TREATMENT. Plant resistant species such as chinquapin, pin, post and Shumard oaks. Treat trees one to two weeks before the buds swell in early spring, using a spray containing captan (such as Orthocide), ferbam (such as Coromate) or maneb (such as Manzate or Dithane M-22).

PEACH LEAF CURL
Taphrina deformans

Throughout the United States peach leaf curl occurs in late spring, usually after cool, humid, rainy weather. Almond, cherry, peach, plum and nectarine trees, as well as some ornamental plants, are susceptible. New leaves on infected trees arch, thicken and pucker. They turn pale green or yellow, then wither and fall prematurely. Heavy defoliation of unsprayed trees occurs in wet weather. Fruit may be scant and drop early, or not appear at all. The fungus that causes the disease is always present on the twigs and bark of susceptible trees. Spores are splashed by rain onto emerging leaf buds and germinate during wet weather. The new leaves develop a silvery coating of multiplying spores. Before the diseased leaves fall, spores are blown onto bark or branches where they spend the winter.

SPECIAL TREATMENT. Choose disease-resistant varieties. Prevent leaf curl with a spray of Bordeaux mixture, ferbam (such as Karbam Black) or lime sulfur applied twice a year— once just at or before leaf fall and again in early spring before buds swell.

LEAF CURL See Leaf Blister and Leaf Curl
LEAF GALL, AZALEA See Gall

LEAF SPOT
BLUEGRASS LEAF SPOT
Helminthosporium vagans

Also called melting-out or foot rot, bluegrass leaf spot is a fungus disease that occurs throughout the United States during cool, wet weather. Damage is most severe in the Northeast, East, and Midwest. The disease first appears on grass blades as brown spots ringed with purple or dark brown. The centers of the spots eventually fade to a straw color. Diseased blades wither and drop, spreading the disease to stems, crowns and even to roots. Weeds invade the disease-thinned locations. In the fall, rain splashes spores onto healthy grass. The fungus passes the winter there and renews the cycle when spring rains come.

SPECIAL TREATMENT. Plant disease-resistant varieties of grass recommended for your area by your local agricultural agent. Lawns of mixed species of bluegrass are frequently more resistant than pure strains. Buy healthy, disease-free seed. Raise mower blades to avoid close cutting and remove clippings if possible. Avoid frequent, light sprinkling. Do not overstimulate lawn growth with excess nitrogen fertilizer. Curb the disease by applying captan (such as Orthocide), or chlorothalonil (such as Daconil).

LILAC SHOOT BLIGHT See Canker, Bleeding
LIMA BEAN DOWNY MILDEW See Downy Mildew

Cautions to observe when using chemicals, page 71.

PEACH LEAF CURL
Taphrina deformans

BLUEGRASS LEAF SPOT
Helminthosporium vagans

FAIRY RING
Psalliota campestris

POWDERY MILDEW OF CUCURBITS
Erysiphe cichoracearum

M

MELTING OUT See Leaf Spot, Bluegrass
MILDEW, DOWNY, OF LIMA BEAN See Downy Mildew
MILDEW, POWDERY, OF CUCURBITS See Powdery
  Mildew
MOLD BLIGHT, GRAY See Blight

MUSHROOM

FAIRY RING
Psalliota campestris, also called *Agaricus campestris*

During wet weather in spring or fall, circles of white mushrooms called fairy rings appear on lawns. Inside and outside these circles, dark green bands of fast-growing grass appear. Close to the rings, the grass dies.

WHAT TO DO. Total eradication may require replacing the lawn. But patches of dying grass can be revived by injecting water 10 to 24 inches into the soil with a root feeder or by using a spading fork to loosen the soil so water can penetrate.

MUSHROOM FUNGUS, HONEY See Rot, Mushroom Root
MUSHROOM ROOT ROT See Rot

O

OAK LEAF BLISTER See Leaf Blister
OAK ROOT FUNGUS See Rot

P

PEACH LEAF CURL See Leaf Blister and Leaf Curl
PLUM BLACK KNOT See Black Knot
PLUM WART See Black Knot
POTATO BLIGHT See Blight

POWDERY MILDEW

POWDERY MILDEW OF CUCURBITS AND OTHER PLANTS
Erysiphe cichoracearum

Most common in the South and along the Pacific Coast but found throughout the United States, various types of powdery mildew injure leaves and stems of nearly 300 plants. The strain listed above attacks the cucurbits—cucumbers, gourds, melons, pumpkins and squashes. Others infect lettuce and potatoes or such ornamental plants as asters, begonias, chrysanthemums, phlox and zinnias. The first signs of this fungus disease appear on the undersides of older leaves as scattered, round white spots. These grow until they merge and cover both sides of the leaf with a powdery web of fungus threads. Infected leaves change from dark green to yellow-green, then brown. The ultimate loss of leaves causes sunscald, a whitening or browning of fruits, or premature ripening. Affected fruits are small and irregularly shaped, with poor flavor and texture. Unlike other fungus diseases, powdery mildew does not need wet weather to spread. The humidity found on leaves in cool, shaded gardens and in crowded low spots with poor air circulation is enough to support its growth. It thrives on dew in areas where cool nights follow warm days. Spores are spread by the wind and on hands, shoes or tools. Spores live only a few hours at 80°, survive the longest around 40° but die at 30° or below. Therefore infections are most serious during cool seasons.

WHAT TO DO. Choose disease-resistant varieties. At the first signs of mildew, check its spread by spraying both sides of the leaves with benomyl (such as Benlate), dinocap (such as Karathane) or sulfur. Repeat at seven to 10 day intervals as needed. Follow label instructions regarding the number of days that must elapse between the last spray and the harvest. To eradicate dormant mildew spores that winter on old stems and leaves, burn infected annuals in the fall.

PRUNUS BLACK KNOT See Black Knot

R

RHODODENDRON DIEBACK See Canker, Bleeding
ROOT FUNGUS, OAK See Rot
ROOT ROT See Rot, Mushroom Root Rot
ROSE BLACKSPOT See Blackspot

ROT

The roots, bulbs, stems, trunks, buds, flowers, fruits and
leaves of almost all plants are susceptible to rots. Found
throughout North America, rots develop fastest in warm,
humid weather. They cause plants to be undersized, with
leaves that turn yellow, wilt and drop early. Parts of an
infected plant may look decayed and have a strong, unpleas-
ant odor. A cottony mold with black fungus spores may grow
over diseased areas. Tiny toadstools or shelf-shaped fungi
may appear at the base of diseased trees or on wounds. Plant
parts die when a rot cuts off their supply of water and
nutrients. A variety of fungi and bacteria cause rots. Rough
handling, storms, insects or nematodes can wound plants and
thus open the way for rot organisms, and contaminated garden tools can spread the disease.

WHAT TO DO. Provide good drainage. Plant disease-free
seed in noninfected or sterilized soil. Space plants widely and
prune trees to permit free circulation of air. Use a mulch,
stake, or wire frame to keep vegetables or fruits up off the
ground. Rotate vegetables on a three-year cycle. Avoid over-
head sprinkling and excess watering or fertilizing. Keep the
garden free of such debris as fallen leaves, dropped fruit and
dead flowers. Control insects that wound plants and carry
disease. Remove diseased plant parts or severely infected
plants and destroy them. Seek professional help to treat
severe infections.

BROWN PATCH OF TURF
Rhizoctonia solani, also called *Pellicularia filamentosa*

Bent, blue, Bermuda, St. Augustine and zoysia grasses are
all susceptible to brown patch during hot, wet weather. The
disease is most prevalent in the South. Brown patch first
shows as circular 1-inch to 3-foot black spots on the lawn.
The grass wilts, then turns a bleached brown. In the early
morning, smoke-colored rings outline the sunken patches.
Brown patch attacks leaves and stems but seldom roots.
Borders of spreading patches stand out as new grass pushes
up in the centers. The fungus remains from year to year in
the soil, attacking lawns when night temperatures stay above
70° during wet periods.

SPECIAL TREATMENT. Ask your local agricultural agent to
recommend a disease-resistant grass for your area. Avoid
watering in late evening. After a late rain in hot weather,
you can swish surface water off the grass with a long bamboo
pole. Be conservative in using high-nitrogen fertilizer. Spray
with a fungicide such as chlorothalonil (such as Daconil),
anilazine (such as Dyrene) or mancozeb (such as Fore or
Dithane M-45) once a week in hot, humid periods.

BROWN ROT OF STONE FRUITS
Monilinia fructicola, also called *Sclerotinia fructicola*

A disease so common that gardeners often call it "the rot,"
brown rot flourishes in warm, humid, rainy regions, particularly in the Southeast. It affects almonds, apricots, cherries,
peaches, plums, Japanese quinces and sometimes apples and
pears. The disease strikes blossoms first, causing them to
brown and stick to twigs. On stems and twigs, the disease
forms brown, sunken cankers that occasionally girdle twigs

Cautions to observe when using chemicals, page 71.

BROWN PATCH OF TURF
Rhizoctonia solani

BROWN ROT
Monilinia fructicola

and kill them. Leaves on infected twigs lose their color, then wither. Wind and rain carry these fungus spores to maturing fruits, where small brown soft spots appear. The spots quickly enlarge and the fruit surface is soon covered with gray, powdery spores. Such rotten fruit may dry on the tree or drop to the ground. Wind, rain and insects also carry spores to nearby fruit and trees. The rot flourishes on overripe, unharvested fruit and remains on twigs, branches and fruit debris until the following year.

SPECIAL TREATMENT. Plant disease-resistant varieties recommended for your area. Promptly dispose of diseased fruit from trees or the ground. Prune off and burn diseased stems and twigs, cutting at least 4 inches below the affected part. To protect stone fruits, use preventive sprays of benomyl (such as Benlate), captan (such as Orthocide) or sulfur (but do not use sulfur on apricots); consult your local agricultural agent about the spray schedule recommended in your area. Handle picked fruit carefully to avoid puncturing the skin, and refrigerate it to slow fungus growth. Pick all ripe fruit.

MUSHROOM ROOT ROT
Armillaria mellea

Also called Armillaria root rot, oak root fungus or honey mushroom fungus, mushroom root rot affects fruit, nut and ornamental trees and shrubs throughout the United States. It is particularly devastating in states west of the Rocky Mountains. Strands of black fungus resembling shoestrings grow through the soil from diseased trees until they penetrate first the roots, then the bark of healthy trees. The first signs of this tree disease are dwarfed, yellow, wilting leaves. The tree loses vigor and drops its foliage prematurely. Infected bark becomes moist, spongy and stringy. Beneath the bark, fan-shaped growths feed on the wood, causing decay. The tree dies of starvation when the fungus infects all of the roots. Clumps of honey-brown toadstools appear in fall around the bases of trees with dead roots.

SPECIAL TREATMENT. Buy healthy trees from reputable nurseries and plant them where the soil will drain quickly. Grow vegetables on newly cleared land for several years before planting fruit trees. If trees become infected, dig down to expose affected parts of the root crown. Cut away diseased portions and apply tree-wound dressing. If toadstools appear at the base of a tree, ask your agricultural agent to have them identified by a specialist. If mushroom root rot is present, remove and burn the tree, the toadstools and as many of the tree roots as possible. Have the soil professionally fumigated before planting trees or shrubs.

ROT, COLLAR See Canker, Bleeding
ROT, CROWN See Blight, Southern
ROT, FOOT See Leaf Spot, Bluegrass; Canker, Bleeding
ROT, STEM See Canker, Bleeding

RUST
Some of the 4,000 species of rust diseases, all produced by fungi, are present in almost every region of the world. Within each species are strains that infect only certain plants. Innumerable plants are subject to rust attack, ranging from garden flowers and vegetables to trees, grasses, grains and other commercial crops such as coffee, corn, cotton, flax, peanuts and sorghum. Rust fungi discolor leaves by producing rust-colored spores in powdery blisters or jelly-like horns. Like many diseases, rust yellows leaves and stunts growth.

Rust has caused severe losses ever since man first began to cultivate crops. The Romans held festivals in honor of the rust gods to implore their forbearance in attacks upon food

MUSHROOM ROOT ROT
Armillaria mellea

crops. That remains about as good as control as any; rust is still largely impervious to modern treatments. Rust typically passes through five spore stages during the life cycle. Some rusts require two host plants to complete this cycle, going through some of the spore stages on one plant, the others on the alternate host. For most rusts, sexual reproduction is followed by a period of dormancy.

WHAT TO DO. Purchase rust-resistant seeds and plants. If the rust needs two host plants to complete its life cycle, eliminate one host. For the ever-increasing number of rust strains, prevention is the best remedy since fungicides cannot control rust infections once they have taken hold.

CEDAR-APPLE RUST
Gymnosporangium juniperi-virginianae

Found generally in the East and Midwest, cedar-apple rust is concentrated in apple-growing regions of Virginia, the Carolinas and the Mississippi Valley. The rust infects eastern red cedar, juniper, apple and ornamental crabapple trees. For most of its two-year life cycle, cedar-apple rust usually remains on cedar trees. At the start of the cycle, spores are blown from apple to cedar trees in summer, where they may germinate or remain dormant until the following spring. The spores produce galls, swellings up to two inches across, on the cedar. The galls grow during the summer and by fall they are brown, bumpy balls. The second spring, warm rain triggers the growth of gelatinous orange tendrils that produce spores that are blown to apple trees. The spores cause lesions on leaves, twigs and fruit. Premature leaf loss reduces the yield and quality of the apples; severely infected trees may not bear fruit the following year. In summer, spores are blown from apple trees back to cedars to begin another cycle.

SPECIAL TREATMENT. Do not plant apple trees and cedar or juniper trees within several hundred yards of one another. If these alternate hosts grow near each other and cannot be removed, plant a windbreak between them to reduce the possibility of wind-blown spore infection. Use a preventive spray of ferbam (such as Fermate or Coromate), maneb (such as Dithane M-22), thiram (such as Thylate) or zineb (such as Dithane Z-78) on apples, or ferbam plus sulfur on cedars. Consult your agricultural agent for the spray schedule for your area. Pick galls off during the winter.

WHITE-PINE BLISTER RUST
Cronartium ribicola

Occurring throughout North America, white-pine blister rust first appears as small yellow or brown spots on pine needles. The fungus grows toward the bark where it creates swollen, spindle-shaped cankers. Trees die when the fungus encircles limbs and trunk, cutting off the flow of nutrients from the roots. Young seedlings can be quickly girdled, but saplings can survive for several years and infected mature trees can live 20 years or longer. Like cedar-apple rust, this fungus has two hosts: a currant or gooseberry bush and any of the eight white pine species. Spores develop on a currant or gooseberry bush and are blown to pines in late summer or early fall. The disease takes three to six years to develop fully on the pines. In the final stages, spores are produced that can be carried by the wind for hundreds of miles to infect gooseberry or currant bushes and renew the cycle.

SPECIAL TREATMENT. Remove all currant and gooseberry bushes, especially wild ones, growing within several hundred feet of white pines. Plant only disease-resistant currant and gooseberry varieties. Destroy diseased bushes promptly, taking care to pull out as many roots as possible. Remove diseased branches from pines, cutting 4 to 6 inches below the

Cautions to observe when using chemicals, page 71.

CEDAR-APPLE RUST
Gymnosporangium juniperi-viriginianae

WHITE-PINE BLISTER RUST
Cronartium ribicola

APPLE SCAB
Venturia inaequalis

COMMON SCAB OF POTATO
Actinomyces scabies

affected parts. Dip pruning shears in 70 per cent alcohol or 10 per cent household bleach between cuts. Strip diseased bark, removing bark 2 to 4 inches around the infected area.

S

SCAB

Affecting fruits, vegetables and some ornamental shrubs, scabs are common throughout North America. Scab diseases cause dark, raised lesions on leaves, stems or fruit. Exactly which diseases belong in this classification is a matter of debate among experts. Diseases formerly called scab on cereal crops, for example, are now termed seedling blight, ear rot, head blight, stalk rot or foot rot. Other diseases once called scab, with similar symptoms, have been reclassified as spot anthracnose. Most scabs, though not all, are thought to be caused by fungi. They are not as damaging as many other diseases of garden plants because they grow slowly and are usually quite small. The fungi rarely penetrate deeply into tissues so most of the infected fruits can still be eaten.

WHAT TO DO. Plant resistant varieties and rotate crops. Remove plant refuse from the garden; prune and destroy diseased parts of ornamentals. For fruit trees, follow the spray schedule recommended by your agricultural agent.

APPLE SCAB
Venturia inaequalis, also called *Fusicladium dendriticum*

Found on apples, crabapples, hawthorns and mountain ashes, apple scab is the most damaging apple disease in the United States, causing the loss of more than 10 million bushels annually. This fungus attacks apple trees from the first leafing until the harvest. Two stages in the life cycle of the fungus spread the disease. The first stage attacks buds, young leaves and blossoms while the second develops during the growing season and infects leaves and fruits.

Spores pass the winter in tiny pouches within growths called fruiting bodies that develop in dead apple leaves beneath the tree. When the leaves are drenched by spring rains, these pouches lengthen and protrude outside the fruiting bodies, exploding when the temperature rises above 40° and the humidity drops. Young leaves and fruit are most vulnerable to the fungus. The fruit develops a thin, corky layer underneath the fungus, cutting off the source of its nourishment. Cracks appear in the corky area. The infection may cause dwarfed and distorted fruit. If leaves or fruits are severely infected, they drop to the ground.

SPECIAL TREATMENT. Clean up fallen leaves and debris in the fall. Use a preventive spray of benomyl (such as Benlate), captan, ferbam (such as Carbamate) or lime sulfur. Consult your local agricultural agent for the spray schedule recommended in your locality.

COMMON SCAB OF POTATO
Actinomyces scabies, also called *Streptomyces scabies*

The fungus that produces common scab of potato lives in the soil in all potato-growing areas of North America. Beets, rutabagas and other fleshy-rooted vegetables are also vulnerable. The scab develops rapidly at temperatures around 70°. The first signs of infection are tiny brown specks that appear on the tubers as the disease begins to develop. The specks grow larger and become slightly raised with depressed centers. Deep corky tissue may cover the tuber's surface. This can be cut off, and it does not spoil the rest of the potato.

SPECIAL TREATMENT. Plant one of the many scab-resistant varieties and purchase certified disease-free seed potatoes. Plant potatoes in an acid soil and rotate crops. Dry soil favors growth of the fungus, so keep the soil moist but not soggy.

SMUT

Grasses and corn are damaged by smuts throughout the United States. Smut has many strains, each attacking particular varieties of plants. The black, powdery masses that give smut its name are live but dormant spores that accumulate òn dead or decaying matter. Thick outer walls enable these spores to stay alive for years until the wind blows them to a host where they can germinate, producing threadlike tubes that penetrate and infect seeds or plant tissues. Smuts enter plants three ways: by infection of seedlings caused by smut spores on germinating seed; by infection of seedlings caused by spores inside the seeds; and by infection of growing plant tissue by wind-blown spores.

WHAT TO DO. Plant resistant varieties and treated seeds in noninfected soil. Destroy diseased plants and debris.

CORN SMUT
Ustilago maydis, also called *U. zeae*

Widespread throughout North America, corn smut is a fungus whose spores survive winter cold in the soil and are blown to corn plants in the spring. All parts of the corn plant above ground can be affected. The spores invade this host, spreading a matted mass of threads through the plant's cells, stimulating them to form growths called galls. Spores develop inside the galls, which range in size from ¼ inch to 6 inches in diameter. When galls first become visible they are covered with a shiny, milky-green membrane. In a short time the membrane ruptures, releasing powdery black spores that the wind blows to other plants. Infection continues to spread in this way throughout the growing season.

SPECIAL TREATMENT. Plant only vigorous hybrid corn varieties. Avoid injuring plants. Do not use manure or infected corn debris as fertilizer. Pick galls off sweet corn.

ONION SMUT
Urocystis cepulae, also called *U. colchici*

Onions, leeks, chives, garlic and shallots are vulnerable to infection by smut, a problem for gardeners in the northern United States and southern Canada where spring and summer temperatures are cool. A seed-borne fungus, onion smut appears on young sprouts or bulbs as dark, thick blisters caused by threads of the fungus that have invaded plant tissue. Long leaves may drop from the weight of the fungus growth. If the plant has not been infected by the time the first leaf has formed, it will escape the disease. Infected seedlings usually die within a month.

SPECIAL TREATMENT. Avoid planting in infected soil. Plant disease-free onion sets or use fungicide-treated seed.

SNOW MOLD

SNOW MOLD OF TURF AND LAWN GRASSES
Typhula itoana

Grasses covered by deep snow for long periods are susceptible to damage by various snow-mold fungi. The variety known as speckled snow mold, typhula blight or gray snow mold occurs mainly in Canada, the eastern United States and the Pacific Northwest. In early spring, a slimy gray mold can be seen at the edges of snow patches. After the snow melts, crusty gray masses of spores are visible. Fungus threads germinate on the grass, producing club-shaped growths that explode and shoot spores into the air. Affected patches of grass, several inches to several feet in diameter, wither and turn light brown. Lawns usually recover from snow mold within six weeks as moisture diminishes and sunlight increases. The disease causes little or no damage.

WHAT TO DO. Mowing grass short in late fall and removing

Cautions to observe when using chemicals, page 71.

CORN SMUT
Ustilago maydis

ONION SMUT
Urocystis cepulae

DOGWOOD SPOT ANTHRACNOSE
Elsinoë corni

ASTER YELLOWS
Chlorogenus callistephi

clippings helps to prevent the disease. If infection is evident or suspected, apply benomyl (such as Tersan 1991) or anilazine (such as Dyrene) before the first snow. If crusty patches of spores appear in spring, break them up with a rake.

SOOTY APPLE BLOTCH See Blotch
SOOTY BLOTCH OF FRUIT See Blotch, Sooty Apple
SOUTHERN BLIGHT See Blight

SPOT ANTHRACNOSE
DOGWOOD SPOT ANTHRACNOSE
Elsinoë corni

Strains of fungi that cause leaf spotting appear on plants everywhere. This classification, spot anthracnose, includes some diseases that were formerly grouped with anthracnose and scab diseases. One characteristic symptom is a slight growth of tissue around a dying spot on a leaf.

Dogwood spot anthracnose affects dogwoods grown in the Atlantic Coast states and has been reported in Louisiana. Flower buds develop spots in spring and either do not open or produce malformed flowers. The disease spreads to leaves where as many as 100 small yellow-to-gray spots with purple edges develop on each leaf. Centers sometimes drop out, giving the leaves a ragged appearance. Severe infection may cause premature leaf drop and possibly the death of the tree.

WHAT TO DO. Apply a spray of zinc ionmanganese (such as Dithane M-45 or Fore), captan (such as Orthocide), maneb (such as Manzate) or zineb (such as Dithane Z-78) at monthly intervals as soon as buds begin to open.

STEM ROT See Canker, Bleeding

T

TOMATO BLIGHT See Blight
TRUNK CANKER OF APPLE See Canker, Bleeding
TURF, BROWN PATCH OF See Rot
TYPHULA BLIGHT See Snow Mold

V

VIRUS
All plants are vulnerable to virus infections. The hundreds of known plant viruses are divided into two categories according to the symptoms they produce: those that cause mottling and those that cause yellowing, stunting, curling of leaves or abnormal branching. Viruses are composed of protein and nucleic acid; the latter substance serves as a genetic blueprint that determines the structure of each virus. A virus reproduces itself by invading a living plant, where the nucleic acid of the virus directs the cells of the plant to recreate the original virus particle. As the virus multiplies, it usually spreads to every part of the plant. Once a plant is infected nothing can be done to cure it completely, but plants often recover through their own healing processes. Most viruses are transmitted by insects, chiefly aphids and leaf hoppers. Mealy bugs, mites, nematodes, thrips and whiteflies also carry certain viral diseases from plant to plant. Infected plants spread the contagion to healthy ones, as do the gardener's hands or tools. Seeds sometimes carry viruses. Dodder, a parasitic vine, can infect the plants it entwines.

WHAT TO DO. Buy only certified disease-free plants, seeds and cuttings. Control insect pests that transmit viruses. Destroy virus-infected plants and weeds.

ASTER YELLOWS
Chlorogenus callistephi

Gardeners in the West combat aster yellows on nearly 200

species of plants. Among the many vegetables it attacks are broccoli, carrots, lettuce, onions, spinach and tomatoes; it infects such flowers as anemones, asters, cosmos, marigolds, petunias, phlox and snapdragons. The virus multiplies within both six-spotted leaf hoppers and plants. Once a leaf hopper feeds on an infected plant it can pass the disease on to healthy plants for the rest of its life. Yellowing of foliage, immature flowers and secondary shoots are the primary symptoms. Plants become stunted and leaves grow upright in rosettes. In young plants, leaf veins disappear, immature leaves become narrow and dwarfed, and the plants do not flower. When the infection strikes mature plants, flowers are misshapen and the seeds are sterile. Infected vegetables ripen prematurely or develop warty skins.

SPECIAL TREATMENT. Destroy diseased plants immediately and eradicate weeds to destroy leaf hopper eggs. Control leaf hoppers with carbaryl (such as Sevin), malathion or methoxychlor (such as Marlate).

CUCUMBER MOSAIC
Marmor cucumoris

A group of virus strains is the cause of this disease in flowers, vegetables and many weeds throughout North America. Dahlias, delphiniums, geraniums, gladioluses, periwinkles and petunias are among the affected flowers; vegetables that harbor the virus include beans, corn, cucumbers, melons, peas, peppers, spinach, squashes and tomatoes. The virus winters in perennial weeds such as catnip, ground cherry and milkweed. It is transmitted by aphids. Leaves that are curled or mottled with yellow and green are characteristic symptoms. Fruits are misshapen and mottled. Flowers become stunted and mottled or streaked. Some plants produce few blossoms and have distorted leaves.

SPECIAL TREATMENT. Use disease-resistant seeds or seedlings. Destroy infected plants immediately and remove the weeds in which the virus winters. Control aphids with malathion or rotenone.

TOBACCO, TOMATO OR PEPPER MOSAIC
Marmor tabaci

Of all the viruses that affect greenhouse and garden plants, tobacco mosaic is the most infectious and the most resistant to controls. The disease is frequently spread to eggplants, peppers and tomatoes by gardeners who smoke. Heat used in curing tobacco does not kill the virus; the cured leaves of an infected plant can carry it for as long as 25 years. The virus winters in perennial weeds as well as tobacco and is carried by grasshoppers and aphids to other plants. It enters plants through small wounds or broken hairs on leaves and stems. Foliage becomes mottled. Blotches develop on fruits and streaks on stems. Young pepper leaves become spotted with yellow and green, curl slightly and wrinkle. Eventually the leaves drop, branches die and fruits also become yellow and wrinkled. Tomato seedlings are usually stunted; the leaves curl and are sometimes misshapen. Although mature tomato plants continue to grow after infection, the yield is reduced.

SPECIAL TREATMENT. Smokers should wash their hands before gardening and should not smoke while they work. Destroy plant hosts. Control insects with malathion.

WART, PLUM See Black Knot

WILT
The drooping, flabby leaves that characterize a plant with wilt disease are caused by fungi that invade the vascular

Cautions to observe when using chemicals, page 71.

CUCUMBER MOSAIC
Marmor cucumeris

TOMATO MOSAIC
Marmor tabaci

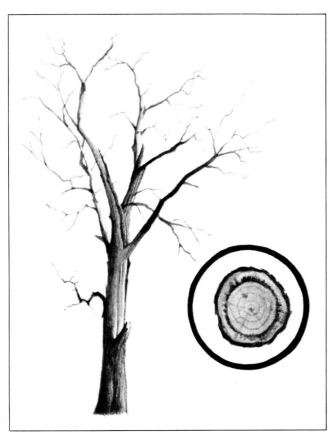

DUTCH ELM DISEASE
Ceratocystis ulmi

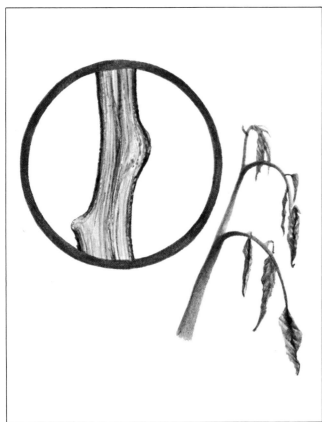

FUSARIUM WILT OF TOMATO
Fusarium oxysporum lycopersici

system that carries water through the plant. A fungus disease can affect water circulation in several ways. Fungus growth can itself block the water flow, or cellular growth triggered by the plant's defense mechanism can block the circulatory vessels. A plant's chemical reactions to fungus sometimes produce gummy substances that plug these tubes. In addition to physical obstructions, the fungus releases toxins that can either destroy vascular tissues or adversely affect transpiration. Wilt fungi are transmitted by insects or are soil-borne.

WHAT TO DO. Wilt diseases are difficult and in some cases impossible to control. Prevent them by keeping plants well fed and watered. Control insect invasions. Choose varieties that are wilt-resistant when they are available. If plants become diseased, remove and destroy them.

DUTCH ELM DISEASE
Ceratocystis ulmi

More shade trees in the United States have been destroyed by Dutch elm disease than any other infection. The fungus is a parasite that thrives beneath the bark of dead branches on still-living trees. Spores of the fungus are carried to uninfected trees by bark beetles that pick them up in their breeding tunnels in infected elms. The small European beetle and the native elm bark beetle are both carriers, but the European beetle does more harm because it feeds on easily infected young twigs and branches. The native beetle bores into trunks but usually not deeply enough to deposit fungus spores in the water-carrying vessels of the sapwood. The disease also invades the vascular system when the roots of an infected tree become grafted with those of a healthy one.

Once in the circulatory vessels, the fungus produces yeast-like spores that are transported by sap. These spores release a toxin and a gummy substance that clog the vessels. A tree usually dies in stages. The leaves of one or several branches wilt, yellow, dry out and fall off. Then the sapwood of the trunk dies. Trees infected late in summer may live until the following year.

SPECIAL TREATMENT. All elm wood that harbors the disease or its carriers should be removed and burned or buried in landfills. When planting new elms, choose such disease-resistant varieties as the European smooth-leaved elm, Christine Buisman elm, Groeneveld elm or the Hanson Manchurian elm. Control bark beetle carriers with methoxychlor (such as Marlate). Preventive measures to protect healthy elm trees include the injection of fumigants in the soil around the trees and chemical injection of the tree itself. Both measures must be undertaken by tree experts.

FUSARIUM WILT OF TOMATO
Fusarium oxysporum lycopersici

One of the most damaging of tomato diseases throughout the United States, fusarium wilt is most active when the temperature is between 80° and 90° and therefore is most prevalent in the South. The fungus can live in soil for years, and light, sandy soil is most conducive to its growth. The soil-borne fungus spores enter the plant at its roots and move up the stem through water-carrying vessels, producing toxins that clog these vessels. The first external symptoms of the disease appear at the base of a plant, where leaves yellow and droop. Seedlings die quickly. Older plants may become infected at any stage, but attacks occur most often when fruit is beginning to mature. The disease may progress erratically, affecting one side of a stem at first or killing a single shoot entirely before the rest of the plant shows any symptoms.

SPECIAL TREATMENT. Start seedlings in sterile soil. Plant fusarium wilt-resistant varieties—all those with the letter "F" after their names in seed catalogs. Rotate tomatoes with other crops on a three- or four-year cycle.

OAK WILT
Ceratocystis fagacearum

Entering trees through any wound that has broken the bark, oak wilt affects 50 species of oak, American, European and Chinese chestnuts, and several apple varieties throughout the United States. Once beneath the bark, the fungus multiplies rapidly in the sapwood, clogging the vessels that conduct water. Red and black oaks are most vulnerable. In the first stage of the infection, leaves at the ends of upper branches turn pale, curl upward and stiffen. Then they turn yellow or bronze from the edges inward to the leafstalk. Heavy shedding occurs throughout the course of wilting and bronzing and even green leaves may drop. From early summer to fall, wilting proceeds rapidly downward and inward. If symptoms appear late in the growing season, a tree may survive the winter and produce dwarfed, short-lived leaves the following spring.

Oak wilt can spread from a diseased tree to a neighbor via roots, especially among red and black oaks growing 50 feet or closer together. The fungus is also spread by nitidulid beetles and oak bark beetles that feed on sap from wounds of infected trees and then move to healthy ones. Oak bark beetles also breed in and spend the winter in infected trees, becoming contaminated with fungus spores.

SPECIAL TREATMENT. No treatment for infected trees is known. Remove and burn diseased trees. Stumps should be poisoned by tree experts and removed. To keep roots of diseased and healthy trees from growing together, the soil can be treated by professionals with Vapam. Or dig a trench 2 feet deep between healthy and infected trees, extending it beyond the branch spread of the diseased trees. To avoid wounds when the fungus is active, prune only from late fall through early spring.

VERTICILLIUM WILT
Verticillium albo-atrum

Some 300 kinds of plants are infected by verticillium wilt, widespread throughout the northern half of the United States and in California. Red, silver and sugar maples and elms are susceptible. Fruit-bearing trees and bushes are also victims, as are a great many annual and perennial flowers including chrysanthemums, dahlias, geraniums, peonies and snapdragons. Among vegetables, eggplants, okra, potatoes and tomatoes are most often affected.

The fungus that causes the disease lives in the soil on dead or decaying matter and may survive for 15 years or more. It enters a plant through the roots and, like other wilt diseases, invades the water-carrying vessels. Toxins trigger growths and gums that clog the vascular system. Leaves yellow and wilt. A portion of a tree may die while the rest of it continues to live. Perennials degenerate slowly. The first symptom of the disease in tomatoes is a yellowing of older leaves and a slight wilting of tips during the day. Eventually most of the leaves die. Although the plants usually live, they are stunted, the branches droop and the fruits are abnormally small.

SPECIAL TREATMENT. Use only healthy plants for propagation and buy resistant varieties whenever possible. Rotate susceptible and nonsusceptible crops on a three-year cycle. Avoid high-nitrogen fertilizers. Destroy diseased plants and prune infected branches from trees. If an entire tree must be removed, do not plant a susceptible species in that spot.

WILT, CUCUMBER See Bacterial Disease

Cautions to observe when using chemicals, page 71.

OAK WILT
Ceratocystis fagacearum

VERTICILLIUM WILT
Verticillium albo-atrum

Appendix

A guide to the enemies of 132 plants

	Ant	Aphid	Beetle	Borer	Bug	Caterpillar	Centipede	Cicada	Cricket	Fly. Maggot	Grasshopper	Leaf Hopper	Mealy Bug	Millepede	Mite	Nematode	Psylla	Scale	Slug	Sow Bug	Thrips	Whitefly	Wireworm
AFRICAN VIOLET		●			●								●		●	●		●					
AMARYLLIS		●	●		●				●				●		●	●		●			●	●	
APPLE		●	●	●	●	●		●		●		●	●		●		●	●					●
APRICOT		●	●	●	●	●			●				●		●		●	●	●				
ARBORVITAE		●	●	●		●						●			●			●					
ASH		●	●	●	●				●						●			●				●	
ASPARAGUS		●	●		●	●	●								●			●					
ASTER	●	●	●	●	●		●				●	●			●			●			●	●	●
BARBERRY		●	●										●		●	●		●				●	
BEAN		●	●	●	●	●			●	●		●	●	●	●	●					●	●	●
BEECH		●	●	●	●	●						●			●			●					
BEET	●	●	●	●	●	●			●	●		●		●	●	●					●		●
BEGONIA		●	●										●		●	●		●	●				●
BIRCH		●	●	●	●	●									●								
BLUEBERRY			●	●		●		●	●			●			●			●					
BOUGAINVILLEA					●							●			●			●					
BOX ELDER		●	●	●	●	●						●			●		●	●					
BOXWOOD					●							●			●	●	●	●					
BROCCOLI		●	●		●					●	●				●								
BRUSSELS SPROUTS		●	●		●	●				●	●				●								
CABBAGE		●	●		●	●				●	●			●	●	●			●		●		
CACTUS		●	●		●							●			●			●			●		
CAMELLIA		●	●		●							●	●		●	●		●		●		●	
CARNATION		●	●		●				●			●	●		●	●		●					
CARROT	●	●	●		●	●			●	●		●		●	●	●					●		●
CATALPA		●		●	●				●			●			●			●					
CAULIFLOWER		●	●		●	●				●	●				●						●		
CELERY		●	●	●	●	●			●	●	●				●						●		
CHERRY		●	●	●	●	●			●	●		●	●		●			●			●	●	
CHESTNUT		●	●	●		●						●			●			●					
CHRYSANTHEMUM	●	●	●	●	●	●			●		●	●	●		●	●		●	●	●	●	●	●
CITRUS	●	●	●	●	●					●	●	●	●		●			●	●		●	●	
COLEUS				●	●							●			●	●		●	●			●	
CORN	●	●	●	●	●	●			●	●		●		●	●	●					●		●
COSMOS		●	●	●	●							●	●										
COTONEASTER		●		●	●		●					●	●		●			●					
CRAB APPLE		●		●	●	●			●			●			●			●					
CUCUMBER		●	●	●	●	●	●		●	●		●			●	●					●	●	
CYCLAMEN		●	●										●		●	●					●	●	
DAHLIA	●	●	●	●	●	●						●	●		●	●		●	●		●		●
DAISY		●	●		●	●									●						●		
DAY LILY		●	●						●			●			●	●		●	●		●		
DELPHINIUM		●	●	●	●								●	●	●	●			●	●	●		
DIEFFENBACHIA		●													●				●				
DOGWOOD		●	●	●	●	●		●		●		●	●			●						●	
DRACAENA			●										●			●					●		
EGGPLANT		●	●	●	●					●		●			●	●						●	
ELM		●	●	●	●	●		●				●			●			●					
EUONYMUS			●										●					●			●		
FIG			●	●		●							●		●		●	●			●	●	●

PLANT	Anthracnose	Bacterial Disease	Black Knot	Blackleg	Black Spot	Blight	Blotch Disease	Canker, Dieback	Clubroot	Damping-off	Downy Mildew	Fairy Ring	Gall	Leaf Blister, Leaf Curl	Leaf Spot	Powdery Mildew	Rot	Rust	Scab	Smut	Snow Mold	Spot Anthracnose	Virus Disease	Wilt
AFRICAN VIOLET		•			•											•								
AMARYLLIS					•				•					•									•	
APPLE		•			•		•	•								•		•	•				•	•
APRICOT		•	•					•					•				•							•
ARBORVITAE		•							•								•							
ASH									•															•
ASPARAGUS	•	•			•				•								•							
ASTER		•			•										•								•	•
BARBERRY		•						•	•															•
BEAN	•	•			•				•	•							•						•	•
BEECH								•									•							
BEET		•			•				•					•				•					•	•
BEGONIA		•			•										•	•								•
BIRCH								•					•				•							
BLUEBERRY		•									•													
BOUGAINVILLEA																								
BOX ELDER																								•
BOXWOOD																	•							
BROCCOLI																						•		
BRUSSELS SPROUTS									•															
CABBAGE		•			•				•	•												•		
CACTUS		•															•							
CAMELLIA		•			•		•							•										
CARNATION	•	•			•												•						•	•
CARROT					•					•												•		
CATALPA					•					•							•							•
CAULIFLOWER									•															
CELERY		•								•					•								•	•
CHERRY		•	•		•			•						•			•					•		
CHESTNUT								•									•							•
CHRYSANTHEMUM		•			•											•	•						•	•
CITRUS		•					•			•							•							
COLEUS		•								•														•
CORN					•													•		•		•		
COSMOS					•											•							•	•
COTONEASTER		•															•							
CRAB APPLE		•				•										•		•	•					
CUCUMBER		•			•					•						•						•		
CYCLAMEN		•																						•
DAHLIA		•			•								•		•	•	•						•	•
DAISY		•			•																	•		
DAY LILY		•																						
DELPHINIUM		•			•					•					•								•	•
DIEFFENBACHIA	•																							
DOGWOOD	•	•						•									•				•			•
DRACAENA	•																							
EGGPLANT	•	•			•					•						•							•	•
ELM								•		•			•				•							•
EUONYMUS		•																						
FIG		•			•			•									•							

151

PESTS

	Ant	Aphid	Beetle	Borer	Bug	Caterpillar	Centipede	Cicada	Cricket	Fly Maggot	Grasshopper	Leaf Hopper	Mealy Bug	Millepede	Mite	Nematode	Psylla	Scale	Slug	Sow Bug	Thrips	Whitefly	Wireworm
FIR		●	●	●	●					●			●		●			●					
FORSYTHIA				●									●	●	●			●					
FUCHSIA		●	●		●								●	●	●			●		●	●	●	
GARDENIA		●	●										●	●	●			●		●	●	●	
GERANIUM		●	●	●	●								●	●	●			●	●	●		●	
GINKGO						●							●		●			●					
GLADIOLUS		●	●	●	●	●				●		●	●	●	●			●		●	●		●
GRAPE		●	●	●	●	●		●	●	●	●	●	●		●			●			●	●	●
HAWTHORN		●	●	●	●	●						●	●		●			●					
HEMLOCK		●	●	●		●							●		●			●					
HIBISCUS		●	●	●		●							●			●		●	●			●	
HICKORY		●	●	●	●	●	●						●		●			●					
HOLLY		●	●		●				●				●		●			●				●	
HOLLYHOCK		●	●	●	●	●						●	●	●	●	●					●	●	
HYACINTH		●	●		●					●	●		●	●				●					
HYDRANGEA		●	●	●	●								●	●	●			●		●	●		
IMPATIENS		●	●	●									●	●	●				●				
IRIS		●	●	●	●				●				●		●			●	●	●	●	●	●
IVY		●	●	●	●						●	●	●		●			●					
JASMINE													●					●		●		●	
JUNIPER		●	●	●	●				●				●		●			●					
LANTANA		●			●				●				●	●	●			●				●	
LARCH		●	●	●	●																		
LAUREL					●								●				●	●					
LAWN GRASS	●	●	●	●	●					●	●	●	●	●	●	●		●		●	●	●	●
LETTUCE		●	●	●	●	●	●					●	●	●	●		●			●	●		
LILAC		●	●	●	●								●		●			●				●	
LILY		●	●	●	●				●				●	●	●			●	●	●	●		
LINDEN		●	●	●	●	●							●		●			●				●	
LOCUST		●	●	●	●	●							●					●				●	
MAGNOLIA		●		●	●								●		●		●	●				●	
MAPLE		●	●	●	●	●		●	●			●	●	●	●			●			●	●	
MARIGOLD		●	●	●	●	●						●	●	●	●				●	●	●		
MELON		●	●	●	●	●		●				●	●	●	●						●	●	
MOUNTAIN ASH		●	●	●	●										●			●					
MYRTLE		●										●	●		●			●			●		
NARCISSUS		●			●					●	●		●	●	●			●	●				
NASTURTIUM		●	●	●	●							●	●	●					●	●	●		
OAK		●	●	●	●	●	●						●	●				●					
ONION		●	●	●					●				●	●							●		●
ORCHID	●	●	●	●	●	●							●	●	●			●	●	●	●		
PANSY		●	●		●							●	●	●	●				●	●			●
PARSNIP		●	●		●					●	●	●			●	●							
PEA		●	●	●	●	●	●		●	●					●	●					●	●	
PEACH		●	●	●	●	●		●	●			●	●	●	●			●			●		
PEAR		●	●	●	●	●		●	●				●				●	●			●		
PEONY	●		●	●									●			●		●			●		
PEPPER		●	●	●	●	●						●	●	●	●	●	●	●				●	
PETUNIA		●	●	●	●						●	●	●	●	●								
PHILODENDRON													●	●	●			●			●		

DISEASES

	Anthracnose	Bacterial Disease	Black Knot	Blackleg	Black Spot	Blight	Blotch Disease	Canker, Dieback	Clubroot	Damping-off	Downy Mildew	Fairy Ring	Gall	Leaf Blister, Leaf Curl	Leaf Spot	Powdery Mildew	Rot	Rust	Scab	Smut	Snow Mold	Spot Anthracnose	Virus Disease	Wilt
FIR																	●							
FORSYTHIA		●			●			●																
FUCHSIA		●															●							●
GARDENIA		●																						
GERANIUM		●		●													●						●	●
GINKGO																								
GLADIOLUS					●												●						●	
GRAPE		●															●							
HAWTHORN		●			●												●		●					
HEMLOCK		●								●							●							
HIBISCUS		●																						
HICKORY		●						●									●							
HOLLY																	●							
HOLLYHOCK					●										●			●						
HYACINTH		●			●																			
HYDRANGEA		●			●												●							
IMPATIENS											●						●						●	●
IRIS		●			●				●															
IVY														●			●							
JASMINE		●			●																			
JUNIPER		●																●						
LANTANA																								●
LARCH								●									●							
LAUREL																								
LAWN GRASS					●							●		●	●		●				●			
LETTUCE		●			●						●				●								●	
LILAC		●						●									●							
LILY		●			●	●		●									●						●	
LINDEN								●																●
LOCUST								●									●							
MAGNOLIA								●																●
MAPLE	●	●						●					●				●							●
MARIGOLD		●			●												●						●	●
MELON		●			●						●				●								●	●
MOUNTAIN ASH		●																	●					
MYRTLE					●																			
NARCISSUS					●												●							
NASTURTIUM					●																		●	
OAK		●						●					●				●							●
ONION		●			●						●									●			●	
ORCHID					●																			
PANSY		●			●																			
PARSNIP		●																	●				●	
PEA	●				●						●												●	●
PEACH		●						●					●	●			●							●
PEAR		●						●									●							
PEONY		●			●												●							●
PEPPER					●						●				●								●	
PETUNIA											●												●	
PHILODENDRON					●																			

153

PESTS

	Ant	Aphid	Beetle	Borer	Bug	Caterpillar	Centipede	Cicada	Cricket	Fly, Maggot	Grasshopper	Leaf Hopper	Mealy Bug	Millepede	Mite	Nematode	Psylla	Scale	Slug	Sow Bug	Thrips	Whitefly	Wireworm
PHLOX		●	●	●	●	●						●			●			●					
PINE		●	●	●		●			●				●		●			●					
PLANE		●		●	●	●						●			●			●				●	
PLUM		●	●	●	●	●			●	●		●	●		●			●			●		
POPLAR		●	●	●	●	●						●	●		●			●			●		
POTATO		●	●	●	●	●				●	●		●	●	●	●		●	●			●	●
PRIMROSE		●	●		●								●	●	●				●		●		
PRIVET		●	●		●		●						●		●						●	●	
PUMPKIN		●	●	●	●	●					●		●	●							●	●	
PYRACANTHA		●	●		●	●									●			●					
QUINCE		●	●	●		●						●			●			●					
RADISH		●	●		●	●	●		●	●					●	●							●
RASPBERRY		●	●	●	●	●			●	●		●	●		●			●			●		
REDBUD		●		●	●							●						●					
RHODODENDRON		●	●	●	●	●			●			●	●		●	●		●			●	●	
ROSE		●	●	●	●	●		●	●	●	●	●	●		●			●			●	●	●
SPINACH		●	●		●			●	●	●													
SPRUCE		●	●	●		●				●					●			●					
SQUASH		●	●	●	●	●					●										●	●	
STRAWBERRY	●	●	●	●	●	●	●	●		●		●	●	●	●	●		●	●	●	●	●	●
SWEET GUM		●		●		●						●			●			●					
SWEET PEA	●	●	●		●	●	●						●	●					●	●	●		
SWEET POTATO		●	●		●				●			●		●	●	●		●			●	●	●
TOMATO		●	●	●	●	●	●		●	●		●	●	●	●	●	●	●			●	●	
TULIP		●								●			●	●	●				●				●
TURNIP		●	●	●	●	●			●	●			●	●							●		●
VIBURNUM		●	●	●	●					●			●		●	●		●			●	●	
VIOLET		●	●			●				●			●		●	●		●	●				
WALNUT		●		●	●	●				●			●		●			●					
WILLOW		●	●	●	●	●				●			●		●	●	●	●					
YEW	●		●			●							●		●	●		●					
ZINNIA	●	●	●	●	●					●	●		●			●							

Acknowledgments

The index for this book was prepared by Anita R. Beckerman. For their help in the preparation of this book, the editors wish to thank the following: Dr. Ross Arnett, *Insect World Digest*, Kinderhook, N.Y.; Robert Bjork, Photo Editor, Agricultural Research Service, U.S. Dept. of Agriculture, Washington, D.C.; Dave Bucher, Grant Heilman Photography, Lititz, Pa.; Dr. Richard Campana, Department of Botany and Plant Pathology, University of Maine, Orono, Me.; John Carter, Nebraska State Historical Society, Lincoln, Neb.; Dennis Ceplecha, Municipal Arborist, Department of Parks, Recreation and Forestry, Evanston, Ill.; Robert Choy, New York City; Dr. John A. Davidson, Department of Entomology, University of Maryland, College Park, Md.; Errett Deck, Environmental Coordinator, U.S. Dept. of Agriculture, Washington, D.C.; Eugene D. Decker, Kansas State Historical Society, Topeka, Kans.; Jay Ellenberger, Office of Pesticide Programs, Registration Division, Environmental Protection Agency, Washing-

ton, D.C.; A. Murray Evans, Department of Botany, University of Tennessee, Knoxville, Tenn.; Fairfax Biological Laboratory, Inc., Clinton Corners, N.Y.; William E. Ferguson, Los Gatos, Calif.; Dr. Allan Fusonie, Rare Book Collection, National Agricultural Library, Beltsville, Md.; Dr. L. C. Gibbs, Program Leader, Pesticide Chemical Extension Service, U.S. Dept. of Agriculture, Washington, D.C.; Henry Gilbertson, Davey Tree Co., Kent, Ohio; Fritz Goro, Chappaqua, N.Y.; Dr. Gary J. Griffin, Department of Plant Pathology, Virginia Polytechnic Institute, Blacksburg, Va.; Herbert Harrison, Office of Pesticide Programs, Registration Division, Environmental Protection Agency, Washington, D.C.; Chuck Herron, Animal and Plant Health Inspection Service, U.S. Dept. of Agriculture, Washington, D.C.; Dr. Francis W. Holmes, Director, Shade Tree Laboratories, University of Massachusetts, Amherst, Mass.; R. A. Jaynes, Connecticut Agricultural Experiment Station, New Haven, Conn.; Dr. David Karnosky, The Cary Arboretum of The New York Botanical Garden, Millbrook, N.Y.; Dr. Waldemar Klassen, Staff Scientist, Pest Management, Agricultural Research Service,

DISEASES

PLANT	Anthracnose	Bacterial Disease	Black Knot	Blackleg	Black Spot	Blight	Blotch Disease	Canker; Dieback	Clubroot	Damping-off	Downy Mildew	Fairy Ring	Gall	Leaf Blister; Leaf Curl	Leaf Spot	Powdery Mildew	Rot	Rust	Scab	Smut	Snow Mold	Spot Anthracnose	Virus Disease	Wilt
PHLOX	●				●											●							●	●
PINE					●				●								●	●						
PLANE																●								
PLUM	●	●			●									●			●							●
POPLAR	●						●							●			●	●						
POTATO					●						●	●							●				●	●
PRIMROSE	●															●							●	
PRIVET	●															●								
PUMPKIN	●				●				●							●							●	
PYRACANTHA	●							●								●								
QUINCE	●							●								●								
RADISH									●	●								●					●	
RASPBERRY	●				●			●								●						●		●
REDBUD								●																●
RHODODENDRON	●				●			●					●			●								
ROSE	●			●	●	●										●								●
SPINACH											●				●								●	●
SPRUCE								●	●								●							
SQUASH	●				●				●								●						●	
STRAWBERRY	●				●											●								●
SWEET GUM								●																
SWEET PEA	●				●											●								●
SWEET POTATO	●				●																			
TOMATO	●				●							●					●						●	●
TULIP	●				●	●										●							●	
TURNIP	●				●				●									●						●
VIBURNUM	●																							●
VIOLET					●																			
WALNUT	●																●							
WILLOW	●							●									●							
YEW																								
ZINNIA					●				●							●							●	

U.S. Dept. of Agriculture, Beltsville, Md.; Dr. Edward S. Kondo, Great Lakes Forest Research Centre, Canadian Forestry Service, Dept. of the Environment, Sault Ste. Marie, Ontario; Raymond E. Landolp, Registration Division, Environmental Protection Agency, Washington, D.C.; Dr. Gerald N. Lanier, Department of Entomology, State University of New York, Syracuse, N.Y.; Dr. Paul M. Marsh, Systematic Entomology Laboratory, U.S. Dept. of Agriculture, Washington, D.C.; Elena Millie, Prints and Photographs Division, Library of Congress, Washington, D.C.; Richard Moorer, Office of Pesticide Programs, Environmental Protection Agency, Washington, D.C.; Mr. and Mrs. Cambell Norsgaard, Lakeville, Conn.; Gerald Odland, Entomological Society of America, College Park, Md.; Dr. James Packer, Entomological Society of America, College Park, Md.; Dr. John W. Peacock, Forest Insect and Disease Laboratories, Forest Service, U.S. Dept. of Agriculture, Delaware, Ohio; Edward S. Ross, California Academy of Sciences, Golden Gate Park, San Francisco, Calif.; Dr. Lawrence R. Schreiber, Shade Tree and Ornamental Plants Laboratory, Agricultural Research Service, U.S. Dept. of Agriculture, Delaware, Ohio; Philip Schroeder, Plant Protection and Quarantine Programs, Hyattsville, Md.; Dr. James L. Sherald, Ecological Services Laboratory, National Capitol Parks, U.S. Dept. of the Interior, Washington, D.C.; Dr. Dorothy Smith, American Chemical Society, Washington, D.C.; Mark Snyder, Ball Seed Co., West Chicago, Ill.; Dr. Roland Jay Stipes, Virginia Polytechnic Institute, Blacksburg, Va.; Joseph Swab, Rare Book Collection, National Agricultural Library, Beltsville, Md.; Mrs. Thedosia T. Thomas, Photography Division, U.S. Dept. of Agriculture, Washington, D.C.; Dr. Eyvind Thor, Forestry Department, University of Tennessee, Knoxville, Tenn.; Frederick Kent Truslow, Charlotte, N.C.; Dr. William M. Upholt, Environmental Protection Agency, Washington, D.C.; Dr. R. N. Waghray, Fairfax County Extension Service, Fairfax, Va.; Walter Waldrop, Office of Pesticide Programs, Environmental Protection Agency, Washington, D.C.; Kenneth C. Walker, Agricultural Research Service, U.S. Dept. of Agriculture, Washington, D.C.; Dr. John A. Weidhaas Jr., Department of Entomology, Virginia Polytechnic Institute, Blacksburg, Va.

Picture credits

The sources for the illustrations in this book are shown below. Credits from left to right are separated by semicolons, from top to bottom by dashes.

Cover—Edward S. Ross. 4—Michael Young; Robert E. Hynes. 6, 9—Charlie Brown, courtesy of U.S. National Agricultural Library. 12—Courtesy of Nebraska State Historical Society (2). 13—Courtesy of Solomon D. Butcher Collection, Nebraska State Historical Society—courtesy of Kansas State Historical Society. 16—©William E. Ferguson. 19, 24, 25—Drawings by Susan M. Johnston. 30, 31—©William E. Ferguson. 35—Robert M. Eginton. 36, 37—A. Murray Evans. 38, 39—Fritz Goro. 40, 41—Ira Wexler (2). 42—Arnold Zann, courtesy of Ball Seed Co. 44, 46—Drawings by Kathy Rebeiz. 49—Drawings by Beverly Jaquish. 50—Drawings by Susan M. Johnston (2)—drawing by Kathy Rebeiz. 53—Ernest R. Manewal from Black Star. 54—Edward S. Ross; ©William E. Ferguson. 55—C. W. Perkins from Animals Animals—Edward S. Ross; ©William E. Ferguson (2). 56, 57—Edward S. Ross; ©William E. Ferguson. 58—©William E. Ferguson (2). 59—Grant Heilman—©William E. Ferguson—Edward S. Ross. 60—C. W. Perkins from Animals Animals; Z. Leszczynski from Animals Animals. 61—M. Stouffer from Animals Animals—John Gerard from the National Audubon Society Collection/PR. 62—Stephen Dalton from the National Audubon Society Collection/PR. 63—Frederick Kent Truslow. 64—Library of Congress. 67, 68—Drawings by Kathy Rebeiz. 74, 75—Drawings by Beverly Jaquish. 79—Richard R. Campana, University of Maine. 80—USDA Forest Service—Horace V. Wester, National Capitol Region, National Park Service. 81—Warren E. Beers for James L. Sherald, National Capitol Region, National Park Service. 82—G. J. Griffin, Professor of Plant Pathology, Virginia Polytechnic Institute & State University. 83—A. Murray Evans (2). 84—Encyclopedia Illustrations by Robert E. Hynes.

Bibliography

Anderson, D. M., *Common Names of Insects*. Entomological Society of America, 1975.

Aphids on Leafy Vegetables. Farmers' Bulletin No. 2148. U.S. Department of Agriculture, 1977.

Arbib, Robert, and Soper, Tony, *The Hungry Bird Book*. Taplinger Publishing Co., 1971.

Borror, Donald J., and White, Richard E., *A Field Guide to the Insects of America North of Mexico*. Houghton Mifflin Company, 1970.

Borror, Donald J., Delong, D. W., and Triplehorn, C. A., *An Introduction to the Study of Insects*. Holt Rinehart & Winston, 1976.

Brooklyn Botanic Garden, *Handbook on Biological Control of Plant Pests*. BBG, 1974.

Comstock, John H., *An Introduction to Entomology*. Comstock Publishing Co., 1940.

Control of Insects on Deciduous Fruits and Tree Nuts in the Home Orchard. Home and Garden Bulletin No. 190. U.S. Department of Agriculture, 1975.

Controlling the Japanese Beetle. Home and Garden Bulletin No. 159. U.S. Department of Agriculture, 1976.

Dahl, Mogens, and Thygesen, Thyge B., *Garden Pests and Diseases of Flowers and Shrubs*. Macmillan Publishing Co., 1974.

Davidson, Ralph Howard, and Peairs, Leonard Marion, *Insect Pests of Farm, Garden, and Orchard*. John Wiley & Sons, Inc., 1966.

Davison, Verne E., *Attracting Birds: from the Prairies to the Atlantic*. Thomas Y. Crowell Co., 1967.

Debach, Paul, *Biological Control by Natural Enemies*. Cambridge University Press, 1974.

Dillon, Elizabeth S., and Dillon, Lawrence S., *A Manual of Common Beetles of Eastern North America*, Vol. II. Dover Publications, 1972.

Farm Chemicals Handbook, 1977. Meister Publishing Co.

Harris, Moses, *The Aurelian*. Privately published, 1766.

Hawley, Gessner G., *The Condensed Chemical Dictionary*. Litton Educational Publishing, Inc., 1977.

Home and Garden Insect Control Guide. New Mexico State University Cooperative Extension Service, 1977.

Horsfall, James Gordon, *Fungicides and Their Action*. Chronica Botanica Company, 1945.

Insect Control for House Plants. Information Sheet 872. Mississippi State University Cooperative Extension Service.

Insects and Diseases of Vegetables in the Home Garden. Bulletin No. 380. U.S. Department of Agriculture, 1975.

Insects: The Yearbook of Agriculture, 1952. U.S. Department of Agriculture, 1952.

Johnson, Warren T., and Lyon, Howard H., *Insects That Feed on Trees and Shrubs*. Cornell University Press, 1976.

Lawn Insects/How to Control Them. Home and Garden Bulletin No. 53. U.S. Department of Agriculture, 1971.

Metcalf, C. L., Flint, W. P., and Metcalf, R. L., *Destructive and Useful Insects*. McGraw-Hill Book Co., 1962.

Mitchell, Robert, *Butterflies and Moths*. Golden Press, 1966.

National Wildlife Federation, *Gardening With Wildlife*. National Wildlife Federation, 1974.

Pflanzenschutz Compendium II. Farbenfabriken Bayer Aktiengesellschaft.

Pirone, Pascal P., et al., *Diseases and Pests of Ornamental Plants*. The Ronald Press Company, 1970.

Roberts, Reed S., *Household Insect Control*. Utah State University Cooperative Extension Service, 1977.

Safe Storage and Disposal of Pesticides. Environmental Protection Agency, May 1977.

Schreiber, Lawrence R., and Peacock, John W., *Dutch Elm Disease and its Control*. U.S. Government Printing Office, 1975.

Shepard, Merle, ed., *Insect Pest Management: Readings*. MSS Information Corporation, 1973.

Shurtleff, Malcolm C., *How to Control Plant Diseases In Home and Garden*. Iowa State University Press, 1966.

Stevens, Neil E., and Stevens, Russell B., *Disease in Plants*. Chronica Botanica Company, 1952.

Swain, Ralph B., *The Insect Guide*. Doubleday & Co., Inc., 1952.

Swann, Lester A., and Papp, Charles S., *The Common Insects of North America*. Harper & Row, 1972.

Tyler, Hamilton, *Organic Gardening Without Poisons*. Van Nostrand Reinhold Co., 1970.

Vogel, Zdenek, *Reptiles and Amphibians*. The Viking Press, 1964.

Waghray, R. N., and Robinson, W. H., *The Japanese Beetle*. Virginia Polytechnic Institute and State University, 1977.

Watson, Theo F., Moore, Leon, and Ware, George W., *Practical Insect Pest Management*. W. H. Freeman and Company, 1975.

Weigel, C. A., and Baumhofer, L. G., *Handbook on Insect Enemies of Flowers and Shrubs*. Publication No. 626. U.S. Department of Agriculture, 1949.

Westcott, Cynthia, *Are You Your Garden's Worst Pest?* Doubleday & Company, 1961.

Westcott, Cynthia, *The Gardener's Bug Book*. Doubleday & Company, Inc., 1973.

Westcott, Cynthia, *Plant Disease Handbook*. Van Nostrand Reinhold Company, 1971.

Wyman, Donald, *Wyman's Gardening Encyclopedia*. Macmillan Publishing Co., Inc., 1975.

Yepsen, Roger B., Jr., *Trees for the Yard, Orchard, and Woodlot*. Rodale Press, Inc., 1976.

Index

*Numerals in italics indicate an
illustration of the subject mentioned.*